LOCATING FILIPINO AMERICANS

In the series

Asian American History and Culture

edited by Sucheng Chan, David Palumbo-Liu,
and Michael Omi

LOCATING
FILIPINO
AMERICANS

ETHNICITY AND THE

CULTURAL POLITICS

OF SPACE

Rick Bonus

Temple University Press

PHILADELPHIA

Temple University Press, Philadelphia 19122
Copyright © 2000 by Temple University
All rights reserved
Published 2000
Printed in the United States of America

Library of Congress Cataloging-in-Publication Data

Bonus, Rick, 1962–
    Locating Filipino Americans : ethnicity and the cultural politics of space / Rick Bonus.
        p. cm. — (Asian Amerian history and culture)
    Includes bibliographical references (p.) and index.
    ISBN 1-56639-778-2 (cloth : alk. paper) — ISBN 1-56639-779-0 (paper : alk. paper)
        1. Filipino Americans—Ethnic identity—Case studies.   2. Filipino Americans—Social
conditions—Case studies.   3. Space and time—Social aspects—United States—Case
studies.   4. Filipino Americans—California, Southern.   5. United States—Ethnic
relations—Case studies.   6. California, Southern—Ethnic relations.   I. Title.   II. Series.

E184.F4 B66 2000
305.89'921073—dc21   99-462220

To my father, Eddie—

Dahil tinuruan mo ako
[Because you taught me]

Contents

Preface

This book is based on an ethnographic study of Filipino American communities in Los Angeles and San Diego Counties from October 1992 to January 1995. Census data reveal a sizable concentration of Filipinos in these areas who do not necessarily represent the bulk of Filipinos in the United States, but whose experiences and formations provide illustrative instances of a specific articulation of Filipino Americanness. This study focuses on commercial establishments (particularly, Filipino "Oriental" stores), social halls, community centers, and media (specifically, Filipino community newspapers) as sites where Filipino Americans publicly construct their ethnic identities in relation to the historical and contemporary conditions they face as members of U.S. society. Through the use of historical data, ethnographic fieldwork, and interviews of more than eighty individuals, I argue that particular practices of community and ethnic identity formations among Filipino Americans in Southern California reflect two things: a need to respond to and resist historical and institutional renderings of invisibility, exploitation, silencing, and racial constructing, and a desire to claim a "space" within the category "American" on their own terms.

The Filipino American population in the United States is predicted to reach more than two million by the twenty-first century. Yet many Filipino Americans contend that years of formal and covert exclusion from mainstream political, social, and economic institutions on the basis of their race and placement in the global capitalist system have perpetuated racist stereotypes about them, ignored their colonial and immigration history, and prevented them from becoming fully recognized citizens of the nation. In light of these experiences, Filipino Americans build communities in alternative ways defined by their critical stances against racism, homogenization, complete assimilation, and exclusionary citizenship, appropriating elements from their former homeland and from their new settlements.

Acknowledgments

I am grateful for the intellectual, financial, and administrative assistance of the faculty and staff of the Department of Communication and the Department of Ethnic Studies at the University of California, San Diego, as well as the Department of American Ethnic Studies at the University of Washington. My professors, colleagues, students, and friends in these departments have been most kind to me over the years. At the University of Washington, I was fortunate to obtain funding and research assistance from the Institute for Ethnic Studies in the United States, the Office of the Dean of Undergraduate Education, and the Office of the Divisional Dean of Social Sciences for the completion of this manuscript. My new colleagues at UW, especially those who are members and affiliates of my home department, the Department of American Ethnic Studies, have been most gracious to me and genuinely supportive of my work. I'd like to thank, in particular, Ana Mari Cauce, Johnnella Butler, John Walter, Tetsuden Kashima, Erasmo Gamboa, Steve Sumida, Michelle Habell-Pallan, Jaime Cardenas, Gail Nomura, Connie So, Seyed Muhammed Maulana, Sam Solberg, Fred and Dorothy Cordova, Patrick Rivers, Betty Salas, Pamela Ralston, Tani Barlow, Jerry Baldasty, and Betty Schmitz. The administrative staff and my students at UW also gave me support, inspiration, and much-needed strength to finish the book. I acknowledge in particular the research assistance provided by Penny Huang, James Dee Regalado, Third Andresen, and Arnel Guzman.

I owe my respondents my sincerest gratitude for allowing me to spend time with them, for welcoming me to their homes and to their gatherings, for inspiring me in the process of writing this work, and for giving me reason to finish it. They trusted me to write something about them, so I hope this book partly repays their generosity and faith.

For guiding me in conducting, writing, and bringing this work to fruition, I thank Vince Rafael, Lisa Lowe, and Yen Le Espiritu. Their patience, generous support, and unparalleled intellectual insights make them the model mentors I aspire to become. I have also benefited from stimulating conversations with Val Hartouni, Dan Schiller, Claudio Fenner-Lopez, Dee Dee Halleck, Herb Schiller, Michael Schudson, Leland Saito, Ross Frank, Paule Cruz Takash, Ramon Gutierrez, Rosemary George, and, most especially, George Lipsitz. For their encouragement during my initial years in graduate school, I thank R. C. Adams, Phillip Lane, and Rita Atwood. For their friendship and crucial contributions to my work, I acknowledge Mariole Alberto, Gary Colmenar (my principal informant) and his family, Eleanor Jaluague, Eric Martinez, Jessica Hagedorn, Roland Tolentino, Nerissa Balce-Cortes, Leny Strobel, Anatalio Ubalde, Tony Tiongson, Liberty Trajano, Nancy Magpusao, Dina Maramba, Linda Maram, Theo Gonzalves, Maria P. P. Root, Emily Lawsin, Daphne Barretto, Cecile Cruz, Roz Partido, Norila Md. Zahari, Riz Oades, and Eydie Detera. And at Temple University Press, I thank Janet Francendese, Michael Omi, and a reviewer chosen by the Press for their most valuable and unwavering support of this project.

I am extremely indebted to Oscar Campomanes for his steadfast nourishment and indefatigable spirit; to Virginia Escalante for her wit, generosity, and unselfish devotion as a study partner; and to Linda Trinh Vo for her remarkable comradeship and loving sustenance. I make special mention of Martin Manalansan, who first convinced me to go to graduate school and who remains a most valuable ally, a consummate supporter, and a true best friend.

Most especially, I am grateful to my family members, who have waited long for this project to end: to my late father, Eddie, and my mother, Miren, for their love, support, and faith in me; to Maritel Naguit, Bobby Bonus, Vida Anderson, Emma Cecilio, Joji Guzman, Veronica Cabrera, Cely Dizon, and their families, and particularly to Marie Nanette Bonus, for their compassion and understanding; to Lucy Tiongco, for her guidance and devotion. *Marami pong salamat sa inyong lahat.* Thank you very much to all of you.

Versions of some chapters in this book have appeared in earlier publications. My appreciation goes to the editors and publishers who granted me permission to reprint excerpts.

Chapter One appeared as "Cartographies of Filipino American Ethnicity," in *Filipino American Architecture, Design, and Planning Issues*, ed. Anatalio C. Ubalde (Berkeley: Flipside Press, 1996).

Chapter Three was originally published as "Marking and Marketing 'Difference': Filipino *Oriental* Stores in Southern California," *Positions: East Asia Cultures Critique* 5:2 (Fall 1997): 643–669.

Chapter Four is revised and reprinted from "Of *Palengke* and Beauty Pageants: Filipino American-Style Politics in Southern California," included in *Cultural Compass*, edited by Martin Manalansan, by permission of Temple University Press. © 2000 by Temple University Press. All Rights Reserved.

Chapter Five appeared as "Homeland Memories and Media: Filipino Images and Imaginations in America," in *Filipino Americans: Transformation and Identity*, ed. Maria P. P. Root (Thousand Oaks, Calif.: Sage Publications, 1997). Copyright © 1997 by Sage Publications. Reprinted by permission of Sage Publications, Inc.

I also wish to thank AT&T and Sprint for allowing me to reprint, in Chapter Five, excerpts from their advertisements.

Introduction
Marking Locations

Pilipino kayo? Taga-saan kayo sa 'tin? [Are you Filipino?
Where are you from in our homeland?]

t has been estimated that by the beginning of the twenty-
first century, Filipinos in the United States will number
over two million.[1] In Los Angeles County alone, 1990
census figures indicated approximately 220,000 Filipinos.
Close by, and rapidly growing, is the Filipino population
in San Diego County, estimated in 1990 at 96,000.
National census figures indicate that Filipinos comprise
the second largest Asian American group in the nation
(the largest is the Chinese), and the largest in California:
the Filipino population as of 1990 was 1.4 million, up 82
percent from the 1980 count.[2] Yet many are quick to
lament that Filipinos are largely invisible in most accounts
of U.S. history and in contemporary scholarship, excluded
from numerous positions of power, and misrepresented
(or not at all represented) in mainstream media, comprising a "silent minority" frequently lumped together with
Chinese, Japanese, Korean, Indian, Vietnamese, and Cam-
bodian peoples under the rubric Asian American.[3] This
kind of categorization may appear harmless or even well-
meaning, especially for policymakers who deal with urban

1

planning, employment opportunities, educational programs, and social welfare. But as a handful of scholars have suggested, this kind of bureaucratic classification has a tendency to conceal stereotypical or racist assumptions about ethnicity and identity that, taken together, have significant repercussions on how power relationships along multiethnic lines get played out.[4] By the same token, this pigeonholing of "ethnic" groups like Filipinos into certain unproblematic designations and unclarified orders ignores both the historical racialization of particular groups against (or compared to) others, and the current racialized experiences of immigrants as active agents in the shaping of their lives in the new nation, even amidst conditions far beyond their control.[5]

Using these criticisms as points of departure, I offer a study of how immigrants from the Philippines are historically racialized and how Filipinos in the United States construct their identities against the racism (along with exclusion and silencing) aimed at them. My purpose is to look at the spaces where the construction of identities, ethnicities, and nationalities takes place—where they are articulated, represented, contested, and denied both by Filipino and non-Filipino Americans. Using Southern California spaces as examples, I analyze the discourses and practices whereby notions of identity and community are mediated.

I cast my work on accounts of identity articulations as significant parts of community formations of Filipino Americanness. A valuable informant once told me: "*Maraming klaseng Pilipino dito ... mahirap intindihin. Pero kung bibigyan mo sila ng chance ... kung kakausapin mo sila nang mahusay, maiintindihan mo rin kung sinu-sino sila, at kung bakit sila ganoon.*" [There are many kinds of Filipinos here ... very hard to understand. But if you will give them a chance ... if you talk to them in a good way, you can then understand who they all are, and why they're like that.]

In this vein, I take seriously the analysis of how Filipinos in the United States construct their identities against historical and contemporary realities to help understand not only the qualifications for who gets to be called Filipino American and on what terms, but also the consequences of defining and negotiating Filipino Americanness on the larger questions of citizenship and national belonging. In other words, I attempt to unravel what it means to be Filipino and American at the same time. I propose that the particular practices of community and ethnic identity formation I uncover represent a need to respond to and resist invisibility, exploitation, silencing, and racial constructing, by history and by institutions, as well as a desire to claim a "space" within the rubric "American" on their own terms.

Fundamental to this study are the recent approaches to ethnicity and space that have stressed reconfiguring the terms and possibilities by which one can speak of community. Beginning with an observation about the rapid flow of migration from peripheries to metropoles, for example, Akhil Gupta and James Ferguson point to the awkwardness and inadequacy of defining nations like the United States as having one fixed and enclosed culture.[6] We must, as they suggest, start envisioning cultures as situated in interconnected spaces, not isomorphically inhabiting bordered places. This idea radically deploys Benedict Anderson's notion of "imagined communities" in which senses of belonging may be founded not on the basis of bounded geographical delineations but on multiple grids of cultural symbols and practices across many interrelated spaces.[7] In light of this thinking, it is necessary to speak of Filipinos as groups of people who not only inhabit the borderlands and the enclaves but also are connected to larger dominant communities within and outside the United States, as well as linked to global capitalist arrangements. And it is also necessary to legitimize particular Filipino cultures that are thought of as unimportant or even excluded from the purview of Americanness.

At the core of this argument is a set of assumptions about identity. What does it mean to have an identity? At a time of globalization due to modern communication and transportation technologies, along with the heightened flow of cultural commodities across nations linked by transnational capitalist arrangements, conventional notions of identity are being radically displaced. Current cultural analyses in various disciplines stress that we can no longer speak of identities as if they are unitary, static, and enclosed in a single space. Rather, identities must be viewed as ever changing, in process, and contingent upon fluid movements between locations. There then could be no

reference to *the* singular Filipino American identity, but articulations
of Filipino American *identities* in specific times and places.

Space as a construct therefore becomes important as a site where
configurations and reconfigurations of identities become possible or
denied. On one hand, space is an arena where contesting definitions,
articulations, and representations of identities are enacted. On the
other, space, or in this case, *re*territorialized space, becomes part of
identity articulation itself, as it brings about experiences of diversity,
displacement, homelessness, and chaos, while opening up possibilities of community and nationhood in unconventional modes.[8] This
is where space, in relation to identity, becomes politicized, as both
contestation and reterritorialization become intimately connected to
the power to define selves and gain access to resources.

I narrowed my focus to three sets of sites to clarify the connections among space, ethnicity, and identities: commercial establishments (particularly "Oriental" stores), social halls or community centers, and community newspapers. I show how each site functions not
merely as a theater where ethnic identities can be staged but as a
meaningful part of identity construction itself. The settings I deal
with are instances of a local and particular set of Filipino American
community formations. I do not intend to paint these sites as
bounded or self-contained. As I will show in the remainder of the
book, public constructions of Filipino American identities are negotiated in spaces that exceed their perceived boundaries.

I conducted the fieldwork for this project between October 1992
and January 1995, concentrating on Filipinos who live and work in
the counties and vicinities of San Diego and Los Angeles. Census data
reveal a sizable concentration of Filipinos in these areas. They do not
necessarily represent the bulk of Filipinos in the United States, but
their experiences and formations illustrate a specific articulation of
Filipino Americanness. I chose to interview and interact mostly with
first-generation Filipino immigrants, who at this time comprised a
significant bulk of the Filipino population in these places. Some were
chosen at random; some were referred to me by colleagues, informants, and acquaintances. I met and conversed with them in stores, editorial offices, and Filipino American community centers. I also spent

significant moments with them in social and political gatherings, in small group interactions over coffee, and in their homes. Most of these interactions were informal and loosely structured, usually conducted in Taglish (a combination of Tagalog and English), and at times one on one. They were recorded either by hand or with an audio tape recorder.

More than eighty individuals agreed to be interviewed in this study, some of them several times, within and beyond the three sites. A little over half of them are men, and close to three-quarters identified themselves as having middle-class backgrounds, while the rest said they were working class or poor. Of particular significance to this ethnography was how they characterized themselves: most said they were "ordinary Filipinos or Filipinas." I took this to mean that they were hesitant to be the spokesperson for their community because most of them did not hold a public office or any position that might encourage them to speak on behalf of the rest, except the newspaper publishers and association officers. I respected this stance, and I opted to pursue a greater number of respondents who were not public figures in their community. This also partly explains why I chose not to identify them by their real names. Yet the responses I gathered from my interviewees did not emanate from purely individual perspectives. As I demonstrate throughout the book, their replies came from positions evocative of both personal and collective experience.

My secondary focus was the fifteen people I interviewed who were second generation; the five who were from earlier generations or "waves," mostly former farm workers; and the twenty-two who were non-Filipino, mostly spouses of Filipinos. Most of my interactions with these groups were minimal, compared to the primary group, and I identify their responses in the study according to how they differ (by generation and by ethnicity or race) from the larger group.

In writing about the people I interviewed, I use the designations "Filipino" and "Filipino American" interchangeably, although the latter more frequently. My respondents only occasionally referred to themselves as "Filipino Americans." More often they used "Filipino" or "Filipina" to distinguish themselves from those (like their offspring) born in the United States.[9] My reason for stressing that they are "Filipino American" speaks to my contention that they are engaged in processes that have implications for being Filipino and American at the same time; almost all of them have settled in California, whether as formally naturalized citizens or as "permanent residents."[10] In addition, while not so often mentioned as a self-referent by individuals, "Filipino American" appears in the names of many sites I visited—commercial establishments, restaurants, newspapers, and video stores—and on organizational banners. I have retained these referents in their original form.

I preserve the exact words of those I interviewed in the retelling and analyses of their stories, whether in Tagalog, English, or both—most of my conversations with them were in Tagalog or Taglish. Tagalog is a language predominantly spoken in many parts of Luzon and Metropolitan Manila. In the communities I went to, it functions, as it does in the Philippines, as a lingua franca. Many consider Tagalog the national language of the Philippines, but Pilipino, a language mostly derived from Tagalog, is the official language. "Taglish" is the popular term for Tagalog and English (and, in some cases, also Spanish) combined. To retain its force and intricacy, I also preserved Taglish, when it was the language spoken. Although I translate the Tagalog and Taglish into English, I do not profess to have caught every thought and nuance, and I have asked some of my respondents and colleagues to verify my translations' proximate accuracy. Still, I bear the responsibility for any mistranslations.

I do not disclose the names of those I quote, honoring the request many made. Beyond protecting their privacy, I also wanted to be sensitive to damaging consequences that might result from the connection of a name with opinions and actions. To ensure their anonymity, I either use pseudonyms or refer to them by general description.

Among Filipino American communities of Southern California, and possibly in many other parts of the United States, it is common to ask a new acquaintance where in the Philippines they are originally from. Situating the other Filipino by some familiar spatial origin establishes a shared sense of history and positionality in chance encounters outside the homeland. This exchange operates not so much to determine where the rest of the conversation proceeds but to set the terrain upon which negotiations regarding Filipino Americanness can be articulated. These terrains of negotiation, the ways they are constituted and thought of—particularly in shaping an understanding of Filipino American identity formations—are the principal focus of this book.

On the surface, questions about geographic origin that start out as small talk among Filipino Americans meeting in some public space like the neighborhood "Oriental" store may appear innocent and inconsequential. After all, they are only passing queries that usually don't last very long and may be answered very briefly—a kind of ethnic curiosity satisfied and acknowledged, the exchange ending with a smile. I argue, however, that these questions and the answers they elicit point to principal indices by which notions about Filipino Americaness can be derived and explained. I consider these identity and community formations both as references to locations and as articulations from a particular set of positions. In so doing, I wish to advance the significance that location plays in charting the historical conditions and contemporary manifestations of constructing Filipino American identities.

My interest in locations, therefore, has much to do with understanding the intricacies and complexities of Filipino American identities over time and space. I say "identities" in the plural to reflect the heterogeneity of this population group, known to have immigrated to the United States beginning in the sixteenth century, along the galleon trade routes that ran from the shores of Manila, California, and Louisiana, and continuing to the present. The arrivals have ranged so widely in age, social status, race, and cultural attributes that one can describe Filipinos as a panethnic group. I believe that it is plausible and reasonable to account for patterns of their identity formations in the United States as not only resulting from these differences but also imposed—in varying degrees, intensities, and emphases—by forces both outside of their group (e.g., colonization, the global economy, the state bureaucracy, media, educational institutions) and within it (e.g., labor movements, ethnic organizations, socioeconomic arrangements, cultural practices). To locate Filipino American identities, then, one must specify these processes of ethnic identity construction as historical and multiconversant with global, national, and local exigencies.

The experience of immigration—of coming to and settling in the United States—affords a myriad of stories, many of which become anecdotes passed from one generation to the next. Some of these tales get written down in history books or expressed in other cultural forms, such as paintings, novels, and dramatic performances. But many have been forgotten, and many more, I presume, have gone untold. On numerous occasions when I was doing the ethnographic fieldwork for this study, I was besieged by respondents who wanted to tell me their stories "so that others will know and remember." There was a need, from their perspective and mine, to inscribe their thoughts via the written word amidst and against experiences of dislocation, marginalization, racialization, exploitation, and, most profoundly, invisibility, in their new country. "No one writes about us," said one of them. *"Dito, hindi tayo importante sa kanila."* [Here, we're not important to them.]

Opinions like this, expressed in different ways in conversations about being Filipino in America by a good number of those I talked to, frequently were voiced not lightheartedly but with great conviction. Over time, I detected the reason for this: to minimize my possibly interpreting such sentiments as those of "victims" in an "us versus them" society. On the contrary, what I heard revealed much about the complex relationships between individual and collective experiences, and the larger political, economic, and social structures that have shaped those experiences. I learned of the shaping force of state-instituted laws, global economies, and media representations, to name a few, that have turned Filipinos into racialized and gendered laborers and service workers to fuel the U.S. economy, but who are otherwise considered "dispensable" or "unimportant." In other words, their comments expose the contradictory placement of Filipino Americans as illegitimate citizens and also as necessary workers who deserve, but do not receive, dignity and equal access to the fruits of their labor.[11]

Many of these stories are also about reworking historical and contemporary realities as mediated through specific individual and group practices. Enacting nostalgic longing for the homeland in song and dance, for instance, helps alleviate the sense of displacement caused by relocation and the "search for a better life." Informal get-togethers among Filipinos—whether they be mah-jongg sessions, prayer meetings, or hometown reunions—are occasions they look forward to for a variety of reasons: to escape the pressures of work, to sustain close relationships with other Filipinos, or to simply take pleasure in "being with people who look and talk like I do," as one of my interviewees said. "No need to translate. No need to be extra careful because some other person might be offended. No need to pretend I'm this or that."

And, as racialization and invisibility have worked to marginalize or exploit Filipino Americans, they have also provided them with a protective coloration that allows them to contest those forces. It has frequently been lamented by many historians and other social commentators that Filipinos (in the United States, the Philippines, and elsewhere) are passive and uncritical, too willing to accept or even deny their realities, and too submissive for their own good. Even some of my respondents echo or agree with these sentiments. Yet, upon close examination of particular practices and during long conversations with interviewees, I witnessed and heard instances that—while not "armed insurrection" or "open rebellion"—question, criticize, ridicule, and, to a good degree, disobey and subvert authority in its various forms.[12] Individual and collective acts of noncompliance with accepted and legitimated norms of political activity, of refusing to be labeled in racist terms, and of nonconformity to standards of selling, trading, and exchanging goods and ideas are just a few examples of these Filipinos' resistance and contestation, whose power largely draws on their ability to go unnoticed by others.

One also hears stories of denial, conformity, greed, and dishonesty, which Filipinos themselves are quick to take notice of. I myself have seen such propensities in action during my fieldwork. But rather than dismiss them as products or effects of what has been called the "poverty of [Filipino] culture," I explain and understand their occurrences as, again, coming from particular "locations"—that is, the position of an individual or group in a particular condition in a given time and space, and against historical structural forces that have left their marks on that condition. In the field, I have found that the tales we weave often hide the positions, strategies, and implicit antagonisms that empower our intentions and acts in the first place. Silence is most often read as passivity, and acquiescence frequently takes the form of surface and uncritical acceptance. But I submit that there are ways of interpretation and analysis that can account for the complexities and nuances of language and practice—precisely the reason why an ethnography, I believe, was an appropriate form for this study.

I do not claim, however, that this ethnography has produced definitive assessments of a complete and impartial body of field accounts. Rather, it is an attempt to specify and analyze moments and "positions" in process, snapshots I deploy to theorize about the intersections of identity formations in their multiple valences with structural forces. In the process, I am aware of the power I have in speaking and writing for others, and I have tried to write with sensitivity and respect for those I seek to represent. Writing an account of my fieldwork, then, has entailed negotiating between overestimating the meaning of others' words and actions and overlooking their import.

I also admit my presence and implication in the ethnography and its interpretation. Many of my interviewees were quite vocal and demonstrative about their willingness to be spoken to at length primarily because they regarded me as a Filipino and an immigrant just like them, because I had a good facility with Tagalog and Taglish, and because I was familiar with or even an active practitioner of their cultures. These forms of cultural membership did open many doors (in the literal and figurative senses) that would have been closed to others. There were also many occasions when my presence in these Filipino communities caused a good degree of tension, especially when I was perceived as not being "Filipino enough" to understand them because I did not speak any of the other Philippine languages and dialects, because I failed at times to speak "the right way" (e.g., differences in pronunciation, choice of words, usage of expressions), and because I came from a more privileged background (e.g., being from Manila, being a graduate student from a research university, being male). I consider these tensions evidence of the different positionalities and uneven power locations that mark this and other ethnographies. I have attempted to integrate many of the tensions in my telling of the tales from the field, while guarding against turning the narratives into overly self-conscious confessionals.[13] I came to the "sites" from specific locations familiar and simultaneously strange to my respondents; they came from locations similar to and distinct from mine. My work speaks to how the tensions of these multiple locations influence each other.

Perhaps the greatest challenge for me was finding points within these tensions at which I could retain a scholar's critical eye while remaining sensitive to the interests and positions of my respondents. More than anything else, this study hinges on these selected points of conversation, included in many of my narratives. And as with any selection, the result can be only partial and incomplete.

This book consists of six chapters. Chapter 1, "Cartographies of Ethnicity," provides the framework for understanding how theories of "location" map historical and contemporary understandings of the notion of ethnicity—particularly in the United States, and with specific reference to Filipino Americans and other groups. It frames and provides the language for specifying ideas and practices of ethnic group formation from selected scholars in the social sciences, ethnic studies, and communication and cultural studies. This chapter also addresses the relationships between ethnicity and racialization, the debates surrounding assimilation and acculturation, and the contestation of dominant social and political constructions of ethnicity and the nation.

Chapter 2, "Filipinos and Filipinas in America" provides the historical and contemporary contexts for the ethnographic work. It charts the history of Filipino American immigration across several themes by connecting the particulars of this immigration to U.S.-Philippine relations from the end of the 1800s, as well as to labor recruitment, racialization, ethnic group formation, and the cultural politics of space in Southern California.

Chapter 3, "Marking and Marketing Identities in Filipino 'Oriental' Stores," probes the kinds of identity articulation and "marketing" of Filipino American identities that are apparent within and around these stores. At these sites, distinctions among the cultural, the political, and the commercial tend to be blurred, and their interrelationships provide the ground on which Filipino Americanness is constantly and creatively recreated. This chapter shows how such stores serve as spaces for negotiating received and dominant identities, and for reconfiguring notions of diversity and commonality along ethnic lines and against practices of consumption.

In Chapter 4, "*Palengke* Politics and Beauty Pageants in Filipino Community Centers," I move on to the spaces that community organizations and community organizing occupy. This chapter locates these spaces in the histories of communitywide organizations of Filipinos in the United States, formed along axes of nationality, labor union activity, social function, gender, age, charity work, province, hometown, school affiliation, political alignments, profession, and trade. It counterbalances these histories with contemporary experience in the home country and in the new enclaves in community centers in Southern California, with specific reference to sociopolitical arrangements (described by many informants as *palengke* style, meaning, conducted like an idiosyncratic Filipino marketplace where anything goes) and charity-driven beauty pageants. The chapter shows that these activities point to particular sites of constant negotiations of Filipino Americanness among the immigrants themselves and in conversation with the larger society.

Chapter 5, "Homeland Memories and Media: Filipino Images and Imaginations in America," indicates that processes of identity and community formation may be located and constituted through media channels. With a focus on community newspapers, narratives of displacement and connectedness relative to Filipino American experiences are explored in the contexts of immigration, U.S.-Philippine relations, cultural commodification, and identity politics. The chapter explains the political-economic structures that affect the visibility of Filipino Americans, the materials that make possible activities of ethnic presentations and re-presentations, and the creative production, reception, and meaning making of cultural symbols by these respondents. It also discusses the implications of the persistence of particular memories of the homeland.

The final chapter, "Conclusion: Re-Marking Locations," emphasizes the contingency of identity articulations of ethnic groups and the contemporaneity of ethnographic projects such as this in mapping the sites and activities of immigrant communities. With specific reference to contemporary Filipino Americans, the chapter recapitulates and underscores the processual nature of claiming spaces, the shifting boundaries of community formation, and the constant negotiation between structural forces and active agents. It reviews the implications of the project for understanding issues of ethnicity, immigration, homeland ties, assimilation, anti-assimilation, alliances with other groups of color, and national belonging.

On the whole, "locating" Filipino Americans for this project is predicated on the term itself: who is Filipino American? Given current recastings of identity and space in the literature, I feel it necessary, on one hand, to consider the diversities and divisions among these people. They vary by sex, age, generation, occupation, status, citizenship, ethnicity, and class. They come from diverse backgrounds, have differing political loyalties and affiliations, live in different locations. On the other hand, they find things in common. They share the same homeland or are descended from people who hail from it. On several occasions, they have mobilized (sometimes alongside other Asian Americans and other groups) against common enemies, such as antiunion employers and policymakers engaged in discriminatory educational and social welfare practices.[14] Most of these Filipinos who live in the United States (and I use this description provisionally) shop at the same stores, see each other in community centers, and avail themselves of the media products that speak of, with, and about them.

Locating Filipino Americans suggests uncovering instances and localities that for others remain concealed or unimportant. Transitory and impermanent as these identity articulations seem to be, they are snapshots of the kinds of possibilities that could be deployed for political ends. In these instances, community—the result of both dissent and contestation due to diversity as well as a sense of belonging to a group or cause—attains prominence, with ramifications for political, economic, and social life. These kinds of processes, indeed, make possible the establishment of communities and commonalities among diverse and scattered groups, as they reconstitute the very terms, conditions, and practices necessary for community building.

1

Cartographies of Ethnicity

Etnik ba talaga tayo? Aba, 'di ba ang mga etnik e 'yung mga Igorot at Mangyan? Hindi naman ako Igorot, a. [Are we really ethnic? Well, isn't it that ethnics are the ones who are Igorot and Mangyan? Well, see, I'm not Igorot.]
—Filipino American interviewee

Pilipino tayo kasi galing tayo sa Pilipinas. At saka ngayon, Amerikano na rin tayo kasi nandito tayo ngayon sa Amerika. . . . Pilipinong Amerikano. O, 'di ba? [We are Filipino because we came from the Philippines. And now, we are also Americans because we are now here in America. Filipinos who are Americans. Well, isn't it true?] It's a problem for others, but it's something I'm proud of.
—Filipino American interviewee

n my fieldwork, my use of the words "ethnic," "ethnicity," and "ethnic group" was usually received with apprehension or, at the least, misunderstanding, as the first quote in the epigraph suggests. For this person, "ethnic" implied "premodern" or "aboriginal." And even though I was not drawing on a similar construct, it was clear that these were markers she opted to keep her distance from. Etymologies of the term "ethnicity" reveal origins and descriptions associated with Greek, Latin, and French, as well as English, usage (*eth-nikos, ethnos, natio,* respectively).[1] Depending on the language diction-ary one consults, its meaning ranges from "people who are heathen" or "pagan" to people who are "members of a religious group" or "parts of a nation." And ethnicity varies not only across linguistic contexts but within local and national communities with geographical borders.

By looking at ethnicity as it relates to the concepts of identity, loca-tion, and nationhood, I here lay the cartographic groundwork for an analysis of ethnic identity formations and constructions among Filipino Americans. I use this three-part framework to establish a conceptual logic that flows from the relationship between ethnicity and identity as historically specific, contextual, and multilayered; to considering the centrality of "location" as both a space and a consti-tutive part of ethnicity; and eventually to conceiving of Filipino American identity formation as a set of claims about ethnicity and nationhood.

Ethnicity and Identity

The connection between ethnicity and identity is not inherent, though it may appear to be. One's ethnicity, however defined, does not unproblematically and automatically refer to one's sense of iden-tity. And one's identity is not only and always defined by one's eth-nicity. In this book, I stress the notion that the relationships between identity and ethnicity are so completely the products of historical and contemporary interactions that the definitions of the terms and their links with each other are always shifting.

The multiple perspectives on ethnicity from the disciplines of sociology, history, and anthropology reflect such shifts, when one examines the nature and causes of ethnic group formation. What is ethnicity? What is it that makes people identify themselves as an ethnic collective? When and how does this happen? The answers to these questions have been generally formulated between two oppos-ing poles, the primordialist and the instrumentalist views.[2] Primor-dialists emphasize that people naturally group themselves together out of a sense of primordial attachment, mostly in the form of original ancestry, culture, and homeland. These bonds are created and maintained through "an array of potent symbols" such as name, language, and religion that, in turn, generate affective sentiments among individuals, holding them together by virtue and through acts of unquestioned belonging.[3] Instrumentalists maintain that having an "identity" in terms of belonging to a group arises from the "circumstantial manipulation of identities" by individuals gathering as one to suit their collective interests.[4] They forge commonality under a unifying ethnic category to promote and protect these shared goals.

From the instrumentalist perspective, when changes in people's social environment disrupt their traditional lives (such as contact with other groups, perceived inequalities arising out of relationships with other people, or movement to another place where other people have already settled), they build coalitions based on identifying and fighting for shared interests. In the process, they struggle to create and sustain common bonds from forged collective affinities, perceiving these struggles as rationally determined.[5] The primordialist stress, however, is on the essential permanence of the commonalities that united the group in the first place. Primordialists explain the nature of ethnicity as a value (or a sentiment, as opposed to an "objective" of the instrumentalists) that has always been held by the people in a group.[6]

Although they differ with regard to explanatory focus, scholars from both perspectives basically concur that ethnicity involves actions predicated on senses of likeness and difference.[7] One may be predisposed to belong to a particular group because of shared features with its other members. Or, based on perceived differences from other groups, one realizes a bond that acts as a glue and sets one's group apart from the rest. Ethnicity, therefore, involves a binary relationship. "Likeness" can be understood or realized only through an understanding and realization of difference. "Difference" carries meaning only as a corollary of likeness. What sets the instrumentalists apart from the primordialists is their contrasting view of the cause or causes of these perceptions of similarity and difference.

To a limited extent, both perspectives also acknowledge that, while attributions of belonging are the same in all ethnic groups, the degree of such attributions may vary *within* each ethnic group, that is, the magnitude and scope of attachments are not always uniform or stable across, for instance, age, sex, and social status differences.[8] In her study of Filipino Americans in San Diego, sociologist Yen Le Espiritu says that for immigrant Filipinos, "ethnicity is deeply subjective, concrete, and cultural . . . [while] for the second generation, it is largely cognitive, intermittent, and political, forged out of their confrontation with and struggle against dominant culture."[9] Generational distinctiveness, in this case, is a function not only of differences in age and life histories, but more importantly, of the sharp contrasts in each generation's allegiance to and immersion in particular cultures. Thus, we have parents who were born and raised in the Philippines immigrating to the United States and professing a Filipino ethnic identity "reinforced on a daily basis"; and we have children who were born and raised in the United States and whose ethnic behavior is "largely symbolic, characterized by a nostalgic but unacquainted allegiance to an imagined past," but nevertheless creating new constructions of both Filipinoness and Americanness.[10]

These findings suggest that the ethnic identification of social actors in a group changes over time. Individuals in the group may profess affinity to an ethnic sensibility along a continuum from "none" (or distanced) to "full" at any given time. This is one of the reasons that one's identity is not always the product of one's conception of ethnicity, and one's ethnicity (say, as defined by a state bureaucracy, regardless of one's affiliation with it in practice) is not always a component of one's identity.

How then do we account for ethnic group construction? What particular forms does it take when people identify as a collective? What do we take into account in these processes of ethnic construction? One source of answers may lie in the notion of "identity" itself, which recent scholars have called "subject position" (see Chapter 6).

We can locate a great deal of scholarship in the social sciences, from both the primordialist and the instrumentalist perspectives, in which much of the focus is on enumerations of various ethnic groups to account for similarities in the ways they pursue collective action.[11] To many of these scholars, identification with an ethnic category meant either an innate and automatic disposition for membership or a linear progression of association that had finite, recognizable, and permanent ends.

With the latter half of the twentieth century, however, came increased global interconnection across national boundaries. Several scholars have theorized this period as a moment (or a set of moments) in which capitalism reaches its full force and extent, so that the world looks and feels tinier, the distances between places much shorter, and the experience of time more compressed and instantaneous.[12] This period wreaks havoc on former ideas about identity because, as some would say, the frameworks that used to hold our concepts of self and community together are being fragmented and destabilized by transnational networks of production and distribution, instantaneous and mass communication, and more emigration and immigration. One code word for such forces and conditions is "globalization," and it has had far-reaching consequences in the ways people conduct their lives. Stuart Hall identifies at least three strands regarding the *nature* of these globalizing effects with regard to thinking about emerging forms of cultural identity in the "postmodern" individual:

1. National identities are being *eroded*. . . .
2. National and other "local" or particularistic identities are being *strengthened* by the resistance to globalization.
3. National identities are declining but *new* identities of hybridity are taking their place.[13]

In light of the transformations occurring on a global scale, the constitution of an "identity" becomes more complex than thinking of an individual as one moored permanently in a closed community (as in a nation), one defined by a stable and coherent self, and one with a fixed and singular identity.[14]

Ethnicity, in this transfiguration, then becomes only one among an array of multiple, competing, and even fleeting identities available (by force, consequence, or choice) to each of us. Along with our ethnic identity, we are also configured (by others and ourselves)—by class, gender, sex, race, and nationality—into a variety of subjects through our positioning in the political economy, in state operations, in public and private discourse, and in media representations. This has triggered studies of identity that take into account the histories, structural forces, local contexts, public displays, everyday practices, and complex sociopolitical processes that impinge on individual and collective lives.[15] Recently, studies of ethnicity have appropriated the lenses of historical dialectical materialism, psychoanalysis, semiotics, regimes of knowledge/truth, and feminist thinking, using tools that borrow from several disciplines at the same time in order to account for ethnic group identification as "multisituated"—traversing, in postmodern sensibilities, contingent, incomplete, open-ended, and unstable subject positions.[16] It is this academic conversation I enter in my study of Filipino American ethnic identities. Moving beyond the strict demarcations and parameters of the primordialist-instrumentalist perspectives, I propose a more complex, nuanced, and dynamic narration of ethnic identity formation.

Ethnicity and Location

The *Harvard Encyclopedia of American Ethnic Groups* notes that, while there is no consensus about the precise meaning of ethnicity, all groups that it included in its study were considered "ethnic" according to some or a combination of the following attributes:

1. Common geographic origin
2. Migratory status
3. Race
4. Language or dialect
5. Religious faith or faiths
6. Ties that transcend kinship, neighborhood, and community boundaries
7. Shared traditions, values, and symbols
8. Literature, folklore, and music
9. Food preferences
10. Settlement and employment patterns
11. Special interests in regard to politics in the homeland and in the United States

12. Institutions that specifically serve and maintain the group
13. An internal sense of distinctiveness
14. An external perception of distinctiveness.[17]

The encyclopedia's intent is, no doubt, to be inclusive, but although it expresses sensitivity to debates over equating "ethnic" and "foreign" (among others), it has no entry for those who describe themselves as "plain" Americans: "There is no entry for '[plain] nonethnic' American, even though their number is undoubtedly large." So, "when a respondent answers 'American' to the question of ancestry, that response is not recorded."[18] To a great extent, this elision of the general category "American" reflects one of the consequences as well as the trajectories of ethnic relations in the United States. For the encyclopedia's editors, being a "white" American, as the classification "plain" may strongly denote, cannot hold categorical weight within the rubric "ethnic." "Whiteness" may indeed be argued to be a racial category, but if "race" is considered by the editors as one feature of ethnicity, why is "white" absent from the book and why are "Asian American," "African American," and "Hispanic" present?

In the United States, race relations are intimately and problematically linked to the process of ethnic group identification, along with their multivalent relationships to issues and positions on the basis of class, gender, and sexual orientation. I draw on these interrelationships to specify how the concepts of ethnicity in my study mark their presences and varied registers. One important way of examining the articulations of these registers in the ethnic group I am studying is through its "locations"—the intersections of the group members' various subject positions that give them a sense of who they are as Filipino Americans.

A recent tendency among scholars is to dismiss "ethnicity" entirely because of its shortcomings as an exclusionary object of analysis and its apparent failure to recognize the interplay of other categorical markers of identity. I take a different perspective. My qualified choice has been to retain this set of markers of identity mainly because it opens up vast and intricate avenues of subjectivity that come into play in individual and group experience. Ethnicity, in this vein, cannot and does not stand outside identifications by race, class, and gender. I therefore seize multiple perspectives on ethnicity—its various tenors and registers in contemporary lives—viewing it as a contingent, unstable, and open-ended site of convergence between individual and society, structure and agency, theory and practice, and accommulation and resistance.

This has primarily meant considering members of ethnic groups as people who are historically positioned and, thus, *located*, by state and society as particular subjects (whether by race, class, gender, or nationality) and also as people who position themselves in various locations and contexts. (I use "locate" in the sense of determining or specifying a position of one thing on another.) Such a perspective also coincides with and renders significant the historical and more recent conditions of immigration and globalization that affect complex and international placements of ethnic identities. From the perspective of Filipino American ethnic identity, for example, I explore where we might locate the various determinants of their identities.

My emphasis on location as a way of studying ethnicity is heavily influenced by the scholarship on *space*. "Oriental" stores, for example, from the outside are racialized spaces, imagined by others as places where one buys Asian goods and sees Asian people shop. But to Filipino Americans, as I show in Chapter 3, these "Oriental" stores are not "Orientalizing" in any derogatory way (for example, depictions of Asians as dirty, exotic, and wily). Along with other spaces, such as the barber shops, beauty salons, and video stores adjacent to these stores, they are spaces where Filipino Americans reconstitute their identities as productive and multilayered, and in active conversation with those who otherwise render them as Orientals. In consequence, they reconfigure the spaces of the "Oriental" stores as such stores become part of their sense of who they are.

Principally, then, "locating" Filipino Americans for this project rests on asking who is Filipino American, and answering this question by sifting through an array of instances and practices of group belonging on a local level.[19] I mean "local" here to include public sites in Los Angeles and San Diego Counties where Filipinos meet each other every day. These are not sites detached from the macrostructures and institutions of society. Rather, they are part of the multiple grids of power relations in local, national, and global contexts—"the place where local struggles and alternative discourses on the meanings of global [and national] conditions are played out."[20] I mean "power relations" to include the range of contestations and negotiations in political, economic, and social situations where multiple and competing ideas and practices of ethnicity and nationhood are articulated. And I mean "practices" to refer to the array of mediated cultural and communicative acts in their specific contexts.

Ethnicity and Nation

Ethnic nationalism is most often associated with the secession of an ethnic group from a nation that results in the creation of a separate independent nation detached from or even within the original nation.[21] One of the initial consequences of this independence, which also assists in sustaining it, is the disappearance of the designation "ethnic" in favor of "nation." I mention ethnic nationalism (and examine it in greater detail in Chapter 6) mainly to make clear my work's distance from it.

Filipinos and Filipinas I interviewed (and on occasion, lived with) had this habit of reminding me, during moments of misunderstanding and debates about what makes them who they are, that I too am Filipino, and that I should always remember that. This seemed to me more than anything else a reminder of how connected our lives are; even though they were the interviewees and I the observer and interviewer, we all come from one homeland and, implicitly, are descended from one ancestry. On one level, this is primordialism in word and in practice. After all the scholarly debates on and realities of ethnic construction and transformation in national and global contexts, I was face to face with a resurgence of primordialist claims, which were supposedly on the wane. Yet such ethnic persistence as a primary anchor of identity is not unique to the Filipino Americans I interviewed. First-generation immigrants in general have been observed to hang on to their homeland's culture in their new settlements for one of two purposes: either to establish a distinguishing ethos, or to mitigate the anxieties they feel in a strange land among unfamiliar and different people.

Such cultural transplanting need not be feared by the dominant culture. (In fact, as many have pointed out, it should be celebrated.)[22] Ethnic attachments will soon diminish through acculturation, which is only one of the early steps on the road to complete assimilation. If ever there is ethnic revivalism—say, among members of the third generation—it only symbolizes an affinity, an appropriation of a once "pure" or "genuine" culture transformed and even influenced by dominant external forces.[23] In the United States, however, there is a volatile view that says ethnic persistence must be contained. Though not altogether new in the late twentieth century, the rhetoric on this front usually coalesces around the issue of the American "nation"— its past, present, and future.[24]

In the United States, owing to its multiethnic history, ethnicization commands particular forms of resistance, from calls to restrict immigration and get rid of affirmative action programs to the dismissal of any institutionalization of multiethnic curricula.[25] Arthur Schlesinger's critique of ethnicity, for example, rests on an accusation that ethnicization leads to the "tribalization" of America.[26] In significant ways, his critique echoes the dominant assessment of ethnic resurgence elsewhere—mostly labeled "ethnic cleansing"—as something to be condemned because it resurrects the marker "tribe" and vies for power.[27] To these critics, "tribe" is a premodern category, an example of "atavistic forces which civilization, in the form of the centralized state, has struggled to expunge or contain."[28]

But what drives the advocates of ethnicization to battle those who insist on unification without question? Perhaps this is the occasion to consider the impetus behind forms of qualified ethnic resurgence among Filipino Americans and other nonwhite groups. Principally, we must not forget that the drive to assimilate into mainstream America remains the dominant force in most immigrants' lives. In many U.S. textbooks, workplaces, and social settings, there is evidence that history is still written from the point of view of the dominant white culture, that American English is the most desirable language to converse in, and that social protocols have to be adjusted in favor of the majority.

One can argue that indeed, such has been the case, and that this is good for everyone because "we are able to communicate effectively with each other."[29] Most Filipino Americans I talked to realize this as well. Theirs is a history of immigration that puts them several steps ahead of their counterparts in the journey to assimilation, mainly because the Philippines was once a U.S. colony. As E. San Juan Jr. puts it, "Long before the Filipino immigrant, tourist or visitor sets foot on the U.S. continent, she—her body and sensibility—has been prepared by the thoroughly Americanized culture of the homeland."[30]

Further assimilation has shaped the lives of many Filipinos in the new country. As one of my informants said: "You only need to make a few minor adjustments—make your English pronunciation more slangy and be more familiar with pop culture. And don't forget, you need to know how those appliances work, and [have]lots of credit cards to buy them [with]!" Social and economic mobility are seen as hallmarks of a "true" American. The end result is, presumably, integration into mainstream society, acceptance as one among the rest, and the legal conferring of the identity "citizen" in the form of a U.S. passport.

Yet many realize that the road to assimilation is not easy, however carefully it may be paved with good intentions. "I have been here for twenty-seven years," said one of my respondents, "and I have a U.S. passport. But still, every now and then, someone would ask me when I am going back. Going back where? This is my home already. Probably, many think I'm still a foreigner." She also told me that *"siguro, dahil may accent pa ako . . . ano sa tingin mo?"* [maybe, it is because I still have an accent . . . what do you think?] I replied that maybe it is not her fault, that maybe she has done her best to adjust to others and it is impossible to control what others might do in return. I remarked to her that this is probably the reason she is so involved in local Filipino American organizations. And her retort to me was, "Of course, *sino pa ba naman ang tatanggap sa atin kundi tayo-tayo lang?"* [who else would accept us other than ourselves?]

Filipino and Filipina immigrants enter the United States as national subjects with Philippine passports. Yet while their incorporation into society emanates from the ideology of, as Schlesinger reminds us, "out of many, one," this incorporation, for people of color, is never a completed or stable project. And we know from the histories of Native American resistance and the Civil Rights movement, for instance, that the ideology itself is prone to contestation.[31] Because the United States as a nation is more or less built on the *submergence of inequalities*, in theory and in practice, it constantly attempts to insulate itself from any *emergence* of inequalities by absorbing them, "ultimately providing some sort of idealistic 'resolution.'"[32] The management of nationalism, then—the attempt to turn immigrant subjects into homogeneous citizens—is always prone to error and disruption, for the realities of inequality and discrimination persist in manifesting themselves.[33]

For many Filipino Americans, these contradictions are too painful to accept. We know this from the literary works they have produced, and my informants surely attest to their consequences on their lives.[34] On a regular basis, markers of difference that should have been sublimated in the process of integration erupt unexpectedly: foreign ("Where did you learn how to speak "), ethnic ("You look exotic"), racial ("Oh, I thought you were black [or Chinese, or Hispanic]"), class ("Aren't you all rich?"), and gender ("Are you a maid too?").[35] In the experience of those I spoke to, being stereotyped not only has been insulting and demeaning but has negatively impacted their political, social, and economic lives. As I have mentioned, the most recent census figures indicate that Filipinos comprise the second largest Asian American group in the nation (after Chinese), and the largest in California. Yet many lament that Filipinos are often lumped together with others as "Asian American." As many of my respondents have suggested, this kind of categorizing often perpetuates stereotypic or racist assumptions about large groups by defining all their members as similar to one another in terms of, say, history, status, and political power.

Filipino Americans whom I have encountered in the United States, therefore, *trouble* the dominant social and political constructions of both ethnicity and nation.[36] They object to determinants of themselves as "ethnic" from at least two vantage points. To a respondent quoted in the epigraph to this chapter, "ethnic" refers to someone primitive or someone who is a member of an indigenous "tribe" from the Philippines, which she said she was not. To me, her assertions were a reminder of tensions of nationhood and nationalism in the Philippines that parallel those in the United States. The Philippines too is a multiethnic and multiracial nation, so the designation "Filipino people" is as problematic as the designation "American people." The Philippine nation too is a product of homogenization that has privileged certain dominant ethnoracial groups and marginalized others.[37] Hence, the Philippines has ethnic minority groups who are indigenous yet not seen as equal to the rest. We see the resulting tensions in, for example, debates over an official national language (one preferred to Tagalog and resistant to other ethnolinguistic groups such as Cebuano and Ilokano); over holding onto southern parts of the country (where there is a strong movement by Filipino Muslims and their allies to secede); and over land ownership (between the state and private firms on one side, and minority groups asserting tribal control of natural resources on the other).[38] Philippine ethnicity and nationalism resurface in the United States in peculiar ways, as we will see in later chapters.

The *troubling* effects of ethnicity have their U.S. context as well. As I have mentioned, there is a strong tendency for state bureaucracies (census takers, for example) to classify these groups of people as *ethnically* Filipino. This is not to say that such a classification is inherently wrong. Grouping people by nationality allows us to measure the breadth and depth of, say, a social welfare program's impact or an educational needs assessment's target with regard to population groups. But these classificatory schemes also have a tendency to label these groups homogeneous—missing, as a consequence, the variety of classes, races, and other differentiating markers. For instance, post-1965 Filipino immigrants have been labeled predominantly middle to upper middle class and therefore not in need of many social programs that could have assisted the poorer sectors of the group. We may also detect anxiety among Filipino activists and scholars about the categorizing of ethnic Filipino Americans as part of racial groups (Asian or, mistakenly, Hispanic, because of Spanish surnames). Such anxieties have manifested themselves historically in Asian American panethnic mobilization movements.[39]

The deeper consequence of ethnic marking for my respondents is that, while they may be referred to as Filipino Americans in the ethnonational sense, the reference is simultaneously race and gender biased. Hence, they see the Filipino American as usually perceived as someone "of color" and male. Here we sense the differences in tenor and impact of the designation of someone as, say, an Irish American or a Filipino American, and as a Filipino American or a Filipina American.

The national *trouble* is a powerful questioning of who can be counted as American, who belongs to the nation, and on what these kinds of belonging should be based. Here we need to pay attention to the difference that underlies being called Filipino *American* as opposed to merely Filipino; the reaction usually expressed by my informants to being called Filipino is "*Amerikano rin ako.*" [I am American too.] It is clear to me that their desire is not to separate from or create another nation within their new nation. Far from it. They want to be included as Americans and entitled to the same rights and privileges as the rest. Schlesinger and his allies will have no quarrel with them in this regard. But what such theorists may oppose is that Filipino Americans who want to be included also want a *different* kind of inclusion, on terms other than full assimilation. They want to be assimilated and integrated, but in ways that will not erase their identities as Filipinos. They want to be included, but in ways in which their representation will also amount to a recognition of them as citizens entitled to an equal share of power. As their identities are transformed in the new place of settlement, they want to transform the ways in which the nation incorporates them. This is the most crucial ground for ethnic identity formation and articulation among Filipino Americans in Southern California. My work is predicated on it, and from it I draw emblems and embodiments of a cultural politics of space.

Documenting these complex issues demands not only precise attribution to identifiable sources but strong, consistent, and verifiable evidence of "real contestation" or "resistance" to "the nation."[40] It is tempting, therefore, simply to let the fieldwork narratives speak for themselves. Yet it is up to me to define the lines of investigation, or themes, of my work. First, I consider the delineations and practices of power from "above," in institutional, structural, historical, ideological, and cultural forms, and, more importantly, from "below," in local social arrangements, economic niches, community media channels, and everyday life. With such a wide perspective, I have learned to be much more sensitive to, for instance, the consequences of systemic racism in the daily lives of both my respondents and myself. But more significantly, I have paid closer attention to the everyday responses of those affected by conditions beyond their complete control. Some activities became significant only in hindsight. One of the angles I only later thought about was that perhaps their seeming insignificance is precisely the measure of their power to elude detection by those who might prevent the activities from occurring. After back-and-forth conversations that often consumed several hours spanning many weeks, a good number of my respondents wondered why it took me so long to figure them out. After all, they said, I was as Filipino as they are.

Beyond a conscious intent to examine power from "below" in a more alert and sensitive fashion, a second line of investigation explores how one might recognize power and therefore be able to name it. This issue has made me think constantly about the warnings ethnographers like myself hear from teachers and colleagues before, during, and after their fieldwork: "Don't stay too close, you might see too much of what's there." Or, its corollary: "Don't stay too far away, you might see too little."

In the "sites" I studied—the "Oriental" stores, the social halls, the community newspapers—I have not witnessed any sustained, open, violent, and direct confrontation with "the nation," usually envisioned as a revolt of the masses with fists raised or with guns pointed at state police. My respondents' activities and practices were much more nuanced and, at times, subtle. For instance, conversations were usually held in Tagalog or Taglish, never entirely in English (except with the second-generation respondents), because, as one said with a snicker, *"Baka may makarinig, heh heh."* [Someone might hear, heh heh.] Often, joking in the forms of word play, satire, and innuendo interfered with or delayed my understanding of the intentions behind it. I detail these and other alternative practices in the ethnography as patterns of interaction or negotiation among Filipinos and with non-Filipinos—the ones whom they perceive to occupy the worlds they also inhabit. Such interactions are the ones I recognize as occurring in different sites of power.

Third and last, my emphasis on these sites of power does not necessarily mean that the Filipinas and Filipinos I write about have become more *powerful* simply because they now have the spaces that previously were denied to them, in the literal and figurative senses. While we must acknowledge and appreciate their efforts in conditions that are not always in their favor, we also must recognize that there is as yet no Filipino American representation commensurate with their numbers in, for example, formal politics in California. One respondent pointed out: "We don't have Filipino producers in Hollywood. No major star to be proud of." And another: "I cannot name a powerful Filipino here." Upon hearing these kinds of comments, my usual impulse at first was to change the topic. Yet often, these people were the very ones who were able to slip from dejection into something more optimistic: "But we're here, anyway, right? We have to do what we can." If one measure of an individual's or group's power is the ability to persist, insist, and trouble another even in the face of probable defeat, then I think it is worth writing about.

2

Filipinos and Filipinas in America

Positively No Filipinos Allowed.
—Sign posted on the door of a hotel in Stockton, California, circa 1930

Filipinos can be found anywhere here. Usually, where there's a military base, you'll find them. Doctors, nurses, engineers. . . we're in California, Washington, Texas, New York . . . mostly everywhere.
—Filipino American interviewee from Los Angeles

he epigraphs—a notice of exclusion from a period of intense nativism in the United States[1] and a comment excerpted from interviews of Filipino immigrants I conducted between 1992 and 1994—frame the ways in which my analysis of historical and contemporary Filipino American identities are implicated within notions of race, ethnicity, and the cultural politics of space in Southern California. And further, how they have been shaped by colonial history, labor immigration, racialization, antiracist struggle, and community settlement patterns in the United States.[2]

31

A History of Colonization

A historical account of Filipino immigration to the United States must take into consideration the Philippine colonial experience and its repercussions on the treatment, movement, and resettlement of its people in particular patterns.[3] This view goes beyond the typical depiction of Filipino immigration as one that is simplistically propelled by the search for the land of milk and honey. In particular ways, the movement of Filipinos both within and away from the archipelago has been encouraged to ensure that the Philippines provides labor for colonial empires.

As colonial subjects of Spain from 1521 until 1898, for example, Filipino shipbuilders and seamen were employed under harsh conditions by the Spanish galleon trade that ferried goods to and from Manila and the New World. Many attempted to escape poverty and harsh treatment by jumping ship when the galleons reached Acapulco, California, and other New World ports, including the French territory of Louisiana. There are scant records as to what happened to them during their resettlement in these places.[4] However, evidence establishes the presence of the descendants of "Manila men" who settled near New Orleans and built their communities there as early as 1763.[5]

During the U.S. war with Spain, Americans, initially assisted by Filipinos, annihilated Spanish military forces, which eventually resulted in Spain's ceding the Philippines to the United States for $20 million in 1898.[6] Immigration to and settlement in America was then encouraged. The possession of the Philippines was crucial to U.S. territorial expansion overseas at the turn of the century. Along with Cuba, Puerto Rico, and Hawaii, the islands provided rich resources for U.S. economic growth and extended the country's political reach as a newly formed empire.[7]

Foremost on the U.S. occupation agenda were the pacification of the rebellious populace through military force, the establishment of a civil government to administer the colony, and the institutionalization of a mandatory public educational system. The justification for such a three-fold project was vigorously articulated, despite opposition from the anti-imperialist voices in the legislative bodies of the United States and from some members of the U.S. public.[8] When U.S. military forces engaged in combat with the local Filipino insurrectionists, they viewed them as "savages no better than [their] Indians" and their engagement with them as simply "another Indian war."[9] In many speeches and debates regarding Philippine annexation, Filipinos were pointedly and consistently labeled "barbarians" in need of "civilization" or people "from an inferior race" who could benefit from skillful and superior American guidance.[10] And, sustaining the analogy with "Indians" and "Indian" territorial conquest, many asserted the duty and the right of white Americans to intervene with, subjugate, and control this "population [that] is as ignorant and savage as the aboriginal Indians."[11]

This civilizing mission was also instrumental in laying the groundwork for a new public school system in the Philippines, shaped in the American way and in marked contrast to that practiced by the Spanish. Before U.S. occupation, schooling was not mandatory, was available to only a few, and was conducted in the local languages. The Americans introduced a free public education system, which opened schools to many who were formerly denied access.[12] The "Americanization" program mandated English as the primary language of instruction in subjects that focused on U.S. history and culture. This kind of education nurtured an idealized picture of America in the minds of students, and they began to perceive the United States as a desirable place to be and Americans in general a desirable people to emulate.[13]

The consequences of U.S. conquest—racialization and "Americanization"—pursued Filipinos as they immigrated to and settled in the United States.[14] For example, beyond instituting a public school system in the Philippines, U.S. colonial administrators also embarked on a project to train their colonial wards in U.S.-style governance by sending them to the mainland, covering their fare, education, and cost of living expenses. The first group to arrive in the United States consisted of Filipino students. Required to return to the islands after their sponsored educational tenure, these mostly male students came from prominent and well-to-do families on whom the management of an independent Philippine state and society would depend. In the United States, these students were known as *pensionados*. Between 1903 and the 1930s, their numbers reached two thousand, scattered in places like Chicago, Seattle, New York, Washington, D.C., and Los Angeles. Eventually, most indeed returned to the Philippines, where secure positions in government, education, and private business awaited them.[15]

During the same period, an additional fourteen thousand Filipinos left for the United States as nonsponsored, self-financing prospective students. To support their studies, many of them worked fulltime as menial laborers in restaurants and homes, going to school (when possible) part-time.[16] But the Great Depression dealt them a major blow, even though some were able to survive the harsh economic and social conditions through mutual support associations and various strategies of accommodation.[17] Still, by the 1930s, the number of Filipinos in school had decreased substantially. Many students went back home. Those who were stranded became "unintentional immigrants" and were forced to take jobs for which they were overqualified.[18]

Some of the *pensionados* joined labor movements to fight against racism and discrimination in work.[19] According to historian Barbara M. Posadas, even though "in Philippine classrooms, American teachers assured eager pupils that those lacking scholarships or family wealth might work their way through school . . . the nature of that work and, more importantly, the role of race in American society was rarely mentioned."[20] This idea of a meritocracy, of success based on individual work without regard to social conditions that might impede a person's life chances, informed many Filipinos' notions of their own possibilities. The meritocracy myth didn't acknowledge or contest the reality that equal chances for all applied only to select groups. As more Filipinos would later come to realize in the United States, school diplomas from home, family social status, and earned money in one's pocket frequently did not guarantee greater opportunities in and acceptance by society.

A History of Labor and Racialization

As is the case for most other immigrants to the United States, the impetus to come to the United States for many Filipinos and Filipinas is closely tied to the desire to seek better work.[21] A corollary to this is the presumed availability of work opportunities made possible by an expansive U.S. economy sustained by a stratified labor force. Most of the Filipinos who immigrated to the United States, especially before 1965, did so under the auspices of recruitment agencies, farm and cannery employment offices, and military bases controlled by U.S. interests. As lower-rung and racialized participants in agriculture, service industries, and armed forces machinery, Filipino workers (mostly male) were exploited and found their mobility restricted, prompting many to seek redress, primarily through unionization on their own and with other racial groups. In the period following World War II and culminating in the Civil Rights movement of the 1960s, Filipino veterans and women entered the United States in limited numbers but found greater opportunities for advancement in work and social status, compared to earlier years, despite covert forms of racism. In these ways, the history of Filipino immigration to the United States is primarily a history of labor and racialization.

The immigrant experiences of those who entered the country as laborers for the farms and canneries were not as promising as those of students. Filipinos were induced by the colonial government to work in the United States primarily to feed its emergent large-scale agricultural industries.[22] The recruitment of the first wave of immigrants began in 1906 and intensified until the 1930s, mainly for plantation work in Hawaii and on the mainland's West Coast.[23] In Hawaii, work was primarily concentrated in the labor-intensive sugar-producing areas, where Filipinos worked alongside Chinese and Japanese farmers even though "planters stratified employment by race and paid different wages to different nationalities for the same work."[24] Filipinos were usually paid the lowest wages, lived in grossly inadequate plantation housing, and performed the most difficult tasks, a set-up designed to create tension among the ethnically mixed laborers and thus prevent them from organizing across ethnic boundaries. Another source of such tension arose from the perception that the Filipinos were in competition with other Asian groups, for they were sent to Hawaii to replace the strike-prone Japanese workers, whose immigration to the United States was restricted by the passage of the "Gentlemen's Agreement" of 1908 and, along with other Asians, the Asiatic Barred Zone Act of 1917 and the Oriental Exclusion Act of 1924.[25]

Recruitment of Filipino farm labor was mainly undertaken by the Hawaii Sugar Planters' Association (HSPA) in partnership with the U.S. colonial bureaucracy in the Philippines. Considered "wards" or "nationals" of the American state at that time, Filipinos were able to travel to the United States without the interference undergone by other foreign nationals, in the form of legal entry and exit processing. The number of recruits grew from 15 in 1906 to a peak of 44,000 in the 1920s, so that by 1932, Filipino sugar-farm workers comprised 70 percent of the total work force in the Hawaiian Islands.[26] Predominantly from the Ilocos, Visayan, and metropolitan Manila regions, these workers were favored over others because of their perceived ability to withstand hard labor and their agricultural experience on local farms. After 1926, when the HSPA stopped active recruitment in the Philippines, many of these farm laborers paid their own ship fare to Hawaii.[27]

On the West Coast of the U.S. mainland, Filipinos were also replacing other Asians (barred by the Chinese Exclusion Act), mainly in the farm labor pools necessary for the burgeoning agricultural industries in Washington, Oregon, and California. A majority of these Filipinos were single young males between the ages of sixteen and twenty-one. Many had come by way of Hawaii, seeking opportunities on the mainland whose working conditions were less oppressive, and often after being blacklisted for actively participating in labor strikes in the islands. Most took work in the fruit orchards, vegetable gardens, and fish canneries of the coastal states and Alaska. These were manual labor–intensive jobs that required frequent movement from place to place, following the seasons of planting, harvesting, and fishing.[28] In 1930, the Filipino population in the United States was 108,260, a four-fold jump from the 26,634 in 1920, and a significant leap from the 2,767 in 1910. Of the 108,260 in 1930,

30,470 were in California and 3,480 were in Washington.[29] Along with Mexican workers, Filipinos on the Pacific coast and in Alaska were considered the most reliable laborers. Yet, instrumental as they were in sustaining the economy of the region, they endured the lowest wages and the filthiest living conditions, much like the situation in Hawaii.

It is not too difficult to understand why Filipinos at this time were bent on moving to the United States, despite formidable odds. The U.S. colonial emphasis on an agricultural export economy (over the internal industrialization that could have prevented the Philippines' later dependence on imports for basic necessities) furthered the fragmentation and displacement of workers begun during the Spanish conquest. More and more people were seeking to escape poverty by moving to urban areas. And the chance to try out life in a foreign land—as a temporary venture, at least initially—must have been attractive, especially in light of the ravages of the Philippine-U.S. war, the letters from relatives and friends that brought news and money from the United States, the schools that touted that country as a prime land of opportunity, the return of the *pensionados* and a few ex-sojourners, and the promises of recruiters. Families were known to pull resources together to help pay the travel expenses of those the recruiters wanted, usually the younger, unmarried males of the household. Women and children were frequently barred by recruiters from traveling with the men; they were likely viewed as burdens that would interfere with the farm work. The prospective laborers' working knowledge of English (learned through mandatory attendance at public schools) and of farm production made them even more worthy candidates for travel and work.[30]

A History of Antiracist Struggle

As important labor recruits in the United States, Filipinos found themselves in a peculiar social position. Although they arrived with U.S. passports (and, therefore, as U.S. nationals, because of the Philippines' status as a colony), Filipinos were ineligible for citizenship and were legally barred from voting, establishing a business,

holding private and public office, and owning land and other property.[31] As wards of the state, however, Filipinos were expected to pay
allegiance to the United States and were subject to the colonial government's jurisdiction and control.[32] As with Native Americans, the
state's rationale for this treatment was fundamentally a result of its
expansionist and imperialist aims—benevolence for "savages" that
needed to be "civilized." A ward, then, was a racialized "barbarous"
subject whose salvation required white domination.[33] This practice
undergirded U.S. exploitation of its colony's raw materials, and, as
in the case of Filipino labor in the United States, the removal of its
human resources to locations outside the Philippines. Productive Filipino laborers in the United States, much like their Asian counterparts, provided important services to the national economy while
being oppressed as noncitizens because of their race.[34] Unlike other
white groups, for example, Filipinos were denied social and economic mobility because of low wages and harsh working conditions.[35]
As noncitizens, they had virtually no protection from labor exploitation because they had no official representatives from their homeland and, therefore, could be threatened with deportation. Male Filipino laborers in California and other states were forbidden to marry
outside their race (most especially, to marry whites) by antimiscegenation laws.[36] Much like other racialized groups, Filipinos found
their rights defined in terms of "separate but *unequal*" status.[37] The
signs posted in front of hotels and other business establishments for-
bidding the entry of Filipinos testify to that unequal status during
this period of intense nativism.

Racial antagonism also erupted in violent confrontations. Displaced by cheap Filipino labor, many white laborers and farmworkers rioted against Filipinos. On top of their racist attitudes against
all Asians, whites perceived Filipinos as greater threats because of
their status as U.S. nationals (they could freely enter the country) and
the lack of immigration restrictions against them. Filipino laborers
were also viewed as "sexual" threats because of their widely known
enjoyment of dancing and other forms of entertainment, and their
frequent companionship with white women.[38] The result was an anti-
Filipino movement that contributed to more riots and later to legis-

lation that strictly limited Filipino immigration. As historian Lorraine Crouchett summarizes it: "This movement to prevent further Filipino immigration, like the agitation against Chinese and Japanese immigration, was rooted largely in the belief that the Filipino workers were an economic threat and complaints that Filipino immorality and unassimilability were detrimental and dangerous to the social conditions."[39]

A number of Filipino farmworkers had to accede to and accommodate the unjust conditions in order to survive.[40] Others saw active resistance through union demands as a tempting alternative, in light of the dependence of growers on their labor. Hampered by the farmworker's nomadic existence, labor strikes were at times unsuccessful. But when their strikes succeeded, Filipinos earned the reputation of being unified and skillful union activists.[41] When their strikes on several occasions paralyzed the lettuce, asparagus, and grape industries around California, they demanded better working conditions and union recognition. They were engaged on several fronts during this period, from all-Filipino organizing (Agricultural Workers League, Field Workers Union, and the Filipino Agricultural Workers Association), to cross-racial (Field Workers Union, with Mexicans) and all-labor coalitions (Filipino Labor Union; United Cannery, Agricultural, Packing, and Allied Workers of America; and Federated Agricultural Laborers Association).[42] But not all labor strikes guaranteed the outcomes strikers sought. Many Filipinos were blacklisted and forced to go elsewhere.

Others ventured outside agricultural and fishing work to find opportunities in the major urban districts of the United States. Mostly concentrated in the service industries, they were hired as waiters, busboys, cooks, barbers, newsboys, bellboys, ushers, attendants, janitors, and domestic helpers.[43] A few were able to advance to skilled and technical positions after further schooling. But with the onset of the Great Depression, jobs available to them grew more scarce. And with the racial tensions due to fewer jobs, Filipinos became more marginalized—excluded from restaurants, clubs, parks, and other public places, and treated like uncivilized beings and animals ("dogs") not worthy of respect.[44]

Concurrent with the recruitment of Filipinos for island and main-land labor was their enlistment into the U.S. armed forces, prima-rily as service workers. The colonial government's installation of mil-itary bases in the Philippines raised the number of Filipinos in these positions—mainly as naval stewards—from less than ten in 1903 to about six thousand by the 1920s and four thousand by the 1930s. After World War I, Filipinos were restricted to work as stewards and mess boys regardless of their educational attainment. Still, the oppor-tunities were alluring enough to risk local careers and family sepa-ration amidst conditions of poverty in the Philippines.[45] When the Philippines gained its independence from the United States in 1946, the Military Bases Agreement signed by the two sovereign nations allowed the U.S. Navy to continue enlisting Filipinos, who were now eligible to become U.S. citizens. Recruitment proceeded at a greater rate from the late 1940s into the 1970s and 1980s.[46]

Settling in Filipino communities in Hawaii and on the mainland, these farmworkers, service industry employees, and naval recruits established mutual support organizations, province- and work-related associations, lodges, benevolent associations, and religious groups. These groups not only fostered self-reliance but provided service sys-tems for those with whom they had common experiences, even if they produced ethnic isolation from mainstream society.[47] Forbidden from—and not being able to afford—living in white neighborhoods, Filipinos were found mostly in urban areas ("Little Manilas"), where temporary spaces in hotels, boardinghouses, and apartments were available. These spaces also proved practical for many who held sea-sonal and migratory jobs. Among the field and domestic laborers, social gatherings took place in taxi dance clubs and pool halls in the rural and urban areas that were more open to a Filipino presence.[48] The *manongs* and Pinoys/Pinays who worked on the farms formed lasting bonds of friendship and support that eventually united them in collective action against unfair work conditions through legal chal-lenges, labor strikes, walk-outs, and employee demands. (Some of them evaded the law, for example, by crossing state lines to marry their non-Filipino partners.)[49] These frequently violent and deadly inci-dents, which were exacerbated by and ultimately increased racial tensions among laborers, found their way into reports and articles in community newspapers published and distributed by Filipinos, and into other literary forms such as autobiographical novels.[50] Such media linked disparate and mobile Filipinos by disseminating information that pertained to their social, economic, and political interests, especially during the period of nativism in the 1930s.[51]

One important consequence of the powerful nativism of the time, primarily coming from white farm and labor interest groups, was the passage of the Tydings-McDuffie Act of 1934, which promised independence to the Philippine colony after a period of ten years. The act also immediately changed the status of Filipinos from U.S. nationals to Philippine citizens of the U.S. Commonwealth. Once they were legally "aliens," Filipinos became subject to exclusionary immigration measures. Excepting U.S. armed force and Hawaiian sugar plantation recruitees, Filipino immigration was limited to fifty per year.[52] Between 1934 and 1946, very few Filipinos were able to come to the United States, nearly damming the once steady stream of arrivals to communities on the mainland.

Another crucial piece of legislation in this period was the Filipino Repatriation Act of 1935, which encouraged the deportation of all Filipino workers. The original plan was to support the return of an estimated forty-five thousand Filipino workers to the Philippines, with the government paying their transportation expenses. The expulsion initiative, however, was only mildly successful, since only about two thousand Filipinos left.[53]

World War II reversed the course of Filipino immigration, as Filipinos were actively recruited once again, this time to serve in the military mobilization efforts against the axis powers. During this war, the Philippine armed forces were incorporated into the U.S. military machinery to fight against Japanese occupation and protect U.S. interests in the colony and elsewhere. A significant number of Filipinos in the United States were also drafted, mostly into the army. Initially, the Selective Service Act could not technically allow the drafting of Filipinos—they were not U.S. citizens. But as the stakes rose (Manila fell to the Japanese in January 1942), the act was modified to allow the enlistment of Filipinos in the United States, but only if grouped in separate units. An estimated eighty thousand Filipinos participated in the war effort as army men, seamen, radio operators, stewards, and war bond investors.[54] News of Filipino and Filipino American wartime service efforts helped ease racial discrimination locally. Subsequently, Filipinos were admitted into the United States with greater facility; these immigrants would later be referred to as the "second wave" and included war veterans, war brides, and male *and* female students, workers, and their dependents.[55] From 1946 to 1965, their numbers reached nearly sixty-five thousand.[56] Many war veterans from the Philippines were promised automatic citizenship, but only four thousand could avail themselves of it before the commitment was rescinded in 1946. This issue would be debated and contested by many war veterans later, from the 1960s to the present.[57]

Meanwhile, significant numbers of Filipinos took advantage of the postwar economic boom in the United States. More opportunities for advancement were available. Several restrictive laws were removed, among them, the alien land laws that had prevented Filipinos from owning or leasing land. Citizenship was made available through the Filipino Naturalization Act of 1946, which permitted the naturalization of Filipinos (forbidden since the Naturalization Act of 1790). As Filipino American citizens, many of them found better-paying jobs that, in turn, enabled them to purchase land, housing, and other properties.[58]

Still, racial prejudice limited their mobility and opportunities during this time. The most widely affected by the false promises of antidiscrimination legislation were those who moved from rural to urban areas. Severe restrictions were still intact, mostly in covert form, in terms of residential choice, jobs, wage scales, and promotion.[59] In 1959, the median annual income of Filipinos was $2,925, compared to $5,109 for male Caucasians.[60]

U.S.-Philippine Relations and Contemporary Movements

The McCarran-Walter Act of 1952, which eased restrictions on Filipino immigration to the United States, provided for the entry of relatives of U.S. citizens (including refugees) as nonquota immigrants. Yet people from Western Hemisphere countries were not subject to the quota of 100 persons per year imposed on countries from the rest of the world. Thus, the act was an attempt to "preserve the ethnic and racial composition of the United States" by limiting the entry of those deemed unfit for that composition.[61] In other words, this act, like its predecessors, set limits on immigrants according to race.

The preference for specific groups of white immigrants was reflected again in the Immigration Act of 1965, as larger but still unequal quotas for each hemisphere were instituted (170,000 places for the Eastern Hemisphere, contrasted with 290,000 for the Western Hemisphere). It placed a cap of 20,000 visas on each country per year and introduced two classes of preferred immigrants: exempted slots outside of the caps for spouses, children, and parents of U.S. citizens (for "family reunification"); and "preferred" categories (with various limitations) within the caps for other relatives, professionals, scientists, skilled and unskilled workers in short-supply occupations as determined by the Department of Labor, and refugees. The intent of the 1965 act was to accommodate the presumed large numbers of European refugees, with the framers estimating that immigration from Asian and Latin American countries would be low, and that the number of nonwhites who could sponsor relatives would be far fewer than potential white sponsors.[62]

But as soon as the 1965 act was in place, immigration from Europe declined, owing to economic prosperity in that region, while immigration from Asia, the Caribbean, and South America rose, comprising three-quarters of the four million immigrants who came to the United States from the 1960s to the 1970s. Toward the end of the 1970s and into the 1980s, Asians (who initially made use of professional immigrant preference slots) and Latin Americans unexpectedly took greater advantage of family reunification nonquota preferences, as chain migration increased (the sending in of relatives from the home country after one family member has been able to resettle). The yearly average of nonquota immigrants before the 1980s was 90,000. In 1980, 796,000 legal immigrants came into the United States, well above the 290,000 ceiling imposed for all immigration by

44   Chapter Two

the Immigration Act of 1965.[63] With the 1960s, then, came another rise in U.S. nativism, as more "undesirable" people—among them, Filipinos—arrived "in hordes."[64]

The McCarran-Walter Act of 1952 and the Immigration Act of 1965 marked turning points in the U.S. political economy and Filipino immigration. The acts came in the aftermath of U.S. participation in World War II, when democracy was being pursued overseas (in order to extend or maintain U.S. interests) and when racism at home was being addressed. The economic boom after the war was accompanied by labor shortages, which were filled with imported workers, mostly professionals and skilled laborers. Moreover, the Civil Rights movement of the 1960s made the quota systems and exclusions of previous immigration legislation seem racist.[65] The 1965 act raised the annual quota for Filipinos from 100 to 20,000, as well as those for other Asians. In succeeding years, both the number and the type of Filipino immigrants changed. Before 1965, they had been mostly students, farmworkers, and military recruits. After 1965, more professionals and other highly trained skilled workers would arrive, as global capitalist restructuring shifted production and manufacturing to the developing countries and concentrated financial and service industries in the developed world.[66] Because of the family unification provisions of the 1965 Immigration Act, these white-collar workers would be joined by another stream of immigrants: family members of Filipinos who had arrived in the United States prior to 1965. Together with the immigrants of the 1970s and the 1980s who also sponsored relatives to come over—the bulk of those I interviewed for this book—they would comprise the "third wave" of Filipino immigrants to America.

From 1966 to 1975, 114,107 Filipinos immigrated to the United States.[67] Many of them were doctors, engineers, and accountants with professional and special technical skills training, ready to be integrated into the highly skilled U.S. work force being developed at the time.[68] More women also came after 1965 (most of them nurses and teachers), significantly altering the previous high male–low female ratio of Filipinos in America.[69] Each year after 1975, more than forty thousand Filipinos were issued immigrant visas to the United States. Filipinos who immigrated after 1965 and well into the

1980s and 1990s comprise the largest number of Asians coming into the United States, and, after Mexicans, the second largest group of immigrants to the nation.[70] Some of those who were overstaying their visas prior to 1982 would avail themselves of the amnesty provisions of the Immigration Reform and Control Act of 1986, and later Filipino arrivals would take advantage of the higher immigrant caps (for both family reunification and occupational categories) stipulated by the Immigration Act of 1990.[71]

Additionally, in California, a good number of middle-aged to senior residents petitioned by their offspring through the family reunification provisions of the immigration acts found employment.[72] This family reunification occurred along at least two streams: immigrants sponsored by relatives already in the United States prior to this period, who were thus likely to have similar socioeconomic backgrounds to their sponsors'; and immigrants petitioned by their children who immigrated as professionals during the period.[73] Many of these parents had less than adequate schooling or below-average qualifications for better-paying jobs. They have taken menial jobs in domestic service, health care (mainly as caretakers for seniors), security, food service, and maintenance (as security guards, cooks, servers, and janitors). Some work in the garment and computer-related industries as assembly-line workers.[74]

The significant movement of Filipinos to the United States during this period has also been attributed to the close and sustained economic, political, and cultural relationship between the Philippines and the United States. The presence of U.S.-controlled military bases in the archipelago until 1992 (when lease between the countries was not signed), coupled with a plethora of business and social networks established even after formal U.S. occupation, have been significant in encouraging Filipinos to immigrate.[75] With modern means of transportation, it has been relatively easy to bring Filipinos to the United States through recruitment and business connections. And all along, there has been the idealization of America as the land of plenty and opportunity—"images of U.S. abundance peddled by the educational system, the media, and relatives and friends already in the United States."[76] At the same time, the Philippines' dependence on external capital, its mounting foreign debt, the depletion of its human and natural resources, and its disequilibrium following global and local inflation resulted in the dislocation of huge numbers of its people. Poverty and unemployment were rampant, and those with educations were seeking better opportunities elsewhere. For them, the United States was an enticing destination.[77] Filipino professionals took advantage of the opportunities opened up by the shortage of white-collar labor in the United States, mainly in the medical field; their primary destinations were the states of the Pacific coast, the Midwest, and the Northeast.[78]

In 1972, Philippine president Ferdinand Marcos declared martial Law and instituted dictatorial rule. During his regime, heightened graft and corruption, as well as unsound economic policies, impoverished the country even further, contributing significantly to the push to live and work elsewhere. During his rule, from 1972 to 1986, approximately 300,000 Filipinos relocated to the United States.[79] It was also during this time that the islands experienced a "brain drain," as skilled and professional "guest" workers (as well as female entertainers and domestic labor), flocked to employment destinations elsewhere: Canada, Australia, Hong Kong, Taiwan, Singapore, Malaysia, Italy, Germany, and the Middle East.[80] They were part of a massive state program to accelerate economic development by easing unemployment and raising foreign exchange inflows. Later on, toward the 1990s, registered permanent emigration of Filipinos to Western countries would reach 1.4 million, and of overseas workers, about 1.2 million. The money they sent back to the islands from more than 130 countries would amount to $3.5 billion.[81] Because of its overseas employment program initiated during the Marcos period, the Philippines in 1990 was the largest source of permanent and contractual migrants from Asia. Their primary destination, as for those before them, was the United States.[82]

From the Marcos-regime immigrants also came active political organizers who campaigned in the United States, through demonstrations and through petition letters in the media and to public offices, against the tyrannical rule of the dictator. Exposing Marcos's unlawful detention of his political enemies and his government's rampant graft and corruption, these Filipino Americans clamored for an end to U.S. support of the Philippine administration in the form of diplomatic and military ties, as well as financial aid. These activists were also instrumental in bringing to the U.S. public the issues surrounding the mysterious deaths of several anti-Marcos elements who were believed to have been assassinated in the United States per Marcos's orders.[83]

It was also during this period that Filipino farmworkers were at the forefront of labor strikes and boycotts of certain agricultural products. These workers and their descendants actively appealed to the U.S. government to help them better their social and economic conditions by allocating funds for the construction of farmworker housing and retirement centers, for medical services, and for employment assistance. In the late 1960s, the Agbayani Retirement Village in Delano, California, and the Roger Terronez Medical Clinic adjacent to it were founded to serve the special needs of the now senior Filipino farm laborers.[84] Working with Mexican/Chicano labor under the leadership of Cesar Chavez of the National Farm Workers Association, Filipino farmworkers led by Larry Itliong and later by Philip Vera Cruz were instrumental in organizing pickets, strikes, and table-grape boycotts that eventually resulted in the improvement of their conditions.[85]

Southern California Locations and Positions

Most Filipinos who moved to the United States during the 1970s to the 1990s chose California as their place of resettlement. Rather than continuing the temporary and migratory patterns of settlement common before 1960s, many who came after 1965 settled more permanently in various states to work in the defense, medical, and service industries. The 1970 census counted 138,859 Filipinos in California, 33,450 of whom were in Los Angeles County and 15,069 in San Diego County (see Table 1). The 1990 census reported 733,941 Filipinos living in California and indicated that Filipinos comprised the second largest Asian American group in the nation (next to Chinese), and the largest in California. Nationally, the Filipino population as of 1990 was 1.4 million, up 82 percent from the 1980 count.[86]

Table 1.   Filipino Population in the United States, California, and Los
Angeles and San Diego Counties, 1960–1990

Year	U.S.	Calif.	Los Angeles Co.	San Diego Co.
1960	181,614	65,459	7,696	3,247
1970	336,731	138,859	33,450	15,069
1980	774,652	338,378	80,042	10,658
1990	1,419,711	733,941	219,653	95,945*

Source: U.S. Census of Population and Housing.

*In the 1990 U.S. Census, Filipinos in Los Angeles County comprised about 2% of the
county's overall population, and 24% of the Asian American population. In San Diego
County, Filipinos were 4% of the county's population, and 52% of the Asian American
population.

Those who could afford to chose California for its ideal climate,
its employment promise (mainly provided by the defense industries),
and the presence of earlier Filipino immigrants. News of California
as a prime relocation destination also reached prospective migrants
by way of letters and visits from relatives and their frequent remittances and shipments of goods via *balikbayan* (homecoming) freight
boxes. Cities in California became either the point of permanent
resettlement or the springboard for other destinations.[87] These cities
are among the most significant of the many sites at which Filipino
labor is recruited for semipermanent or permanent jobs. Other places
include Malaysia, Singapore, Hong Kong, Japan, Australia, India,
Saudi Arabia, Kuwait, Italy, and Germany. Filipino workers, most of
them women, are estimated to number upward of four million and
can be found in more than 130 countries, remitting to the Philippines billions of dollars annually.[88] But on the whole, years of colonial capitalist links between California and major cities in the Philippines have perpetuated migration streams that move labor power
from peripheries to centers.

That movement persists to this day. In Southern California, as in
many other places, Filipinos with relatively high educational attainment are encouraged to work outside the Philippines in service-ori-
ented jobs and in production lines, as well as in technical and man-
agerial positions, in contrast to the farm labor jobs prior to 1965 (see

Tables 2 and 3). Concurrent with these changes in occupational placement have been shifts in settlement patterns. The "Manilatown" of the 1920s and 1930s in downtown Los Angeles, which used to be the hub of Filipino commercial and recreational activity for mostly working-class service workers, is no longer the premier site of Filipino settlement in the area. Rather, it is one among many, as Filipino families have moved to outlying areas and suburbs such as Glendale, Eagle Rock, Silver Lake, Carson, Long Beach, Cerritos, West Covina, Walnut, Rowland Heights, and Diamond Bar. Even though Manilatown still bears remnants of the older Filipino community (restaurants, social agencies, and community centers) and even has newer commercial establishments (stores, beauty salons, bakeries, and video stores), there are also numerous Filipino-distinct businesses and social halls in the suburbs where more middle-class and middle-aged Filipinos have settled.

The enlargement and spread of Filipino communities are also noticeable in San Diego County. Earlier communities of mostly naval employees are still evident in National City and Miramesa, but suburbs such as Rancho Peñasquitos and Poway have their own pockets of Filipino residents and entrepreneurs now. Both San Diego and Los Angeles Counties display a more diverse scattering of Filipino settlement, particularly in working-class and mixed-income neighborhoods. Yet, if one looks closely, many of these spots are identifiable as Filipino mainly because of their proximity to work sites (as in the

Table 2.   Educational Attainment of the U.S. Filipino Population of Persons 25 years or Older, 1990

Education	% Native Born	% Foreign Born	% Total
H.S. Graduate	4	12	16
Some College	4	14	18
Bachelor's Degree	3	29	32
Advanced Degree	1	7	8

Total of U.S. Filipino population of persons 25 years of age or older (1990) is 865,308 or 61% of total U.S. Filipino population (1,419,711).
Source: U.S. Census of Population and Housing.

Table 3.   Occupational Distribution of U.S. Filipino Population of Employed
Persons 16 Years or Older, 1990

Occupation	% Native Born	% Foreign Born	% Total
Technical, Sales, and Administrative	8	29	37
Managers and Professionals in Specialty Occupations	5	22	27
Precision Production, Operators, Fabricators, and Laborers	4	14	18
Service	3	14	17
Farming	0.3	0.7	1

Total of U.S. Filipino population of employed persons 16 years or older is 750,613 or
53% of total U.S. Filipino population (1,419,711).
Source: U.S. Census of Population and Housing.

naval communities in National City and Long Beach, and the health
profession communities in East Hollywood, with its many hospitals),
their concentration of commercial establishments owned and patronized by Filipinos (as in downtown L.A., Cerritos, and Miramesa),
their previous histories of Filipino presence (as in Carson and San
Diego), and their proximity to long-established and growing Catholic
churches.[89] It is in these neighborhoods that Filipinos from of all generations, new arrivals and established families, find spaces to work,
live, go to church, shop, and socialize with each other.

Despite the easing of discriminatory immigration legislation, the
institutionalization of affirmative action for a few years, and the formal
removal of overtly racist laws, however, many Filipino third wavers
have been subjected to covert and indirect forms of discrimination.
One of the foremost of these is the practice of "almost insurmountable"
licensure policies for Philippine-educated professionals, particularly in
the medical fields.[90] Most who found it very difficult to pass licensing
examinations were not able to practice their professions and were forced
instead to accept jobs for which they were overqualified or outside their
field. Many of my respondents believe that, since they come from a
Third World country, Americans falsely perceive them to have had an
inferior education. This situation has surely hampered their opportunities to pursue desired careers and has prevented their mobility.[91]

A more insidious racism, however, has made itself felt in their everyday lives. Said one respondent: "It's here. It happens daily, even though many people won't care to admit it." Many of them have been faulted for speaking English with an accent, for behaving "too much like a Filipino" and presumably too little like an "American," for conversing in their native tongue in the workplace, or for simply being "too successful." Parking her Mercedes Benz at the shopping mall one time, a Filipino American told me, she was accosted by a white man who suspected her of stealing the car, as if, she said, "It was a crime to enjoy the fruits of my labor." I have also heard of accomplished doctors and dentists who lost non-Filipino patients upon their learning during the initial consultation that they are Filipino. And then there are Filipinos who have attempted to purchase houses or open up businesses but were suspiciously barred from doing so in certain neighborhoods. "Many people think of us as foreigners or, sometimes, even strangers and visitors," remarked a Filipino I interviewed,

> because they find it very hard to place us. We get mistaken for Chinese, Japanese, Korean, Thai. We're Asians, but we're different Asians too. Some of them think we're black or Hispanic, or even [American] Indians. Occasionally, someone would ask, "Are you Filipino?" The moment I say yes, somehow I get the feeling the person was really asking, "Are you like them?" Meaning, "Are you just like the other coloreds?" I think this is why racial discrimination is so *matindi* [virulent] even though we have these nice houses and cars.

These examples show the ways in which class status may not necessarily or automatically translate into the erasure of racial identities, and how the "lumping" of Filipino Americans into the Asian American category (or other racial categories) may be fraught with tension.[92] As an interviewee cited in this chapter's epigraph implies, even though Filipinos may be found almost everywhere in the United States these days, their perception is that they remain marginalized, excluded, or invisible to others.

Many observers have also noted the very small number of Filipino Americans in public office despite their numbers and concentration in a community. True, some Filipino Americans have successfully occupied elected and appointed positions in Hawaii, California, and the federal government.[93] But, looking at the aggregate figures for all Asian and Pacific Americans, Harold Brackman and Steven Erie conclude that "historically, Asian Pacifics have been highly underrepresented among voters and elected officeholders."[94] As a result, Filipinos have resorted to a "politics by other means" (such as monetary contributions to candidates' coffers and panethnic coalition building), which, in turn, has intensified nativist hostility and intergroup tensions.[95] The low political participation of Filipino Americans (for example, only 27 percent of the eligible Filipino American voters were registered in Los Angeles County in 1984) has been explained primarily as the result of their immigrant status, which prohibits them from voting or running for office.[96] But as one study has shown, the reasons for such a phenomenon may have deeper or hidden causes. For many Filipinos, past and present structural and financial constraints, as well as discriminatory barriers to political participation (fueled by persistent racism in overt and covert forms), have had longlasting effects on their ability to become politically involved. They have thus distanced themselves from active participation primarily because they have been discouraged from participating.[97]

This is not to say that Filipino Americans have chosen to be completely silent and passive on all political matters affecting their lives. Facing a different set of conditions and circumstances than those experienced by the previous generation, many of them have been involved in issue-oriented causes such as voter registration, affirmative action, bilingual education, workplace discrimination, and citizenship entitlements. Along with other Asian Americans, Filipino Americans confront civil rights issues that involve hate crimes, access to police protection, educational opportunity, employment discrimination, health care, media representation, violence against women, and religious freedom, among others.[98] The most common perception among Filipino Americans I talked to is that more covert forms of racism exist particularly in job promotion and the curtailment of language rights in the workplace, and in access to higher-level educational opportunities.

The economic participation of Filipinos after 1965, however, is another story. According to the 1990 census, Filipinos are more likely than the population as a whole to participate in the labor force. They have the highest labor participation rate among all Asian Americans (75.4 percent of Filipinos sixteen years old and over) and the most families with three or more workers (29.6 percent) compared with other Asian Americans. Most Filipinos are high school graduates or possess higher degrees (82.6 percent; third after Japanese and Asian Indian Americans) and are managers or professionals; in technical, sales, and administrative support; and in service.[99] But these figures may not entirely coincide with their perceived "economic success." Five percent of the Filipino American labor force is unemployed (close to the 6.3 percent unemployed figure for all Americans), and 6.4 percent is considered poor. And even if many are in occupations that are deemed higher paying, Filipinos' average per capita income was only $13,616—lower than that of all Asian Americans ($13,806).[100] These figures suggest the diversity of the Filipino American population and, possibly, the underemployment of its professional pool.

The extent to which the Filipino American population today is principally a labor force and marginally a political force is testament to the continued dependence of the United States on a racially stratified and gendered labor pool that is at once treated and perceived as, or desired to be, silent and docile.[101] Filipinos occupy peculiar niches in the U.S. terrain. Encouraged to immigrate as vital and integral components of the nation's economy, they are simultaneously marked and placed as outsiders, alien, or foreign to such an extent that their historical presence in the educational, political, and social realms is marginalized or even erased.[102]

Because of or despite these conditions, many Filipino third wavers try to ignore or brush aside the impact of racism on their lives by living apart from mainstream society and working long hours or taking extra jobs to gain greater financial security. Many also try to "pass" by "acting like an American," as several respondents have said, paying the price of forsaking their native culture. A number of them, for instance, have chosen to speak to their children in English exclusively to protect them from possibly being maltreated in school and other public places. The common perception is that they run the risk of being "punished" if they continue to act like the Filipinos that they are.

"This race thing is new to us," said one interviewee. "We never learn this from the TV shows we saw back home. But we know how to survive. We know how to make it. We'll even exceed what they can do."

To many of those I talked to, there is a dark side to assimilation. Even the formal conferment of citizenship by way of naturalization and a U.S. passport does not guarantee full acceptance into society.[103] To them, these can indeed be giant strides in terms of being able to vote and have a voice in how the nation is run. But they know that these are also but small (though significant) steps on the long road to visibility and recognition.

In the meantime, a good number of Filipinos today have found refuge in places where they can be among and enjoy the company of people who are like them and therefore are likely to treat them in more positive ways. Many of them are beginning to realize that their common experiences of racism and invisibility have roots that span generations of contact between their former colonizers and their nation of origin or descent. In places where they see other Filipinos, the stories that they exchange with each other often reflect this shared historical and contemporary experience.

These places include churches, commercial centers, and community halls, which become venues for Filipino American gatherings, meetings, and regular interaction. Filipino American social and political organizations, some of which were started by first- and second-wave immigrants decades ago, continue to flourish and thrive in support of local needs and interests.[104] Commercial establishments like stores, restaurants, beauty and barber shops, and video rental stores dot a number of neighborhoods to cater to Filipinos' demands. Community newspapers, as well as statewide and nationwide magazines, link disparate population groups and provide spaces for conversing with each other on matters affecting their interconnected lives.[105] These are the kinds of spaces that have bridged a diverse and heterogeneous population, across generations and subgroups, against shared experiences of racism.

Filipino American settlements today are multiple, scattered, diverse, and heterogeneous. To refer to a Filipino American community, one must include men and women who came to the United States at different times; who were born in the United States and who were born in the Philippines; who are unskilled, semiskilled, and professional; who are and are not educated; who came from and live in urban and rural areas; who came in as parents and as children; and who are offspring of both early and recent arrivals. In other words, the breadth and variety of Filipino immigration to the United States necessitates the signification of a Filipino American community in the plural.

Such a plurality is evident in the Southern California Filipino American communities I have studied. Both the Los Angeles and San Diego Filipino population groups are predominantly third wavers as opposed to oldtimers (as first and second wavers are locally called). There is also substantial representation of parents of professionals who are retired or working menial jobs, of second- and third-generation offspring of earlier immigrants, and of skilled workers in the military (primarily in San Diego, since its naval stations and their outlying environs have been home to many recruits). Parts of the counties have also preserved in varying degrees the communities of earlier immigrants, whose members have had limited interaction with those I interviewed. The 1990 census counts 219,653 Filipino Americans in the county of Los Angeles and 95,945 in San Diego County.[106] They have settled in a variety of neighborhoods, depending significantly on their class status.

I hesitate, however, to claim that Southern California Filipino Americans—the subjects of this book—are representative of Filipinos in the United States. Doing that would gloss over the differences across this multifaceted group at the least and establish Filipino American identity as a singular formation at most. Rather, I explore instances of Filipino American identity construction in Southern California as examples of the wide and complex array of Filipino American ethnicity over time and space. This has meant considering the specifics of Filipino Americanness in their Southern California locations, with their traces of past and contemporary immigration, and the emergent forms of ethnic identification among their Filipino American inhabitants. And even though these communities differ from other Filipino American settlements in terms of number, character, or sentiment, this study shows the ways in which all of these communities exist in relation to each other as they share a common history and as they experience, in varying degrees, contemporary forms of marginality. I position this study of Southern California Filipino Americans, then, as an index both of the labor-specific and colonized/racialized history of Filipino movement to and settlement in the United States, and of the kinds of identity construction and community formation that provide the grounds for questioning, challenging, and acting upon such a history.

3

Marking and Marketing Identities in Filipino "Oriental" Stores

In the world through which I travel, I am endlessly creating myself.

—Frantz Fanon, *Black Skin, White Masks*

o shop in an "Oriental" store is to experience, literally and figuratively, a different world. From the outside, "Oriental" stores are natural-looking components of ethnic enclaves or ubiquitous corner establishments at once familiar (they have always been there) and strange (they just look "different"). But inside, the stores are far from ordinary—the prospective shopper sees a dazzling display of fresh and preserved goods and bric-a-brac, imported magazines and local trade papers, cashiers and salesclerks speaking in alien tongues, Oriental muzak blaring from rusty speakers, and fellow shoppers whizzing about. To the tourist, this is unfamiliar territory. Yet to the regular patron, this other-worldliness is immediately apprehended not only as demarcating a space of one's own within a larger unfamiliar world, but as reclaiming once familiar territory—a piece of home from the past—

where the shopping experience can be enacted, reformulated, and (to extend Fanon's insight), *recreated* in many different ways.

Examining the shopping experience at "Oriental" stores is paramount to understanding how difference gets played out for Filipino Americans in particular sites of consumption—a kind of difference that is centrally *ethnic* but also configured along intra- and interethnic, racial, class, generational, and gender lines. By "ethnic," I mean a sense of belonging to a group having a common homeland that individuals in these sites refer to. By "shopping experience," I refer to a set of social practices performed within and around particular stores, and across linguistic and economic configurations. "Oriental" stores are social spaces where ethnic differences are publicly displayed and enacted in ways that reveal certain processes of ethnic identity articulation over time and space.

My analyses of stores and shopping are based on historical and ethnographic accounts of selected "Oriental" stores in Filipino immigrant communities in Los Angeles and San Diego Counties. I concentrated on stores wholly or partly owned by Filipinos, whose clientele were mostly Filipinos. In Los Angeles County, I focused on twelve stores, in San Diego County, eight.[1] I conducted interviews, mostly on an informal and loosely structured basis, of seventy-four Filipino first-generation immigrants who are regular "Oriental"-store patrons and business proprietors in these areas. Of these, thirty-eight were female and twenty-six were male. Close to three-quarters of the respondents identified themselves as having middle-class backgrounds, while all but ten of the rest said they were working class.[2] (I also interviewed twenty-two non-Filipino spouses of the respondents.) I use their responses to illustrate the commonalities and varieties of "Filipino Americanness" in Southern California. These interviews form the basis for my definition and interpretation of identity construction in the activity of shopping.

Filipino "Orientals" and "Oriental" Spaces

In demonstrating how Filipinos in the United States express their contestations of Oriental*ism*, I take seriously the provenance of Oriental*ist* gestures of representation in general and patterns of Filipino immigration to the United States in particular. Edward Said's landmark study of Orientalism points to representations of peoples and places outside the West that are designed not only to demarcate boundaries of otherness but to manage and keep the other in place.[3] Notions of the Oriental as passive, submissive, and exotic that appear in official documents and literary works justified to an extent Orientals' subjugation and containment. Instances of such subjectification have persisted from the first efforts at classifying the population of the Middle East to latter-day representations of Asia and Asians.[4] The Filipinos were not exempt from these attempts. Certain government agencies' lists and U.S. census accounts of the immigration and naturalization of Asians from 1870 to the 1950s routinely classified Filipinos as Orientals because their numbers were apparently small.[5] Popular culture, as expressed especially in the mass media, propagated the idea of Filipinos as Oriental and further submerged their ethnic existence by sometimes explicitly, more often implicitly, placing Filipinos as *essentially* similar to the Chinese and Japanese, since "they came from the same place."[6] Such treatment resembles the erasure for convenience and efficiency employed in census taking. In a sense, therefore, Filipinos acquired a marginality, characterized as submissive Chinese/Japanese Orientals.

The study of "Oriental" stores in these Southern California enclaves can also indicate the ways in which economic niches of minority populations are created, managed, and sustained. A small amount of sociological scholarship has detailed the success of ethnic groups in establishing trade associations and rotating credit systems formed along ethnic-specific lines and around goals of self-sufficiency.[7] On one hand, these studies demonstrate how sites of production and consumption are intertwined not only with local ethnic ties (since most of the sellers and patrons are members of a particular ethnic group) but also with the larger network of producers and distributors outside their states and country. On the other hand, such instances of small market trading in specific places provide new ways of defining ethnicity: the dynamic processes of identification with a group.[8] These are the spaces where the economic, the social, and the political converge. For not only do these stores provide a site for economic exchange, they also are sites where social relationships and political alliances are formed on the basis of a common ethnicity.

Marking Difference

The most salient claim to cultural difference in "Oriental" stores is rooted in territoriality. As Mang Ambo, a Filipino American store manager and owner said, "I own this establishment. This is mine." While this may be read as a declaration of "official" ownership (Mang Ambo is the legally registered owner of the business), its cultural ramifications spring from a recognized difference between self and other defined in terms of power relations that are spatial. Ownership of territory is important for Mang Ambo because it signifies and makes concrete his power relationship with others. Mang Ambo's position is, thus, based on who he is (the owner of the place) and who he is not (the patron).

This position is extended by store owners like Mang Ambo along axes of racial and intraethnic class differences. *"Iba ito kaysa sa mga tindahan ng mga puti"* [This is different from the stores owned by whites], says Lydia, who has owned and managed a store in National City, near San Diego, for six years. "At least, I have managed to start up a business on my own. *'Yung ibang mga Pilipino, siyempre, hindi nila kaya.* [The other Filipinos, of course, cannot do the same.] It takes a lot of money." That Lydia was able to put up a business of her own despite being a Filipina in a predominantly white (and male) society is anchored to a kind of spatial identity that makes a distinct demarcation not only between whites and Filipinos but among Filipinos. Both Mang Ambo and Lydia understand their store ownership as an assertion of their own standing and that of their racial and ethnic group in relation to the more powerful white community. Yet, while this conception of difference by race prefaces the description of her store, Lydia follows it up with a more particularized difference by class. Not *all* Filipinos can do what she has done. She had the resources to invest in this business, to set up the store. Coming from a middle-class background in the Philippines gave her an edge on disrupting an established economic arrangement. Space, in this instance, is emblematic of differentiation across interethnic and intraethnic lines.

The point of such spatial demarcations on racial grounds becomes more clear as store owners and shoppers describe their territory:

Iba dito. [It's different here.] You can buy the things you can't find in Von's or Lucky.

Mas maiging mag-shopping dito kasi nandito lahat. [It's better to shop here because everything's here.]

Marami dito, hindi mo makikita sa iba. Sa Oriental store lang. [Most of what's here, you can't see anywhere else. Only in an "Oriental" store.]

Such descriptions articulate the stores' differences, qualified again in terms of relationships between particular spaces and through components within space: this is a store that is "different" from others. Note that the recognition of "difference" here is based on observation and the marking of tangible objects within a visible space. And the fact that there is some hard evidence to support this contention of "difference" allows one to separate and distinguish this space from the rest along a presumed system of hierarchy. These are spaces seen to be superior to ordinary stores; their function and uniqueness give them a special place in the owners' and shoppers' minds.

Most of the "Oriental" stores I visited were strategically located in strip malls along the peripheries of shopping centers and in pockets of Asian American communities. But they are positioned alongside other "convenience" stores (7-Elevens, Circle-Ks, and the like) or even close to larger franchises and outlets (K-Marts, grocery chains, and auto parts and repair centers). It is rare to find "Oriental" stores standing alone or with other "Asian" establishments only. Yet it is easy to recognize them. Or, more specifically, it is not difficult for Filipino Americans to recognize them among non-Oriental businesses. Banners that scream "Oriental store" or "Oriental market" are iconic symbols that point to their differences.

"Oriental" stores are equally distinctive inside: sacks of rice, fresh fruits and vegetables (usually of the "exotic" variety, such as plantain, jackfruit, guava, papaya, bok choy, Baguio beans, yam, ginger, sweet potato, and *kang kong*), spices, sweets, meats (usually a lot of pork), poultry, dairy products, seafood (often arranged on display stands separate from the meats and consisting of different varieties of fish, squid, shrimp, oyster, crab, mussels, octopus, and turtle), beverages (local as well as imported), and frozen items (including cured meats, preserved fish, and banana leaves). Most of the nonperishable items are imported: canned goods, noodles, kitchen utensils, cookware, small appliances, chop sticks, cosmetics, pharmaceuticals, medicinal herbs, slippers, shoes, raincoats, candles, and toiletries. More specialized products include gossip magazines, local newspapers, cassette tapes, stickers, memorabilia, souvenirs (from "back home"), delicacies, trinkets, religious items, and home ornaments.

As one shopper said: *"Alam ko kung ano ang mabibili dito . . . kung ano ang mabibili sa iba."* [I know what can be bought here . . . (and) what can be bought in other stores.] What is available in these stores is clear only to the stores' regular shoppers; the products are perceived to be in the "right" location. How do they come to know this? Responses to this question were almost acrimonious, which I attribute to the respondents feeling that I should know better, since I'm a Filipino who also patronizes the stores.

> *Siempre, 'yung mabibili dito e mga Pilipino products. E 'di kung gusto mong bumili ng sabon o toothpaste, doon ka pupunta sa Lucky.* [Of course, the things you can buy here are Filipino products. If you want to buy soap or toothpaste, you go to Lucky.]

> *Ano ka? Hilo? Bakit ka pupunta dito kung ang hinahanap mo e 'yung mga nabibili sa Von's. Doon ka pumunta. Doon ka mag-shopping.* [What are you? Crazy? Why would you come here if what you're looking for are things you can buy at Von's. Go there, then. Go and shop there.]

In these cases, articulating difference or identity depends on recognizing differences in store products. On the basis of local knowledge, shoppers are aware of the kinds of products that are available only in these kinds of stores. They are products that are recognizable because of their origin ("Made in the Philippines") and, more specifically, because of their association with life and things in the homeland. Such commodities then become expressions of, or even sources of, one's ethnicity. Often, simply the labeling of products mediates between object and experience. The label "Made in the Philippines" triggers a connection that may have been physically severed but one that is reestablished by the product's availability in the new settlement. Labels are used as a basis for remapping one's sense of displacement.

Respondents also mark the differences among products based on "genuineness." Labels signify this quality in its most direct sense: a product came from, and therefore was made in, the Philippines. To say that the products are genuine because they come from a certain place (the "homeland") invites a sense of relationship to such products that one does not have with "other" products that one can buy from other, bigger stores. They are special. Their value is unlike that of other products precisely because of their difference in origin and their imagined qualities. Some of these products (such as sardines) are similar to locally made goods, but those from outside the country are regarded much differently. As Eva, a shopper, said: *"Yung sardinas sa Von's, iba 'yun sa sardinas na gawa sa atin."* [The sardines at Von's are different from the sardines that are made in our country.] The qualities of the imported goods at the "Oriental" stores help mark differences that, as we shall see later, produce relationships and practices that are unique among shoppers. That is, the assignment of certain values and properties to specific commodities (according to their perceived qualities and referents) becomes a point of articulation of otherness—transcending what may be the "objective" properties of such commodities. These are products that are redefined by "use" value rather than merely "exchange" value, as they are mobilized in the service of ethnic formation.[9]

The processes involved in recognizing how the origin and quality of products demarcate differences, however, are not limited to simple association or identification by contrast. For example, some say:

> *Maganda dito kasi sariling atin 'yung mga nabibili. Galing pa sa Pilipinas.* [It's nice here because we buy what's ours. They come from the Philippines.]

> *Nakakatuwa kasi 'yung mga nabibili sa Pilipinas e mabibili din dito. Para kang nasa Pilipinas nga eh.* [It's fun here because what you can buy in the Philippines, you can buy here. It's like being in the Philippines.]

Iba yung mga nabibili dito. Para bang mas-espesyal kasi genuine, galing talaga sa Pilipinas. Tingnan mo, talagang "Made in the Philippines." [The products you can buy here are different. They seem to be more special because they are genuine, really "Made in the Philippines."]

Para ka na ring nasa Pilipinas, kasi 'yung mga binibili mo e 'yun ding binibili ng mga kapwa-Pilipino. Para ka na ring nasa atin. [It's like being in the Philippines, because the things you buy here are the same ones bought by other Filipinos. It's like being in the Philippines.]

Here, a kind of ethnic fetishism is foregrounded in the sense that goods seem to trigger images and memories of a time and place associated with the original homeland. It is as if products mimic the objective existence of immigration while charting a different geography: the Philippines is simultaneously "here" and "there." Looking at these products and shopping for them becomes an exercise in nostalgia, so that a specific "identity" is built on a kind of longing for what is missing and attempting to fill that space. Nostalgia, elicited through shopping for these specific goods, is of primary importance in dealing with displacement—being separated from one's original place—and in purposely reordering present disruptions. In a sense, nostalgia eases the trauma of immigration because it provides some degree of comfort or security, some feeling of being "at home."

This comfort-producing nostalgia occurs in three ways: by distinctive smells, by reference to the store's counterpart in the homeland, and by recollection of a specific shopping practice known as the *"suki"* system, in which shoppers are accorded special treatment by vendors.

Iba ang amoy ng tindahan dito. Amoy tindahan talaga. Medyo marumi, pero ganoon naman talaga ang mga maliliit na tindahan sa atin, 'di ba? [The smell of this store is different. It really smells like a store. It's a bit dirty, but it's really like that in the small stores we have back home, right?]

Alam ko kung saan pupunta. Madali lang naman hanapin 'yung mga kailangan mo dito, 'di ba? Iba kasi talaga, pati ang amoy. Amoy tindahan talaga. Mabaho. (laughter) *'Yung mga malalaking tindahan, amoy gamot. Sobrang linis kasi.* [I know where to go. It's really easy to find the things you need here, isn't it? It's because of the difference really, even the smell. It smells like a real store. Smells bad (laughter). The other big stores smell like medicine. It's because they're overly clean.]

These responses are rooted in the idea that "Oriental" stores have been transplanted from back home into a new place, including their very smell. Odor also offers a different way of organizing the senses in terms of their importance in articulating specific identities. That the sense of smell is accorded a particular weight alongside the sense of sight and the other senses makes this kind of cultural practice quite unique in its own right, especially in contrasting spaces. As mentioned by the shopper just quoted, the big stores are less enticing, particularly because of the way they smell. Moreover, smell permits a ranking of stores. For a lot of these shoppers, stores that exude the "correct" odor (most often characterized as "fishy" or "*amoy tsinelas*" [smells like slippers]) rank as "better" or "more trusted" as compared with mainstream stores, which arouse suspicion by how "clean" or "medicinal" they smell.

Beyond the nostalgia produced by odor, respondents nostagically connect stores in the homeland to the "Oriental" stores in the United States. Almost all of them talk about how these stores remind them of those back home, the *sari-sari* stores that, like the ones they have here, are neighborhood retail establishments on quite a small scale. *Sari-sari* stores, begun by Chinese merchants in the eighteenth-century Philippines, sell goods in small quantities.[10] As in the Philippines, for the convenience of shoppers, some of the "Oriental" stores here sell some products by the piece or by weight, such as one cigarette instead of a whole pack, or a pound of rice instead of a prepackaged sack. This allows more convenience for the buyer because of necessity and economic constraint. Moreover, what I term "shopping practices" in these stores include more than Western shopping conventions allow. Although "Oriental"-store shoppers generally shop in the same ways as non-Filipinos, most respondents say that they go to the stores not only to shop but to socialize, a practice common in the *sari-sari* store. Here they meet other Filipino Americans, "hang out," and engage in small talk. These activities eventually turn the "work" of shopping into a collective pleasurable practice, removed from the realm of the mechanical and the industrial nature of the bigger stores. Especially for some Filipino American homemakers, this combination of socializing and shopping has been a longstanding practice.

Masayang mamili dito kasi may halong kuwento. Nakikita ko 'yung mga kakilala ko. Tapos, hayun, kuwentuhan kami. [It's enjoyable to shop here because we can mix it with conversation. I see those I know. And then, we tell each other stories.]

Okay lang. Mamimili ka, tapos makikita mo 'yung mga kaibigan mo. [It's okay. You shop, and then you see your friends.]

Parang 'yung mga dating tindahan din sa Pilipinas. May halong tsismisan sa tindahan. Madalas, ganun dito. [It's like what used to be the kind of stores in the Philippines. There's a mix of gossip in the stores. Often, it's like that here.]

The third way "Oriental" stores feed the nostalgia of Filipino American shoppers is through a practice in which shoppers *(sukis)* are given special attention by owners and their employees: the butchers, seafood "cleaners," cooks, salesclerks, cashiers, security guards, and bag persons.

Suki na ako dito. Lagi kasi akong nandito. Buti 'yon, magandang baboy ang binibigay sa akin. [I'm a *suki* here. It's because I'm always here. It's good, I get good pork parts from them.]

Pag pasok ko, hinahanap ko na 'yung tagalinis ko ng isda. Magaling siya e, tapos may dagdag pang hipon kung minsan. [When I come in here, I look immediately for the one who cleans the fish. He's good, and then, there's additional (free) shrimp sometimes.]

The *suki* system has its origins in the Philippines. Pioneered there by the Chinese in the mid–eighteenth century, "suki" refers to a system of seller-shopper exchange that is more intimate than usual. It involves having a store owner or store clerk accord special privileges to a regular client to encourage that client to continue patronizing the store. Privileges can range from reserving scarce items in the store for a particular shopper to offering select goods at discounted prices. The principle here is that both owner and shopper obtain benefits by going beyond impersonal exchanges. This system, "transplanted" to Southern California, allows owners to make their stores even more attractive to Filipino American shoppers. The shoppers who participate in the system find shopping in these stores comparatively better and more economical.

Nostalgia here is experienced by a group of Filipino American shoppers who share a conception of "what it must have been like" to order "what it is now." As Susan Stewart proposes, nostalgia is an essential narrative particularly for displaced people because it calls into action a kind of language and practice that make possible a common frame of meaning. For her, it dramatizes aspects of a "fluid and unnamed social life . . . in the mode of 'things that happened,' that 'could happen,' and that 'threaten to erupt at any moment.'"[11] Nostalgia, therefore, becomes a key element in what Hamid Naficy calls communal cohesion and ethnic solidarity, because people from the same group have common referents to a past that bear on current symbolic and material goods and practices.[12]

Nostalgia also figures prominently in language—here, the use of Taglish as a principal form of communication in the stores. Taglish is a popular term for a kind of speaking and writing that combines Tagalog and English (in some cases, also Spanish). Conversing in it takes a particular facility, for it is not an arbitrary combining of two or three languages. Spoken mostly in Metropolitan Manila, Taglish is employed by Filipino Americans in the stores as a way of talking "just like we do [or did] at home." For example, phrases like *"mag-shopping"* [to go shopping], *"Pumunta tayo sa store"* [Let's go to the store], *"magkano ang selling price ng mga ito?"* [What is the selling price of these?], and *"Buy ka na lang dito"* [Just buy here] can be overheard in the stores. Even some product labels and signs appear in Taglish: *"patis sauce"* [fish sauce], *"maanghang vinegar"* [spicy vinegar], *"chismis magazines"* [gossip magazines], and *"Dito kayo mag-line-up"* [Line up here]. The use of Taglish is an example of the past recurring in the present, and the "far away" being situated in the "here." It is an attempt to trace and articulate both historical memory and current situation. When I asked several patrons why they spoke in Taglish, they said:

Aba bakit? Masama ba? Ganyan tayo mag-salita 'di ba? Parang sa Pilipinas din. Halo-halo. 'Di ba nagpunta rin sa atin ang mga Kastila? E di marunong din tayo ng konting Kastila. Tapos, nag-aral din tayo ng Ingles dahil sa mga 'Kano. Tapos, marunong din tayong managalog. Hindi natin nakalimutan ang mga ito, 'di ba? [Well, why? Is it bad? That's the way we speak, isn't it? It's like in the Philippines too. Mix-mix. Didn't the Spaniards go to our place?

Then, we do know some Spanish. And then, we also studied English
because of the Americans. Then, we also know how to speak Tagalog. We
didn't forget these, right?]

*'Yung Taglish e matagal na nating sinasalita. Mabuti nga iyon, pagdating natin
dito, pag tayo-tayo lang e tayo-tayo din ang nagkakaintindihan. Aba, e paano
mo i-ta-translate ang patis? Fish sauce daw? Parang hindi patis iyon, 'di ba?
Parang gawa dito pag sinabi mong fish sauce.* [Taglish is something we've spoken for a long time. It's good, when we arrive here, when it's just us and
we who can understand each other. Well, how do you translate *patis*? Fish
sauce, they say? That's not like saying *patis*, is it? It's like it's made here if
you say fish sauce.]

*Nakakatawa kasi pag ganoon tayo mag-usap. Minsan may hindi marunong
managalog pero nakaka-pick-up . . . 'yung bang mga bits and pieces . . . like, da-
da-da-da-da bananas . . . da-da-da-da-da five dollars. Siempre, por que nandito
tayo, dapat ba e makalimutan natin iyon?* [It's funny when we speak like that.
Sometimes, someone who doesn't speak Tagalog is able to pick up . . . the
bits and pieces . . . like, da-da-da-da-da bananas . . . da-da-da-da-da five
dollars. Of course, just because we're here, is it right to forget it?]

*Lalo na sa tindahan. Paano ka maiintindihan kung iisa lang ang alam mong
language? Lalo na kung Pilipino ka.* Well, you can pretend. *Pero, and samang
pakinggan kung puro Ingles o puro Tagalog. Pabili nga ng peytis?* O kaya e, can
I buy some fish sauce? Fish sauce? Patis iyon, 'di ba?* [All the more in the
stores. How can you be understood if you know only one language? Especially if you're a Filipino. Well, you can pretend. But, it's awful to hear if
it's pure English or pure Tagalog. May I buy *peytis* (pronounced with a
mocking accent)? Or, can I buy some fish sauce? Fish sauce? That's *patis*,
isn't it?]

A specificity of Filipino "Oriental" stores also lies in the fact that
the language most appropriate to them is Taglish. It is a language that
goes beyond both the national (Tagalog) and the imperial (English
and Spanish) languages: it is not purely Tagalog, English, or Spanish, but all of these at the same time, in different combinations, and
in varying relation to each other. Taglish tries to circumvent the hierarchies between and within these languages, so that one is not privileged over the others.[13] In fact, Taglish registers a refusal to translate certain Tagalog words into the mainstream or dominant language
mainly as a marker of Tagalog's (and English's or Spanish's) insistent
presence in the speech, labels, and writing in the stores. Thus, the

use of Taglish is not only a nostalgic evocation, but a sign and practice of movement or mobility across linguistic boundaries.

But the power of group nostalgia has certain limitations as well. To an outsider, nostalgic practices embedded in "Oriental"-store shopping may appear homogeneous and fixed, as if all Filipino Americans have the same versions of the past. To an extent, this is true: all of them come from the same homeland. But if one looks closer, subtle differences in invoking the past reveal the group's heterogeneity. A working-class Filipino, for example, would tend to reconstruct his country of birth in ways that reflect his family's poor living conditions. The *sari-sari* stores for him are mostly rundown shacks where one can buy "cheap beer." Several working-class Filipinas said they preferred these stores over others because "everything was cheap." For a middle-class male respondent, the *sari-sari* stores were more the "concrete" and "nicely constructed" ones that are there primarily "for others." Although he is familiar with how they look, he does not patronize them that much, owing perhaps to a class standing that affords him a different quality of life with a different set of social expectations. Women in this group also tended to have recollections of these stores as "alternative" stores or "stores for convenience only," where they "just go to buy sugar or candy." Most of their shopping was done in the bigger stores. I do not deny that *sari-sari* stores in the Philippines come in many shapes and sizes. Rather, I wish to point out that, even if collective memory refers to a *kind* of store in the homeland, the particular configurations of that store tend to vary across, in this case, class and gender within the same group.

Even the practice of speaking in Taglish is not without its tensions. Taglish is spoken in many different ways by different Filipinos and, like most languages, is open to change over time and space. As one Filipino American said:

> The Taglish that we speak here is medyo [somewhat] different from that in the Philippines. *Siempre, may dagdag din tayo. Kaya baka akalain noong mga bisita dito e mga mayabang tayo.* [Of course, we've also added to it. That's why people who are visiting might think we are boastful (or braggarts).]

Then, there are those who remark that some kinds of Taglish reveal where a speaker comes from, in terms of class position and (U.S. and Philippine) location:

Sabi ng iba, 'yung Taglish natin dito, iba kaysa sa ibang parte ng 'Tate. Siempre, dito sa San Diego, may halo na rin ng ibang words from the people in the Navy. Galing sa mga sundalo 'yung mga ibang dugdug. [Some other people say that our Taglish here is different from the other parts of the United States. Of course, here in San Diego, it's mixed with other words from the people in the navy. The other additions are from the soldiers.]

'Yung iba diyan, isip mo mga colegiala. Mga isnabero. Mayaman kasi, eh. "Tusok-tusok da fish balls." Nakakabuwisit pakinggan! [The others here, you'd think they are college students. Those snobs. It's because they're rich. "Put the fish balls on the skewer." It's so disgusting to hear!][14]

Depende rin naman. May iba, isip mo kung magsalita e may mga mansiyon sa Pilipinas. Pero okay lang, nagkakaintindihan naman tayo. At least, kilala mo kung saan nanggagaling. [It also depends. Regarding others, you'd think from the way they speak that they have a mansion in the Philippines. But it's okay, since we can understand each other. At least you know where they are coming from.]

Nostalgia, as a significant deployment of a particular common past, tends to obliterate these variations in favor of demarcating differences across other races and ethnicities. You have to be a Filipino ("*galing sa atin*" [from our place]) to perform this kind of nostalgic exercise. Or, as those I interviewed said in many instances, "You have to be like us . . . Orientals" to be able to shop in these stores with ease. The marking of the site not only seeks to be exclusive, but attempts to be inclusive. This is where notions of ethnic difference come into play. When asked who they think patronizes the stores, respondents answered by qualifying shoppers by ethnicity—which kinds of people shop in the stores, and which do not. This double-edged marking of "difference" by identifying groups of people is articulated by both owners and shoppers:

Mostly, Pilipino at saka Intsik ang nagsho-shopping dito. Tayo lang naman ang nakakaalam kung ano ang mabibili dito e. [Mostly, Filipinos and Chinese shop here. It's only us who know what can be bought here.]

Obvious ba? 'Yung asawa kong puti e maliligaw dito. Hindi niya alam kung ano ang kukunin niya. [Isn't it obvious? My white husband would be lost here. He wouldn't know what to get.]

Tayo-tayo lang naman ang nakakaintindi kung ano ang nabibili dito. 'Yung iba e walang alam. [It's only us who understand what can be bought here. The others don't know.]

Ang tindahang ito e para lang sa atin. 'Yung mga puti, bihira mo lang makikita dito. Marami, hindi lang Pinoy, pati Intsik, Koreano, mga taga-Thailand. 'Yung iba e sa ibang malalaking tindahan lang. [This store is only for us. The whites, you rarely see them here. Many of us, not only Filipinos, even Chinese, Koreans, those from Thailand. The rest can go to other big stores.]

These are quite vivid descriptions of difference that situate the shopper vis-à-vis ethnic identities: these specific spaces are only for specific people. In this case, Filipino "Oriental" stores' clientele is primarily Filipino but includes other Asians and excludes whites, who are among "other people" viewed as either lost or "just looking."

Karamihan diyan, tumitingin lang. Minsan bumibili, pero wala yatang regular customer. [Many of those (others) just look. Sometimes, they buy; but they seem not to be regular customers.]

'Yung mga puti na nagpupunta dito, usually asawa o kamag-anak ng mga Pilipino. Bihira 'yung nag-iisa. [The whites who come here are usually the spouses or relatives of Filipinos. Seldom do we see them alone.]

'Yung mga ibang taong nandito, patingin-tingin lang. Hindi bumibili. Pero ine-entertain din namin sila. [The others who are here, they just look. They don't buy. But we entertain them too.]

Space offers a means by which identities and counteridentities can be articulated publicly, and not only vocally. As Aling Myrna, another store manager, explained:

Wala namang nagsasabing bawal pumasok ang iba dito. Walang "Do not enter." Pero siempre, alam natin na ang tindahang ito e para lang sa mga katulad natin. [Nobody says the others could not come in here. No "Do not enter." But of course we know that this store is only for people like us.]

Demarcating the site requires very little manifestation of physical difference. Although the stores have obvious tangible boundaries and signs that identify them for what they are (Asian Market, Paradise

Oriental Store, Maynila Oriental Store, Cham Song Oriental Supermarket, Makati Supermarket, etc.), we find no clear borders or check-
points that regulate entry—anyone can come in. The more powerful
and provocative point is that people *know*, without being told and on
the basis of local knowledge, whether they should come in or not. The
spaces themselves act as regulators whose seemingly invisible signs and
rules control traffic to and from their confines. Space in this case,
therefore, is itself the central articulator of identity differences. Moreover, the fact that these are implicit markings forces shoppers to confront the contours of identity difference. They must recognize these
identities within the site in order to shop there. Otherwise, they can
go to another site where shoppers, goods, and shops are more familiar and, therefore, manageable.

The non-Oriental shopper in an "Oriental" store is inundated
with rows and rows of strange goods, as several non-Filipino respondents made clear:

> This place is so confusing. I'm at a loss every time I'm here.

> Most of the stuff here, I don't know what they're for. My [Filipina-Amer-
> ican] wife picks whatever we need.

> I'm lost. I need a guide to help me shop here.

> Only you guys know what to buy here.

Clearly, these assertions reflect the identity markings just discussed.
But the politics of difference also come into play in the ways shoppers
relate to the objects for sale. For non-Orientals, the products are mere
goods, often goods that are unrecognizable and, therefore, meaning-
less or at least "confusing." Even if most of the labels for the goods have
English translations and accompanying graphics, their meanings are
often unclear. Only the seasoned shopper knows what the goods really
are, and what they are for, as Marilou, a regular shopper, indicates:

> *E kung magluluto ka ng dinuguan o kaya e kare-kare o adobo, alam mo ba kung
> anong sangkap ang kukunin mo? Siempre, kahit may translation, mahirap ding
> intindihin.* [Well, if you have to cook *dinuguan* or *kare-kare* or *adobo*, do
> you know which ingredients you need to get? Of course, even with trans-
> lation, it's hard to understand if you don't know what's being translated].

In a world in which many objects have multiple signifiers, the ability to match meaning to object is a survival skill. In this context, it is another indication of how "Oriental" stores have made possible a marking of difference along consumption, cultural, and identity lines.

Marketing Difference

The initial point of marking difference in spatial terms constitutes a somewhat easily detectable and observable series of movements on site. A more implicit set of territorializing processes reveals indirectly attempts to address the very conditions that account for marginalization by twisting these conditions around to achieve other specific purposes. The process does not begin and end by merely defining differences. It takes off again by capitalizing on the power that was gained in marking by "talking back," reasserting differences outwardly, and opening up new avenues for contestations of identities. Space here becomes crucially reterritorialized. My term for this activity is "marketing differences."

For most "Oriental"-store proprietors, ownership of a business has, first and foremost, a concrete objective—to do business. The bottom line is to make money, to earn a living:

> *Tinayo ko itong tindahang ito kasi gustong kong magkaroon ng business.* [I built this store to have a business.]

> *Ako ang nagmamay-ari ng tindahang ito. Okay naman, minsan maunlad, minsan gipit. Dati nagtatrabaho lang ako sa Navy, pero naisipan ko na mas mabuti kung magpatakbo ako ng sarili kong tindahan. Okay naman.* [I am the one who owns this store. It's okay, sometimes it's prosperous, sometimes it runs low. I used to work in the navy, but I thought it was better if I run my own store. It's okay.]

Their explanations of how they got to be in this business show how the history of business in these communities is linked to the history of Filipino immigration to California and perhaps even to immigration policies.

> *May mga fifteen years na ako sa business na ito. Noong una, puro bahay lang dito. Ang mga Pilipino, nagkumpol-kumpol dito sa National City. Ewan ko ba,*

siguro dahil malapit sa Thirty-eighth, sa navy shipyard. Pero hindi rin, dahil ang hirap bumili ng bahay sa ibang lugar. Tapos, naisip ko rin, e kung mag-tatayo ako ng Filipino store, e di doon na sa lugar kung saan maraming Pilipino. Siempre, sila din naman ang bibili ng mga ititinda ko. Tapos, tulong-tulong kami. May mga distributor sa L.A., pinag-commit ko sila. Aba, e ang hirap mag-import noon. Katakut-takot na bawal. Kesyo bawal ang may buto, bawal ang buhay na isda. Kaya ang bangus, hindi namin matinda. Tapos, may mga per-mit dapat. Mga Magnolia, Newton. . . . 'Yung permit sa tindahan, inayos ko rin. Naku, ang dami palang kailangan. Matagal din bago kami nagbukas, at maliit 'yung una naming tindahan. Ngayon kita mo, nakapag-expand na ako. [I have been in this business for about fifteen years. Before, there were only houses here. The Filipinos clustered around National City. I don't know, prob-ably because it was close to Thirty-eighth (Street), the navy shipyard. But not really so, since it was hard to buy a house in other places. And then, I thought that if I have to build a Filipino store, it had to be in a place where there were a lot of Filipinos. Of course, they are the ones who will buy the goods I will sell. And then we helped each other. There were dis-tributors in L.A., I asked them to commit. Alas, it was hard to import (goods) at that time. A lot of restrictions. Restrictions on seeds (or fresh fruits with seeds), restrictions on live seafood. And then we had to have permits. Magnolia (ice cream), Newton (preserved fruit). . . . The permit for the store, I fixed it too. There were a lot of requirements! It took some time before we opened, and our first store was small. Now, you see, I was able to expand.]

Kilala ko lahat 'yung mga may tindahan dito dati. Ang balak ko talaga, mak-isosyo. Pero sayang din. Nandito na tayo sa Amerika, why not? Nakipag-con-tact ako sa mga kaibigan ko sa Pilipinas. Pero sa una, puro isda lang ako, at saka baboy, gulay. . . . E may tindahan ka nga, wala namang iba pang mabili. Siempre, gusto ng mga Pinoy, nandito na lahat. Kaya hayun, dinagdagan ko na lang nang dinagdagan. Tahimik dito noon, kanya-kanya. Pero ngayon kita mo, maunlad. Only in America! [I knew everyone who owned stores here before. My original intention was to be partners with others. But I couldn't miss the chance. We're already here in America, why not? I contacted my friends from the Philippines. But at first, I only sold fish, pork, vegeta-bles. . . . But I had a store where you can't buy other things. Of course, Filipinos want to buy everything here (in one store). That's why there, I added and added. It was quiet here before, each to one's own. But now it's prosperous. Only in America!]

In National City, the Filipino American communities formed around military (particularly, naval) work sites, when droves of Filipinos were recruited to work in the navy. This wave of immigration started in the

1950s and reached its peak in the 1970s as more and more Filipinos served as nonenlisted seamen (often as "mess boys") aboard U.S. military ships. Around Los Angeles, during the same period, Filipinos who immigrated were mostly professionals (particularly in the medical and allied health services), who lived in small enclaves in the downtown and suburban areas. Although it is reasonable to assume that the stores were purposely built at sites where Filipinos worked, and thus where prospective customers would be located, it is tempting to draw parallels between "ethnic" clustering and city zoning policies. As several store owners recount, it was difficult to settle anywhere other than where most Filipinos were already situated. I would argue that assignments of inhabitable and commercial spaces masked as formal zoning policies reflected the underlying racism of those in authority. In the city of San Diego, for example, evidence of racial discrimination in housing was rampant until the 1970s. Calling for more "ethnically balanced communities," the 1971 Fair Housing Committee Report for that city pointed to an "alarming tide of latent exclusivity inherent in real estate practices which use prohibitive costs of new housing" to keep minorities away from certain neighborhoods. Even those new immigrants who had enough money to purchase or rent housing in predominantly middle-class areas were unable to do so because of discriminatory action.[15]

The locating of "Oriental" stores in strip malls, usually adjacent to shopping centers, especially in Southern California, is also worth noting. Shopping centers did not become popular in the United States until after World War II, when automobile ownership greatly increased and a massive nationwide population movement to the suburbs took place. In Los Angeles and San Diego Counties, shopping centers sprouted near postwar suburban communities as opposed to older, more centralized cities. As some urban historians have suggested, small shops like "Oriental" stores, while unable in most instances to afford locations in a shopping center, often tried to locate nearby and capitalize on the center's attractive force. Small retailers banded together and put up strip malls, blocks fronting main streets that positioned several small stores right next to, or in front of, ample parking.[16]

These "pirating" stores, as they were once known, rode the coat-tails of the shopping center's publicity, the pulling power of its big-ger businesses, and the changes in traffic patterns connected with its construction. These stores openly, but subversively, took advantage of the otherwise threatening competition of the shopping centers. One city planning study in 1960 details how shopping center man-agers opposed the "uncontrolled and chaotic" character of strip mall development, which counteracted efforts of the shopping centers themselves to present a "pleasant" appearance in the surrounding residential areas. Owners of big businesses even ascribed to "pirat-ing" stores the "deterioration of surrounding residential property values, the impairment of the visual quality of the neighborhood, and the blighting of surrounding areas."[17]

Conditions were further confounded by the immigrant entrepre-neurs who moved to the suburbs and capitalized on the small-scale investment requirements and ideal locations of the strip malls. More-over, the restructuring of the U.S. economy created opportunities for small investors to compete against the remaining large department stores in the cities. The combination of big department and chain stores leaving the inner cities and their inability to adapt quickly to a new and more diverse clientele allowed recently arrived entrepreneurs to establish small and medium-sized businesses, especially in minor-ity-populated neighborhoods. (In some ways, these businesses helped revitalize depressed communities that were victims of deindustrializa-tion.) Immigrants in urban areas capitalized on these opportunities, along with other entrepreneurs.[18]

Included in the Filipino American store owners' accounts are memories of what they call the "nonbelievers"—those who told them their stores could not succeed.

Akala nila e hindi namin kaya. Walang naniwala sa akin noon, kundi kapwa Pilipino lang. . . . Kaya hayun, sabi ko bahala na. Nagsikap talaga kami. 'Yung ayos ng tindahan, pinlano ng anak ko. Tapos, gusto rin namin maiba. Hindi naman namin puwedeng parisan 'yung mga malalaking tindahan. Pero inayos namin ng mabuti para medyo maganda naman. [Before, they thought we wouldn't make it. Nobody believed in me, except Filipinos themselves. . . . We really strove. The way the store was arranged, my offspring planned.

And then, we wanted it to be different. We can't match the (big) stores. But we fixed it well so that it will look pretty.]

Oo nga, maraming nagsasabi noon, walang mangyayari dito. Paano, ang big-pit-higpit, tapos ang dami pang kumpetensiya, mga malalaking tindahan ng mga puti. Tingnan mo ngayon, may nagsasalita ba? [Yes, many said before that nothing would happen with this. Because it was so restrictive, and then there were a lot of competitors, big stores owned by whites. Look now, is anyone saying anything?]

In these narratives, one hears the value placed on succeeding against tough odds. These struggles are particularly important to the store owners, since implicitly they are struggles against oppression aimed at them because of their ethnic or national origin. It was the non-Filipinos who did not believe at first and were eventually proven wrong. These narratives also reveal subversions of Orientalist assumptions about the store owner's character and position in society. No, they are not submissive, voiceless, lazy creatures. No, they are not unimportant and inferior. They can rise above these mistaken notions, and the "proof" of their success is their lucrative business. Space has become the evidence.

What stands out in these accounts is that, even though these owners had problems establishing a business, they were able to challenge authority with much success. In their "assigned" places, they were able to carve out a creative and productive existence by invoking the support of allies from within and outside the country. Owners were reluctant to depict their histories as individual struggles. Rather, they credited business connections, kinship alliances, and community support for enabling them to build a lucrative enterprise. Managers often speak of this web of production and distribution networks, whose participants are mostly Filipino or other Asians in the United States and in the homeland. It provides them easier access to in-demand goods such as candies (Storck, White Rabbit, *titina*), particular staples (Nestlé Cream [for fruit salad], *queso de bola*, canned Kraft cheese), and fresh produce (bok choy, *kang kong*, laurel) that customers know can be bought only at their stores. The result is a reterritorialized space—a direct transformation of their space's function from keeping them marginalized to declaring their difference despite their position at the margins of society.

The kinds of community socialization that occur in these sites make a strong case for "Oriental" stores as more than money-making ventures. Although emphasizing the socialization aspect of shopping might be considered a ploy to attract more customers, I suggest that—while the bottom line for the shop owners is to make a profit the businesses are tied to a very localized and ethnically bound circulation of capital. Store owners are supplied goods by Filipino and other Asian merchants in the United States and overseas. They deal only with wholesalers and distributors who are Filipino. Their stores are mostly patronized by people of their kind. In short, business owners decide whom to deal with inside a very tight web of ethnic interconnections and economies of mutual interest. For instance, when I accompanied a Filipino store buyer to the Los Angeles Merchant Exchange (a market exclusively for store owners and their bulk buyers), I noticed that he always opted to purchase goods from the Filipino and other Asian sellers, despite the presence of many non-Asian merchants who were selling goods at the same price, "to keep it in the family," as he said. "Besides," he continued, *"hindi ka lolokohin ng mga ito* [you won't be fooled by these people]. I trust them. And they're good to me. So we just help each other." These networks of buyers and merchants also exchange goods on a credit basis with relative ease, compared to other options.

Many business owners I talked to have refused continuing offers from the big supermarkets to buy them out, with promises of increased patronage and higher profits. In my second year of fieldwork, 1993, larger "Oriental" stores were beginning to sprout near the smaller stores, posing a threat to their business. Ranch 99, once a medium-sized grocery in Monterey Park, was setting up branches in San Diego and in other parts of Los Angeles, forming a chain of stores financed largely by Taiwanese capital. These stores offered more space and a wider variety of products than did the smaller "Oriental" marts, arranged mostly by national origin. And as in the mainstream groceries, price scan machines and mechanisms for charge card purchases became standard features. They also housed eateries, bookstores, pet shops, banks, and specialty merchandise stores. "It's getting harder and harder to do business here," said one "Oriental"

store owner. "These are bigger chains with lots of capital from everywhere in Asia. Many have already asked me to join with them. You
know, the market is expanding and expanding. But no way will I be
eaten up. I don't want to give up my store. I worked so hard for it
already. *Sayang eh* [I don't want it to go to waste]. The customers still
come . . . so we help each other *na rin* [also]."

Increased competition has brought mixed results for both owners
and shoppers. It has made many proprietors develop new ways to
keep their regular customers and to attract those who now have more
shopping choices. Side stalls within the stores have lately been filled
with specialty brand-name goods bought through direct suppliers
from the Philippines. These include Goldilocks pastries, now sold in
franchise stores and bakeshops in the United States, Magnolia and
Selecta ice cream products from home, and Regal and Viva movies
from Filipino-owned film production outfits. Reflecting the expanding transnational marketing ties of U.S. and Philippine-based cor-
porations, these products appeal to prospective shoppers' associations cultivated outside the United States. To attract those who
usually don't enter their stores, particularly second-generation Filipino Americans whom I've seen waiting outside or in their parents'
cars while their parents shop, store managers have begun promoting
audio cassettes and CDs of Philippine-based popular music artists by
playing their songs in the stores and posting their album jackets
prominently. On the other hand, competition and expansion have
forced many of the "Oriental" stores to look for ways to keep over-
head costs to a minimum. Owners have resorted to hiring mainly
Mexican American maintenance personnel willing to accept low pay
for their service. While their presence in the stores is strikingly apparent, many of those I talked to were reluctant to identify any racial
tension that might exist.[19]

Nevertheless, for these "Oriental" stores, participating in a
transnational marketplace does not necessarily mean surrendering to
the dictates of big business, where decisions are based solely on profit.
As several owners emphasize, the desire to keep their businesses
small-scale and attuned to local community interest has always been
paramount. One of them told me: "I try to give back what I can. Our

store sponsors many Filipino events. We donate prizes and we serve refreshments for free in many of the fiestas. We try to serve our clients [beyond] . . . selling them things." In these ways, "Oriental" stores are able to resist the encroachment of profit-driven corporate strategies in the places where they operate.

Even the use of "Oriental" as part of many stores' names may be read as contesting Orientalist assumptions. As most respondents would say, "The store may be called Oriental, but I am no Oriental." What for you is an Oriental? I would ask. "An Oriental," one said, "is someone who is deceitful but very quiet, submissive, lazy, smells bad, talks bad, cannot be trusted." In short, "you don't want to deal with any Oriental, and I'm far from smelling bad." But why do you call your store an "Oriental" store? I ask. "Well, that is a different Oriental," was the response. "That is an Oriental place, not a place in the *Orient*, but a place here where you can be comfortable, where you can be your own self, buy the best goods that you need, those that you cannot find anywhere else, where you can feel okay because you buy them from people you know and can trust." What I read from this and similar responses is a recognition of the negative connotations of the word "Oriental"—and a pointed refusal to be called one. But the same word may be used to refer to a condition of a space—a kind of Oriental space that is not Orientalizing in its original arcane sense.

Labeling an enterprise an "Oriental" place is indeed part of a business strategy—a mark of difference meant to attract those who think of themselves as Orientals and even continue to call themselves by that term. These stores play up the ways they contrast with the large groceries: small size, minimal lighting (as opposed to bright fluorescents), few and noncomputerized cash registers (and no price "scanners"), and general untidiness. But inside the stores, as noted earlier, the term "Oriental" takes on multiple meanings. Presumed homogeneities are fragmented as Filipino Americans of varying race and class distinctions appear, along with Chinese, Koreans, Indonesians, Thais, Malaysians, Singaporeans, and even Mexicans, Nicaraguans, and some African Americans. The shop owners recognize these differences; that is why they place piñatas alongside woven baskets, audio cassettes of

Thai singers with Filipino recordings, statues of Buddha together with those of the child Jesus. Even detergents made locally (and sold at large department stores) occupy spaces with kitchen utensils manufactured in Taiwan. Dry goods of a variety of Asian origins share aisle spaces with herbs and spices for Mexican dishes, arranged alphabetically. Where is the "Filipinoness" of these stores? Conventional cultural boundaries are blurred and identities become multivocal. Both Orientals and non-Orientals confront and are confronted by their differences. Again, this could be read as part of the continuous shaping and reshaping of Oriental identities.

But in spite of these distinctions, many owners and shoppers still perceive the stores and the goods displayed in them as predominantly Filipino (defined as "originating" from the homeland), and non-Fillipino goods as of secondary importance, even though they are shelved together (Mexican products, Japanese goods, etc.). As one shopper said:

> *Itong mga tindahang ito e talagang pam-Pilipino. Iyung mga ibang nabibili dito . . . katulad ng mga piñata at saka mga spices ng ibang tao e nandito lang para convenience ba. Since nandito ka na, e di bumili ka na noon, keysa naman papunta-punta ka sa iba. Pero ang karamihan dito, talagang pam-Pilipino lamang. 'Yong mga hindi Pilipino, pumupunta dito kasi gusto nilang bumili ng mga Pilipinong produkto.* [The products here are really for Filipinos. The other products which can be bought here . . . like the piñata and spices used by other people are here only for convenience. Since you are here, why not buy them then, instead of going to each and every store. But most of the goods here are for Filipinos only. Those who are not Filipino come here because they want to buy Filipino products.]

During my first few visits to these stores, owners insisted on giving me a "tour," a tradition, they said, to welcome those who may be new to the area. Usually, our first destination was the meat section, where the owner would proudly show me how different the store was from any other store because it carried fish heads, bulls' testicles, pigs' penises, and other *"lamang loob"* (animal entrails) not normally sold anywhere else. "Do you eat these?" one owner asked me. When I hesitated, he said, "Are you sure you're Filipino? You must try them. They're good. Makes you feel more Filipino."

"Hey, we eat everything," another store owner remarked. "We come from a poor country . . . nothing's wasted."

"Oriental" stores also offer services not available in other stores, such as descaling, cleaning, and deep frying fish, or custom cutting meat for "*adobo*" or "*sinigang*" (native dishes). Said a shopper: "I like the service here. *Walang ganito sa iba.* [This doesn't exist anywhere else.] They do all the dirty work for you. And they are real good experts."

To many of the shoppers, the classification "Filipino" cannot also sustain its presumed homogeneity in the stores, as reflected in the variety of the products being sold there. The availability of certain goods marks not only the colonial history of the Philippines, but its multicultural facets as well.

> *E ano nga ba ang Pilipino? Hindi ba halo-halo tayo? Kaya meron diyang mga produkto na pang-Intsik. 'Di ba may dugong Intsik din tayo? Tapos, 'yung mga ginagamit ng mga Meksikano, katulad ng achuwete at iba pang mga spices . . . at saka 'yung dila ng baka . . . 'di ba ginagamit din natin iyon. 'Di ba galing din iyon sa Spain? Pilipino rin iyon ah. Nagugulat tayo . . . pero nagugulat din ang mga iba sa 'tin.* [Well, what is Filipino anyway? Aren't we all mixed? That's why there are products here that are for Chinese. Isn't it trye that we have Chinese blood? And then, those which are used by the Mexicans, like *achuete* and other spices. Didn't that come from Spain? That's also Filipino ah. We're surprised . . . but others are surprised at us too.]

> *Itigil na nga iyang mga pagtanong-tanong mo kung ano ang Pilipino at kung ano ang hindi! That goes to show na marami talaga ang hindi nakakaintindi sa 'tin. Akala ng mga Amerikano e kung ano na lang tayo. Diyos ko! Akala nila e mga Intsik tayo kasi galing tayo sa Asia. Oo nga, marami sa 'tin mukhang Intsik pero mga Pilipino din iyon. Ang mga apelyido natin, sound like Spanish. Kaya marami ang nagkakamali. Pero mga Pinoy tayo. Hindi ba nila maintindihan iyon?* [Put a stop to those questions regarding what is Filipino and what is not! That goes to show that many really don't understand us. Americans think we're just whatever. My God! They think were Chinese because we came from Asia. Well yes, many of us look like Chinese but they're also Filipino. Our surnames sound like Spanish. That's why many are mistaken. But we're Pinoy. Don't they understand that?]

Clarifications like these were almost always included in the responses of Filipinos I talked with in the stores, addressing the neverending assumptions that Filipinos are Chinese (or Orientals) or Mexicans, and the misunderstanding of their culture as well. The mix of products in the stores mirrors the heterogeneity of Filipino culture, something apparent to its Filipino patrons but not to others. Filipinos view the stores themselves as integral to Filipino identity in the United States. That identity takes into account the displacement and alienation of self brought about by settling in a new country, so that being Filipino American, in this case, is about bridging the past and the present, the distant and the nearby. "I don't think we think [of these products in the stores] this way in the Philippines," mused one shopper:

> There, canned goods are just canned goods. *Iba sa America. Mas nakikita mo 'yung kaibahan kasi ang layo na ng pinanggalingan mo, tapos biglang eto na sila, nandito 'yung mga galing doon. Siempre, iba ang pakiramdam mo. Nasa Amerika ka pero ang feeling mo, nasa Pilipinas ka rin.* [It's different in America. You can see the difference more because you came from a very distant place, and then suddenly they (the goods from the Philippines) are here. Of course, you feel differently. You are in America but you feel you are also in the Philippines.]

Additionally, what makes the stores *Filipino American* to the Filipinos who shop there is their belief that such stores won't be found anywhere but in the United States:

> *Filipino American? Siempre, nasa Amerika tayo. Wala naman yatang Oriental store sa Pilipinas.* [Filipino American? Of course, we're in America. I don't think there is an Oriental store in the Philippines.]

> *May Oriental store sa Pilipinas? Kung meron man, I don't think katulad ng mga nandito. Kaya nga 'yung mga ibang tindahan dito, ang tawag nila e Filipino American Oriental store. 'Yung iba, Filipino store lang ... kasi obvious ba? Nasa Amerika naman 'yung tindahan. Bakit pa kailangang ilagay?* [Is there an Oriental store in the Philippines? If there is, I don't think they're like what we have here. That's why with the other stores here, they call them Filipino American Oriental store. The others only put Filipino store ... because isn't it obvious? The store is in America anyway. Why the need to say it?]

> *May Oriental store ba sa 'tin? Siguro Chinese store. Pero, dito lang may Pilipinong Oriental store ... sa Amerika. Ibang klase 'no?* [Is there an Oriental store in our homeland? Maybe, a Chinese store. But, it's only here where there's the Filipino Oriental store ... here in America. A different kind, no?]

Beyond arranging their products according to varying practices of classification, "Oriental"-store owners also emphasize the social relations their stores create and reshape. For them, the store is not *just* a store. Unlike the bigger groceries, the stores are also meeting places and centers of information—these marketplaces of goods are also marketplaces of ideas. Plastered on the walls are notices of upcoming concerts, social affairs, beauty pageants, community/organizational meetings, job openings, properties for sale, and get-togethers (picnics) of family or regional groups, along with posters of political candidates or persons or animals missing and birthdays of senior citizens. Racks of magazines from the Philippines and newspapers published in San Diego and Los Angeles line entrance and exit points. "Ethnic" phone books are distributed free alongside counters of "home-cooked" hot meals. These stores are ideal places for socializing and networking—ethnically specific public spheres. Both men and women—as in the sari-sari stores back home—catch up on the latest gossip, engage in everyday bantering, exchange cooking tips, discuss politics, haggle over buying a specific ingredient for a dish, look for dates, or just enjoy small talk. For them, it is the *sosyalan* [socializing] that makes the difference.

> *Masarap mamili dito kasi may halong kuwentuhan. Nakikita ko 'yung mga kilala ko. Tapos, nagku-kuwentuhan kami.* [It's enjoyable to shop here because we can mix it with conversation. I see those I know. And then, we tell each other stories.]

> *Karaniwan nga, and akala ng ibang mga tao e pambabae lang ang shopping. Hindi oy! Ang asawa ko, lagi kong kasama. Marunong din iyan mag-grocery. Dito, ke babae, ke lalaki, marunong mamili. Hindi lang iyung mga housewife.* [Ordinarily, many other people assume that shopping is just for women. Not really! My husband is always with me here. He also knows how to do the grocery shopping. Here, both women and men know how to shop. It's not only for the housewives.]

> Shopping? *Pambabae lang?* [Only for women?] No. Sometimes, it's my husband or my brother who does the shopping. There's no difference. We share the chores here in the States.

> *Well, nakikita mo yung lahat ng mga Pilipino dito. Minsan nga, nakakasuka. Kahit mga mag-kaaway e nagtatalo dito. Nagsisigawan sila, nagbabatuhan ng*

prutas sa mukha. Ah, nakakatuwang manood! [Well, you see every Filipino here. Sometimes it's sickening. Even enemies confront each other here. They yell at each other, even throw fruits at each other's faces. Ah, this is so much fun to watch!]

The opportunities for *sosyalan* attract Filipino Americans, in both Los Angeles and San Diego Counties, who live twenty miles and more from the stores. "I can take the sacrifice," said one. "It's worth it. I go to this store because I can buy the things I really want. And with people I am comfortable with. This doesn't happen in Von's [a local supermarket chain]." Many encounter friends and acquaintances who are Filipino, and a good number use the stores as meeting places, combining shopping and socializing.

Because many Filipinos know that "Oriental" stores serve the needs of those who are like them, they also use them to alert others to shared interests, from the cultural to the political. For example, I saw several postings of Filipino cultural programs and celebrations to observe or commemorate events relevant to Filipinos. Many people I spoke with believed these would not have been posted in mainstream newspapers or announced in other media. *"Dito mo lang makikita ang mga iyan ... kasi wala namang paki 'yung mga hindi Pilipino sa ganiyan. Sayang, pero buti na lang meron tayong board dito."* [It's only here where you can see these things ... because those who are not Filipino don't care about them. Too bad, but its good we have a (bulletin) board here.] I also saw flyers of Filipino candidates vying for positions on school boards and other local offices, as well as position statements by local Filipino political organizations, including panethnic groups, on ballot measures that affect Filipino Americans.

During the time of this fieldwork (1992 to 1995), for instance, I saw statements about Propositions 187 and 209 tacked on bulletin boards fronting two of the bigger "Oriental" stores in San Diego, and three stores in downtown Los Angeles. The statements detailed how Proposition 187, for example, would make it difficult for "illegals" to get medical care. Those on Proposition 209 (one of them was written in Tagalog) explained how Filipino Americans and the rest of U.S. society are benefited by affirmative action, which the proposition was seeking to abolish. According to the people I talked to, they would not have known otherwise what these propositions were and how they would affect them, had it not been for the postings in the stores.

In these cases, the stores participate in and expand the realm of "politics" for their patrons, providing access to a notion of political power or a voice in determining how the larger society ought to work. The stores themselves represent a product and an ongoing process of attaining public visibility in the marketplaces of both goods and ideas. They operate on both symbolic and practical levels, because they offer concrete opportunities to participate and a vivid access to resources. Stores also offer public spaces for initiating, discussing, and negotiating political interests, thereby encouraging their patrons to be informed decision makers and savvy participants in conversations about issues that directly affect their lives. The spaces within and around these stores, then, act as seedbeds that nurture proactive political communion in society.

Some older patrons also reminded me that *sosyalan* in the stores has included some colorful events. "I've seen many fights here," an older generation patron said. "You know, when enemies confront each other. He-he-he. But things turned out okay. They patched up later." A Filipina remarked:

> Oh, you don't know how important these stores are to us, especially when we need to let other people now about what's happening. See these [Filipino American] newspapers? That's why they're here. Many Filipinos know they can be picked up here. *One time, nakita ko 'yung isang naka-headline ... inaway niya 'yung reporter na nakita niyang nagsho-shopping dito.* [One time, I saw someone who was in the headlines (of the local newspaper) ... he fought with the reporter, whom he saw shopping here.] That's good. Sometimes, I think those of us who fought against Marcos during the 1970s should have used these spaces to get people together [to fight for our cause].

Spaces in front of "Oriental" stores have also been used for a variety of purposes. Occasionally, I saw booths for voter registration and for hawking products like phone cards and insurance plans. A number of senior men use the benches outside the stores for playing chess or *dama*, a native game of checkers. And store owners have capitalized on the attraction of these environs by setting up picnic tables with umbrellas to serve those who want to snack on pastries and coffee bought at the stores. In these ways, "Oriental" stores bring people together, especially those who feel disconnected from other Filipinos because of work or residence. Both the inside and outside of these stores evoke such familiarity and comfort that some Filipino Americans who are not from Los Angeles or San Diego make it a point to visit the stores when they are in town, to "bring back memories" or "to feel at home again."

Connections along common ethnic lines are amplified as store owners battle for social prominence. Most of them try to be as visible as they can to attract business. They try to outdo each other since, as Mang Ambo would say: "This is still business. *Siempre, may competition.*" [Of course, there is competition.] True, many stores try to form cooperative relationships with each other by sharing capital, business know-how, distribution of goods, and clientele. But they also compete with one another for more favored customers with lower prices and promotions. Many compete by expanding the scope of their stores' offerings:

Marami dito, consignment. Nagdadala sila ng mga kakanin. . . . Sige lang, pasok nang pasok. [Many (items) here are (sold) on a consignment basis. (The consigners) bring delicacies. That's all right, we keep on permitting this.]

Itong tindahan namin, madalas sponsor ng mga kung anu-ano diyan . . . mga concert, mga palabas, mga charity. Buti nga 'yun, pampalaki 'yun ng business. [Our store often sponsors a variety of events . . . concerts, shows, charity projects. It's good because it increases our business.]

Nagpo-promote din ako ng mga show. Nagpo-produce naman 'yung misis ko. 'Yung mga ticket, dito na rin tinitinda sa amin. Balak din namin, mag-tayo ng restaurant. Kasi 'yung iba, malakas ang tindahan nila kasi may pagkaing luto nila. [We promote shows too. My wife acts as producer. The tickets . . . we sell them in our store, too. We also plan to put up a restaurant. Because the other (restaurants) do good business, since they also offer meals they cook themselves.]

Bukod sa pagtitinda, may pautang din ako. 'Yung misis ko e alahera. Kung minsan nga, para na rin kaming pawnshop. Pero ayaw ko rin 'yung nag-papautang. Delikado. Sa mga kakilala ko lang talaga. Alam mo naman, parang Pilipinas din dito. Little Philippines nga, kung tawagin nang iba. [Aside from selling, I also offer loans. My wife is a jeweler. Sometimes, we're like a

pawnshop. But I don't really like lending money to people. It's dangerous. (I loan to) only those whom I really know. You know, it's like being
in the Philippines here. Little Philippines, as many would call it.]

The preceding quote is striking for the way the respondent invokes
images of the homeland to refer to sites and activities in the adopted
country. Impressions of how it was back home, even if geographical
boundaries have been crossed, persist in the new nation. Many of
these sound mythical and seem to evoke idealized locations and experiences. Most have been reconstructed to "fit" new surroundings. In
such spaces, where many voices speak about diverse experiences and
conditions, identities have taken on many sets of markings.

"Oriental" stores are the transplanted spaces of uprooted migrants.
In these establishments, Filipino Americans have recreated the places
where they used to be. They have also extended the borders of "Oriental" stores far into other commercial spaces. Amid other businesses, such as restaurants, video stores, barber and beauty shops,
dental and medical clinics, these people have formed communities
of identities that have traveled, stayed, and changed over and over.

My reading of "Oriental" stores as spaces in which identities are contested and articulated regards space as a kind of social text that could be
historicized and materialized to reveal the conditions under which it
exists and the creative actions of its inhabitants. Rather than imagining
these commercial sites as bordered places that enclose hermetically
sealed cultural elements, I propose that they are stores/spaces whose
borders are porous and fluctuating. "Oriental" stores do not occupy
spaces only of Filipinoness, however its variety is defined. Other cultures,
images, and attributes flow in and out of their tentative boundaries.

This exploration of "Oriental" stores reveals elements of the relationships possible between conventions of consumption and cultural
practices that relate to identity and power. The intimate link between
such stores and identity indicates that meaning making is relational
and processual. In the stores, people's actions subvert notions of unitary, fixed identities embodied in Oriental*ist* discourse. They show
how identities are constructed in and through fields of power dif-
ferentials. People have used these spaces as sites of cultural contes-

tation—constantly seeking to include as much as exclude selves and others. They have claimed venues for the presumed voiceless—providing opportunities for challenging authority that seeks to marginalize and exclude them. They are the "others," speaking out through performance against a marginalizing condition.[20]

As sites in which reassertions of displaced selves take place, "Oriental" stores have assumed a key role in these Filipino Americans' lives, paving the way for marking and marketing different articulations of otherness. In these communities, where depictions of what Salman Rushdie calls "imaginary homelands" vary by ethnicity, race, class, and gender, commonalities that transcend such demarcations are difficult to isolate.[21] Yet Filipino Americans have been quick to identify what makes them different from the others, and what makes them similar to each other. Such an awareness has, in many ways, alerted them to think of themselves not as isolated individuals but as members of a group who can protect and work for their common interests.

Filipino Americans have been criticized for not being "unified" enough to have a political voice in the larger communities, even though they comprise a significant number among minorities. But unity in order to engage in political activity does not and will not work in communities with multiple voices and contingent cultures. On one hand, one can say that one intent in locating identity is to try to fix it in a world of flux and contingency. On the other hand, being alert to the contingent rather than the essential character of identity leads to a different kind of politics of unity, one that favors coalition over tribalism. Here, a parallel between spatial politics and popular culture criticism, which Henry Louis Gates Jr. writes about, is particularly instructive. Quoting Stuart Hall, Gates states that

> an overemphasis on the contingency of culture can be a problem: but to forget the contingency of culture can have hazardous consequences. His [Hall's] response is to call for a 'politics of articulation,' a kind of Pompidou Center politics with all of the innards—the wiring, pipes, plumbing—worn on the outside. The idea is that you should know always what you're getting yourself into. . . . What's clear is that an awareness of contingency, the artifactual nature of our social identities, need not lead to political paralysis.[22]

My interpretation of practices in "Oriental" stores reveals a kind of political articulation of identities that are contingent, yet forceful. In these sites where identities are produced and reproduced, are expressed and become expressive, dynamic articulations take place. In my interviews, one common referent Filipino Americans mentioned was an identity defined by place of birth: the Philippines. Beyond this, they expressed similar notions of identity in terms of race, class, and ethnic commonalities.

This study also shows that the ontological boundaries of a Filipino identity are not preordained, nor are they static in theoretical, pedagogical, and everyday representations. The immigrant moment provides an occasion, however fleeting, for articulating different ideas of identity. I now see how such articulations take place in the everyday world and in specific times and places. But I also recognize and acknowledge the tensions inherent in "articulating the articulations" and accounting for the active, self-conscious intents of my respondents. I stress, therefore, the partiality and selectivity of my respondents and of my reporting and interpretation of their practices. I also suggest that, regardless of whether or not my respondents self-consciously intended their actions to be perceived as, say, contestations, their overall significance in the uncertain, dynamic, and continuous processes of creating identities cannot be minimized. As Judith Butler has proposed, one needs to consider disruptions in the performance of "acting out" an identity, whether intended or not, as possibilities that eventually disrupt such essentializing expectations.[23] As ethnically demarcated activities, these disruptions reveal the potential power in moving from creating "senses of belonging" or having "spaces of one's own" to mobilizing group efforts to gain access to larger social, material, and political resources.

I also suggest that these practices of identity articulation have their limitations. Nostalgia can be powerful in enunciating cultural difference as a way of engaging with the present. But it can also motivate idealized constructions that may reveal often concealed or unacknowledged intraethnic differentiations by class, gender, or generation.[24] Exclusionary practices that are part of defining and delineating cultural difference may also hinge on current debates in identity politics, a feisty component of which persists in asserting that "nobody else can speak in my behalf except those from my own group, community, race, gender, or ethnicity." Of course, one always speaks from a certain position and makes a claim with a particular stake in mind. But one cannot also assume an all-knowing position that claims complete and final authority. In light of the instabilities, ambiguities, and contradictions of both pedagogy and performance, I acknowledge using specific lenses that permit reading the everyday as temporarily definable. I also recognize its complexities, and its fleeting, everchanging quality.

Because people and their cultures are continually redefined and rearticulated, the "Oriental" stores of today show signs of change. Alongside small "Oriental" stores are new large "Asian" markets that mirror the more conventional department stores.[25] Here, the ways goods are arranged, displayed, and organized are slowly becoming indistinguishable from those of "Oriental" stores, as these larger stores attempt to copy them. What probably remains are ideas or imaginings of how "Oriental" stores are supposed to be, for these immigrant communities. Like identities, the roles that "Oriental" stores perform, as well as the meanings they evoke, are not definitive or static. They are fluid, everchanging, and provisional. As such, their existence is contingent upon their time-tested ability to provide spaces that open up possibilities for articulating identities.

4

Palengke Politics and Beauty Pageants in Filipino Community Centers

t is already 7:45 P.M., but the Council of Pilipino American Organizations of San Diego County, Inc. (COPAO), House of Delegates meeting scheduled for 7:30 shows no signs of opening formally. Men and women, all Filipinos, chat in small groups as if at a cocktail party, only instead of champagne glasses, some hold Styrofoam cups of water or soda. The rented meeting hall, south of San Diego in a National City community center, is bright under fluorescent lights, with ceiling fans rotating at low speed to circulate the air and disperse the cigarette smoke. Smoking is prohibited in the room, but smokers gather on a balcony, separated from nonsmokers only by a narrow walkway. Several other groups are still assembled on the parking lot below.

With a capacity of about two hundred, the room is arranged with rows of chairs facing a long table with reserved seats for officers. Two cubicles along one wall provide office space for the secretary and chair of the organization. Now many in attendance have seated themselves. Glancing at their wristwatches, some call on others to defer their little debates and beauty pageant ticket selling for a while. When I look at my watch too, a woman

sitting beside me mutters, "Filipino time, huh?" I smile. She asks me
what organization I represent, and I say I don't represent any, I am
just there as an observer. "For what?" she presses. "To look at how
we do politics here? And *gulo 'no?* [It's a mess, isn't it?]" We both look
around the room as the sound of laughter and conversation escalates.
She giggles. "*Nakita mo na . . . 'di ba parang palengke? Anong say mo?
Bukas, lalo na! Coronation ng Miss Philippines-San Diego USA!* [So you
see . . . isn't it like a marketplace? What can you say? Tomorrow,
even more! It's the coronation of Miss Philippines–San Diego USA!]"
She wants to tell me more, and her hands fish for something in her
purse; I suspect she is about to sell me some tickets. But a loud voice
and a gavel's bang interrupts us. "Attention everybody! The meeting
will come to order!"

Palengke-style Politics

In many encounters I have had with first-generation Filipino Americans in San Diego, our conversations about "politics" would center
on what happened in the latest get-together of COPAO's House of
Delegates, which met the second Thursday of every month. An
umbrella organization that brings together more than 125 Filipino
American associations in and around San Diego, COPAO centralizes
and coordinates community projects and events for its members as
well as for others in the communities who have an interest in Filipino
American activities. Its voting members are the senior officers of Filipino American social associations, organized on the basis of common
ties traced to Philippine towns, cities, regions, and provinces. Many
other Filipino American organizations are organized as alumni associations, by gender, occupation, profession/trade, and recreational
interest. Their members are overwhelmingly post-1965 middle-class
professionals, with a good number of senior citizens (mostly parents
who were petitioned over once their immigrant children had permanently settled), working-class factory workers, and older generation
immigrants (who are now, usually, citizens).

Filipino American styles of politicking are principally geared
toward creating and maintaining spaces where Filipinos can actively

engage each other in the pursuit of shared interests in local political representation, in the protection of their civil rights, and in the improvement of their well-being. These common concerns are significantly bound by their emphasis on recognition and group action: "Doing politics" for them is always an effort, first, to calculate and respond to the effects, in the past and present, of having no representation in mainstream politics and no access to it, and second, to facilitate the establishment of self-reliant networks of support and mutuality—appropriated from the homeland—as alternative spaces of collective action. In these ways, Filipino American "politics" is constituted in and through maps of historical memories of immigration and settlement, of links between original homeland and new destination, of mainstream and informal/alternative political practice, and of "Filipinoness" and "Americanness."

Whenever conversations with my informants turned to what they thought about politics, I got responses about topics that ranged from presidential performance to what was on TV last night. Occasionally, I would get blank stares or queries in return: "What do you mean by politics, *hijo* [son]? What are you thinking about? Are you referring to what people do out there in Congress and the White House? Or, do you mean the weekly meetings we have here in National City?"[1]

Even though I almost always made it a point, when I referred to "politics," to quickly add "whatever that means to you," many respondents who live around San Diego would mention something about COPAO, the local site of Filipino American politics. "What you need to see," said Roger Alano, "if you really want to see the politics we have, is to go to COPAO meetings at the community halls, the *palengke* of FilAm politics, *'ika nga* [as they say]."

"What do you mean by *'palengke'?*" I asked. "*Palengke* ... e *'di parang palengke!*" he answered. "*Nakapunta ka na ba sa palengke sa atin? Ganoon! Labu-labo! Kaniya-kaniya.*" [*Palengke* ... well, it's like a marketplace. Have you been to a marketplace in our country? It's like that! It's a melee! To each his or her own.] I began resurrecting memories of *palengke*s in the Philippines—fresh produce markets in the city where tons of fresh produce would be hawked by sellers scream-

ing for attention, yelling out prices of goods, names of vegetables and
fish just delivered, meat that just came in; of vendors and buyers haggling at all hours of the morning; of filth and stench; of edibles and
garbage inches away from each other. I was appalled for a moment.
Roger Alano continued:

> You should go and attend the meetings we have. People from as far as
> North County [north of San Diego] all the way to the [Mexican] border
> make it a point to be there. You'll get to see how we do our own kind of
> politics here. You'll get to see these personalities and celebrities—oh, they
> could be real dirty there, you know. Plus, you'll get the latest gossip, and—
> God knows what's the next thing they're up to. Most of the time, there's
> so much yelling, screaming, and—what do you call that? feuding—public
> feuding. It's really a *palengke*.

My initial shock quickly turned into a mixture of excitement and
apprehension. I had heard about COPAO through articles in community newspapers and also by word of mouth through several key
informants. Many other interviewees had referred to COPAO as some
sort of *palengke*—an idiosyncratic Philippine wet marketplace where,
according to them, "anything and everything goes." But Roger Alano
added spice to the description. When he revealed to me, moments after
the conversation I just quoted, that he happens to be an officer of
COPAO, I asked him about his "negative" portrayal of the group.

> Oh, was I painting the organization in a negative light? *Hindi oy.* [Not
> really.] I was merely describing how we do our own stuff here. *Siempre,
> maraming sigawan.* [Of course, there's a lot of yelling going on.] But I
> think we get things done too. Why do you think I remain [committed] to
> the group for over five years now? *Siguro* [perhaps] you're thinking about
> the congressional and Senate meetings you see on C-SPAN which, by the
> way, has a lot of screaming too. Well, we do it the same way . . . and in
> different ways too. You should go and see us. Even if we're not in Con-
> gress yet, you'll see what we're doing.

Indeed, I *had* been looking for a version of C-SPAN politics, where
leaders held institutionally sanctioned positions and deliberated in
some orderly fashion. Obviously, Roger Alano recognized this. To
him, "politics" is "of our own," something that is markedly Filipino
(through, for example, the invocation of a place that originates in the

homeland—a *palengke*) as well as a process by which "we get things done," not in spite of but through the idiosyncrasies and apparent disarray of the *palengke*.

The assurance Roger Alano gives about how "we get things done" is important, since we both do have some understanding that in a *palengke*, market transactions are usually undertaken with a lot of hawking and screaming. On the surface, one could easily ask how things could possibly get accomplished in the midst of the chaos and confusion associated with the *palengke* atmosphere. But to these Filipinos, it is precisely the place where things do get done. One arrives in a *palengke*, screens the goods, participates in some haggling and gossiping, and eventually makes a purchase. To someone unfamiliar with the *palengke*'s "hidden transcripts," it is difficult to imagine how one arrives at a productive end via such bewildering means, how there can be a kind of order in the midst of confusion, and how the practice makes such good sense to those who engage in it that it is imported and transformed in the new place.[2]

"There's just too much preoccupation with order here [in the United States]," Rose Sison said. As a former officer and current active delegate of COPAO, Sison, in her words, "has gone through thick and thin" despite the seeming *"kaguluhan* [disarray] of FilAm politics here." And through it all, she claimed:

> I have seen the best and the worst *sa mga meeting* [in the meetings]. Sometimes, *magulo* [it's in disarray]. *Pero kahit magulo, alam naman ng lahat kung nasaan ang mga limits.* [But even if it's in disarray, everyone knows where the limits are.] We always try to be *desente* [decent] with each other. *Pangit naman 'yung sobrang maayos.* [It's not nice if it's too orderly]. *Siempre, tayo-tayo, nagkakaintindihan kung ano ang babagay sa atin.* [Of course, we know what will suit us.]

Here, Sison's characterization of the meetings' apparent disarray is emblematic of the *palengke*'s surface appearance of frenzy. But the transcript of knowing "where the limits are," known only to those who regularly attend and opaque to non-Filipino guests, transforms this marketplace of excess into a productive endeavor in which the understanding of "decency" toward each other establishes a baseline of social conduct. Complete order, in this case, becomes a suspicious and repulsive exercise ("it's not nice"), something that is marked as alien and out of place in the meetings and therefore appropriately replaced or often supplemented by moments of disorder, undergirded by a standard of decorum based on the assurance that "we know what we're doing."

Again, as in the "Oriental" stores (see Chapter 3), language plays a key role in conjuring up this ordered confusion in *palengke* politics, with Taglish as the lingua franca of COPAO's participants. In "Oriental" stores, Taglish marks "Filipinoness," in nonhierarchical relationship to "Americanness," appropriate to the activities of shopping and socializing. In the community centers, we see a parallel significance. As a primary mode of communication among the *palengke* participants, Taglish brings decorum to the meetings by taking the focus off the hierarchies among languages and among speakers and listeners in acts of speaking both Tagalog and English (as well as some Spanish). Speaking in Taglish, then, gives rise to, or evokes, democracy and understanding among participants—an experience that the meetings and exchanges themselves attempt to elicit. And in these exchanges, one senses the threat of chaos (represented by the *palengke* atmosphere) that the practice of "decency" tries to diffuse. Taglish represents that threat as much as it simultaneously contains the possibility of democratic exchange going out of control.

"We try to keep things in perspective *naman* [even then]," added COPAO secretary Daisy Perez. "We make sure we record meetings ... we also make sure we have an agenda that's distributed to members before the meetings." A casual perusal of the minutes of previous meetings reveals a concise but comprehensive listing by issue of previous activities and discussions. And in meetings I attended, organizers always made sure copies of the agenda were distributed that listed the order of activities for the 7:30 P.M. deliberations. Always, the agenda began with "Call Meeting to Order," because before 7:30, members would slowly walk in and engage in discussions with each other. Meetings rarely commenced on the dot. "Filipino time," yet another component of *palengke* politics, has little regard for the temporally specific. People knew such meetings regularly start late and almost always joked about it as something one could expect in any Filipino gathering. Tardiness was viewed not as bad behavior but as normal behavior when the strict observance of rules was not a top priority. As one member said: "It's okay to be late. We allow these things because we're really like this. We need to talk to each other first . . . and [being late] is not a crime. *Magh-intay sila!* [Let them wait!] We'll get there when we want to. *Humi-nahon kayo! Mag-uumpisa 'yan kung kailangan nang mag-umpisa."* [Lighten up! It will start when it needs to start.] In affirming the practice of "Filipino time," members affirm a sense of time at odds with the discipline of normative clock time. Official time is thus rearticulated and redeployed as a marker of ethnic difference rather than a standard into which one is assimilated.

When the presiding officer steps up and announces that it's time to settle down, members and guests dutifully oblige, some more hastily than others. The meeting then proceeds: an "Opening Prayer," "Introduction of Guests," and "Approval of Last Meeting's Minutes." When it gets to the central issues on the agenda, delegates begin voicing their opinions, questions, and suggestions about the items listed. "That's the time when you see this [kind of] *palengke* rolling along," Perez added. "So there's order and disorder at the same time."

Of course, understanding and working within and through these polarities demands a particular facility in social relationships of this nature on the part of players and attendees, something that the minutes of any COPAO meeting find difficult to capture. While "knowing what we're doing," keeping things in perspective, and "decency" serve as indices of social behavior in the meetings, they are most often silent indices. If they are ever mentioned, in a rare instance of outright public misconduct, it is in the context of delegates reminding one another that "decency," for example, is something that is expected and assumed as a prerequisite for participation. Two meetings come to mind as illustrations.[3]

In one instance, a delegate from one of the associations suddenly raised his hand and, when acknowledged, said that he wanted to start a discussion on an issue different from that under discussion. The chair responded by referring to the agenda, which was made public beforehand, and assuring him (as well as everybody else) that matters not on the list would be accommodated after the agreed-upon activities were deliberated and settled. "You are out of order," he said to the man. "And you should know how we do business here." The rest of the audience, including myself, hissed the chair for a moment, until one of us said out loud, for a moment appearing also out of order, "*Pasyensya na kayo, baguhan lang siya!*" [Be patient, he's just new!][4] "Well, then, he should brush up on our rules. Give him a copy of our by-laws!" retorted the chair. "*Maging maayos naman po tayo. Konting decency naman ho.*" [Let's be orderly. A little bit of decency here, please.][5]

A call for "order" also came during another delegates' meeting, when members of the audience, including myself again, persisted in talking to each other during the deliberations on the floor. Here, the apt word is "*chismisan,*" or gossiping, which especially angered the officers because the topic being discussed related to suspicions that COPAO funds had been pilfered and embezzled by certain members. The handling of the organization's money has traditionally been a contentious issue, and COPAO's history, as revealed in minutes dating back to the 1970s, has been fraught with incidents of funds lost, stolen, or embezzled. Members have a good sense of this history and regard it with contempt, especially as they see the graft and corruption prevalent in the Philippines find their way to the new land. The urge to make side comments about this issue, as it was being formally discussed by the officers, was too strong to resist.

To contain this *chismisan,* about to reach disastrous proportions, one COPAO officer yelled out: "*O, chismisan na lang ba ang gusto natin? Itigil naman po natin iyang mga chismis na iyan. Maging desente naman tayo sa isa't isa.*" [Oh, is it just gossip that we want here? Let's please stop that kind of gossiping. Let's be decent to one another.] This man's voice was so forceful that everybody immediately stopped speaking. In a way, his interjection defined the limits of disorderly conduct, articulated in the gossiping that ensued for a moment and was quickly quelled in the name of decency. People afterwards resented the way he had raised his voice but understood that he did it for a reason. A delagate said: "*Siempre, baka mauwi na naman tayo sa palengke. Kaya niya ginawa iyon. . . . Atin 'to. Dapat lang pag-ingatan natin ito. Sayang din naman. Konting gulo, okey lang. Pero konting ayos din, mas maigi."* [Of course, we might end up as a *palengke* again. That's why he did that. . . . This is ours. We ought to take care of it. Let's not put it to waste. A little bit of disorder, it's just okay. But a little bit of order, it's better.]

Yet, what appears to be chaotic *palengke* "politics" has its historical roots in the social and political conditions of Filipino immigration to and settlement in the United States. It is demarcated as both characteristic of Filipino "politics," which includes "frequent yelling," and a kind of "politics" that Roger Alano casually defines as American—which "has a lot of screaming too." Evident here is not only the synergy of "politicking" culled from at least two different systems, but one forged out of a relationship of exclusion ("we're not in Congress yet") that makes possible an alternative form of politics in the absence of more legitimate avenues. This relationship of exclusion is understood by many as intimately tied to a history of exclusion by race. Said one participant:

> Had we been white immigrants, it would [have been] a different story. We try very hard, but we also inherit these years and years of not being able to [become] citizens simply because we were Filipinos and considered alien . . . not being able to vote, not being able to run for office. . . . The first ones who came here, they didn't stand a chance because of all these laws. That's why it's so hard for us because even if these laws are not here anymore, their effects are still with us. Very strong. We are starting late too.

Years of racial exclusion from the mainstream political process definitely inform and motivate these participants' local political activities. "I don't think they're ready for us," quipped another frequent COPAO delegate, who explained that

> they won't take us right now. Some of us try to join these big political organizations . . . but all they want is our money first before we could even get heard. *Pera kaagad!* [Money up front!] And then, when I joined one of them, they just want me to sit down and be quiet. They want me to speak perfect English. *Aba, Amerikano rin ako!* [Well, I'm an American too!] Why won't they hear me out too? They just want me to be one [among] the many. You know, they want me to be like them—*puti* [white].

And they're corrupt too. *Maraming dayaan.* [There are many fraudulent activities.] *Iba talaga* [It's really different] when you are with people who speak and act like you . . . who will listen to you and treat you with respect.

Here, she has summed up what may be the most important rationale for contemporary Filipino American "political" activity: the perceived inability of the traditional political organizations to include minority voices and their reluctance to take them into their folds. And if access is indeed offered, it requires assimilation—melting into the pot and discarding difference—by keeping silent, speaking in "perfect" English, and behaving like a "white" person. To those who do not choose to participate in these traditional avenues of politicking, assimilation is too high a price to pay for inclusion, especially when cynicism regarding mainstream politics is rampant and the prospects of being heard are dim.

Yet their desire to be included ("I'm an American too") is strong enough to lead them to seek out alternative channels of participation that would be resistant to or critical of assimilation and more conducive to acceptance. According to Kiko Beltran, a younger and recently inducted officer:

That's why we have these meetings of our own. Where else could we go? Many ask . . . why do these meetings? We got jobs. We got families. But we set aside time for these. Who else would? Chinese people and Korean people have these too. Well, they are also outsiders, right? We see how it [local political organizations] benefits them. Why not us too? Many think it's our fault that we don't join these big [political] parties. That we're no good or stupid. But they [the big political institutions] have to do the adjusting too. They need to include us as part of the system. It's not always us all the time [acceding to their wishes].

Here, we see how Filipino American politics is born out of exclusionary conditions and the necessity for self-reliance ("Who else would?") that are shared with other racialized Asian American groups. The presence of these other ethnic-based groups gives impetus to organizing community associations as examples of alternatives that can work outside the system. Part of their intent is also to be included in that system of mainstream politics—but only on their own terms. These terms involve an openness to their voices, a recognition of their needs, and the pursuit of their interests.

"We want to be heard as Filipinos and Americans," clarified one delegate:

> We want them to consider us as equal [partners] in America, but we also want them to . . . not forget that we've been here for a long time, and that people like us have been forever outside . . . or foreign . . . just because we are not like them. That is the first step. If they could see us as the same . . . but also different, then they [will] be able to listen to us. We want to be represented . . . and we want money for our sick and disabled, for our kids . . . and we want . . . our rights advanced and protected.

Another delegate, who had been listening to our conversation, chipped in: "Wow! *Ang bigat naman niyan!*" [That's very heavy!]. "But I'm serious," the first respondent replied: "We do take these things seriously. If this is the politics you are asking about, I'll say . . . this is the politics we have been fighting for. It's just that many times, they get hidden or . . . just simply understood [as that] . . . no need for . . . open declaration. You have to be Filipino to get it, *'di ba?*" [isn't that so?]

I nodded my head in agreement. Indeed, *palengke* politics or doing "politics Filipino-style" makes sense only if one knows what it means to be a Filipino in the United States as far as these respondents are concerned. It assumes an understanding that the local ("Filipino") strategies—like *palengke* politics, Taglish, decency, and self-propelled action—serve common aims.

These Filipino Americans have resorted to using the spaces of the community centers to organize themselves and build networks of mutual support outside the traditional or mainstream political venues that usually exclude or marginalize them. Said one senior officer: "These centers [where] we hold our meetings . . . you can see that they're just rooms and buildings. *Mga kuwarto lang iyan.* [They are just rooms.] But they mean so much more to us. They symbolize what we can do, what we're doing, and what we hope to do. See that Filipino flag over there? And the American flag beside it?" He points to the flags flying outside the building. "We want to show everyone that we are Filipinos and Americans . . . that we meet here and talk about Filipino things . . . and that we belong to America . . . and that we exist so others will know. It's also an invitation."

In these ways, community centers represent and constitute Filipino American politics to the degree that they serve as sites for articulating a kind of politics that may fall outside the state but adamantly part of the nation. Beyond their surface attributes of physical space, these public spaces express the historical record and, indeed, proclaim a brand of politics unique to people like Filipino Americans. Again, such a politics is a response to the unwillingness and limited ability of the state to serve their interests. And it is a politics that nevertheless attempts to retain and sustain its ties with, not separate itself from, both Filipino and American realms.

"We can only work through little steps, one at a time," mentioned one respondent. In significant ways, these "little steps" have manifested as increased participation. Attendance in COPAO has grown over the years since its formal organization in 1971. "Built from the bottom," as one founding member said, COPAO started with a few community leaders of several provincial and professional organizations. In the 1960s and 1970s, when the number of Filipinos in San Diego grew as a consequence of the military and industrial development of the place, associations defined by Philippine hometown origin arose primarily to bring together people from the same town or province who happened to share the fate of moving and settling in the same city. Aida Santos, a member of the San Diego Cavite Association since 1968, remembers how isolated and lonely she felt upon coming over to work as a nurse in a local hospital. "I was looking all the time for people who looked Filipino," she said.

> I really wanted to see someone familiar. I was so sad being with people who didn't look like me. Then, I met this man whom I recognized as someone from a town near where I grew up. He's from the navy, he said. Just seeing and talking to him did a lot to me. He said there are a lot of Caviteños [Filipinos from the province of Cavite] here. So I met them all in a party. Diyos ko! [My God!] I was so glad to be with them . . . and I really had a nice time. Just being there with all those people from Cavite. . . . At that time, it was just party-party. Then, we decided to be more formal. . . . They set up this thing called San Diego Cavite Association . . . and I became an official member later on.

Like most early immigrants, Aida Santos found in her association of province mates a community bound by a common thread of dislocation and misery mitigated by the comfort and security of being with people of the same ethnicity. These kinds of associations would later flourish, especially within Filipino American communities elsewhere.[6] "We are known for having a lot of organizations, I think," Ben Vargas, a Filipino community paper editor told me. "We have a lot . . . and we have too many." According to his estimate, in 1992, there were more than 150 organizations in San Diego County alone, and more than 200 in the Los Angeles area.[7] "We even have an association of associations!" Vargas added. Referring to COPAO, he further mused: "We just can't get enough. But also, we want to be organized. You know, [we want to] organize the organizations!"

"Why do you think we have so many associations?" I asked one interviewee. "Well," she said, "because we love company. We like being with each other. These are [bonds] that are like family. It's a way of keeping together what is often broken. You know, we travel a long way. Then, we go here alone. These people are like family to us. We don't have anything like this back home. I mean, there are just so many!" Many respondents told me that associations of Filipinos in the United States outnumber those in the Philippines, and some are found nowhere else—province- and town-based associations would be the prime examples. These groupings reflect the heterogeneity of the Filipino American population: ethnic identity is determined not only in relation to other ethnic and racial groups in the United States, but by population subgroups in the Philippines. These include the place-specific associations and those organized along generational and religious lines.

In the midst of these multiple, diverse, and heterogeneous associations, umbrella organizations like COPAO provide a more centralized and organized space of unity. In the COPAO House of Delegates meetings I attended, drawing a quorum was never an issue. Over the years, COPAO has accommodated its member groups' shifting interests and conditions. Early on, there was a focus on alleviating poverty, the effects of the Vietnam War on the Filipino community, and the plight of Filipino American farm workers. In the 1980s and 1990s, with new leaders coming in and new issues affecting the communities, civic programs targeting the health and well-being of senior citizens and pursuing the welfare of the youth took center stage.

"Operation *Kalusugan* [Health]," which provided financial and medical resources to young adults and older members of the population, was so successful in raising funds and reaching its audience that a newspaper reporter told me, "It's a project that should serve as a model for all kinds of community work among all groups." "We really helped each other out here," said one volunteer. "And it's still ongoing. It's amazing what community participation can do." Additionally, the organization has sponsored voter registration drives and occasionally reserved time and space for local political candidates, both Filipino and non-Filipino American, despite the officers' hesitation in advocating particular candidates for fear of losing the group's city and county funding. "They prohibit us from endorsing candidates," mentioned an officer:

> It's really hard . . . *parang* [like] catch-22. We can't get the funding if we register as a political organization. Like Democrat or Republican. But see, we need the money to do politics *na rin* [also], so even if we register as a social organization, we invite these people . . . and then we pretend that we don't endorse them. But if you can read between the lines, it's *parang* [like] endorsement *na rin* [too]. *Iba tayo eh. Nakakalusot pag minsan. O, huwag kang maingay!* [We're different, eh. We can wing it sometimes. Oh, don't you tell!]

COPAO has been instrumental in calling the attention of lawmakers and law enforcement officers to the perceived violation of the civil rights of several Filipino Americans. One recent case involved the wrongful imprisonment of a former U.S. Army lieutenant whose case in court was financially, legally, and morally supported by council members because they believed him to be a victim of racial discrimination and harassment. Said one informant: "We rallied for him not as an individual, but as a member of our group. We have been victimized many times already . . . and this is one clear example of how we can fight this thing together."

But COPAO's primary goals have always been clear and consistent: "to build and support networks of alliance among ourselves," said one of its officers. And further, as the slogan accompanying its letterhead affirms, "community development through self-reliance."

This impetus for self-reliance draws its intensity from the specifics of Filipino immigration history. Here, I make a brief digression to provide the historical context in which this discourse of self-reliance operates. Sociologist Elena S. H. Yu, in an article that traces the nature of Filipino migration and patterns of community organization in the United States, claims that the varying characteristics of each migratory wave of Filipinos and their differing adaptation experiences have resulted in fragmentary, unsustained, and unorganized Filipino communities.[8] The mobile character of first-wave agricultural contract laborers (1900s to 1930s), who for the most part depended on migratory work on the West Coast, for example, deterred them from settling permanently in any one place to establish longlasting affiliations. The second wave of migrants, who enlisted mostly in the U.S. Navy and Army (1940s to 1960s), also had difficulty in sustaining ethnic organizational ties owing to their regimented and mobile tours of duty. And with the professional immigrants of the 1960s and onwards, Yu points to career orientations (usually, earlier, in the medical field) that necessitated dispersal into and confinement in urban and suburban locales. There are clear divisions by generation, class, and gender (the first and second waves were comprised predominantly of males) across these temporal swells, which Yu identifies as factors that have made Filipino community formations in the United States quite peculiarly disaggregated.[9]

I would suggest, however, that what complicates this history of migration further are the social-political conditions in the United States that Filipinos faced upon arrival—conditions that rendered them racialized subjects (Orientals, little brown people, etc.) regardless of generation, class, and gender and that bridged their migratory differences.[10] I am not implying that a single form of racism met all three waves, nor that all Filipinos who came to America experienced racism in the same way, if at all. But for many of my respondents, as I have mentioned earlier, there is an acute consciousness of racism as either personally experienced (and oftentimes, painfully told) or known to have happened to some other Filipino in recent or long-term memory. The Filipino immigrants in Southern California that I talked to are familiar with the oppression of Filipino farm workers, the strikes and boycotts these laborers led and participated in, restaurant and grocery store signs that used to announce "No Filipinos and Dogs Allowed," and the Hollywood depictions of the "wily" Filipino in old movies. *"Alam ko lahat ng mga iyon* [I know all of that]," says Daisy Perez. *"Hanggang ngayon, malakas pa rin ang dating nila. Ang tingin ng mga puti sa atin, kadalasan e itim, o kaya e Mexicano o Intsik. Pati accent, kundi ka slang e masama ang tingin sa iyo."* [Even now, their force is still great. Whites see us as black people, or Mexicans, or Chinese. Even our accent, if you don't speak like them (using slang), they look at you in a bad way.][11]

Contemporary Filipinos' knowledge of these historical "incidents" of racism may not have the detail of scholarly texts, but a significant awareness of past and present injustices does enable them to find common ground with those who are generations apart from them. COPAO, like many Filipino organizations established before and contemporary with it, seizes these shared narratives of racism that have rendered Filipino Americans marginal or invisible by deploying the virtue of self-reliance; that is, as Roger Alano pointed out: "If we're always left out, if we are always cast aside, who else can we turn to except ourselves? Who else can we rely upon to make a decent living here except our very own people?"

I have heard sentiments articulated along similar lines in smaller organizations, both in San Diego and Los Angeles. COPAO's northern counterpart, the Filipino American Community of Los Angeles (FACLA), prides itself on being the catalyst for unifying and servicing Filipino immigrants based in California primarily through *sariling pagsisikap* [individual/collective diligence]; that is, according to one of its members, through the "efforts of our own little groups."[12] But again, what seems to make them cohere regardless of generational and class disparities is their awareness of the shared fate voiced by a longtime FACLA officer: "We have come to this nation to seek new or better lives but we have found, instead, a lot of difficulty and a country that mistreats us; since we are on our own here, we can only rely on ourselves." To be sure, there are many ways in which racial exclusion is collectively experienced, but in the realm of what these Filipinos view as politics, the fundamental evidence lies in the absence of any political representation of their group in most public offices— or consistent failure in attempting to get such representation— despite their numbers and presence since before the turn of the twentieth century.

In response to these overdetermined conditions, the *palengkes* of Filipino American politics have served both as avenues for rectifying exclusion as well as venues for practicing a kind of politics on their own terms. I am not implying that these Filipinos have merely reacted to conditions thrust upon them. Rather, I am suggesting the force of agency that drives *"palengke* politics" in the instances I mentioned, as these Filipino Americans shore up what's familiar to them, adjust it to suit their needs and limitations, and ultimately use it to access a kind of power. This is where I situate a specific style of politics that my informants recognize both as Filipino and American. ("This is what makes us Filipinos . . . and Americans too.") According to a FACLA member:

> *Maganda nga 'yung parang palengke kasi at least, kahit sino, nakakapagsalita. May demokrasya baga. Kung meron kang gustong sabihin, sabihin mo kaagad . . . kaya minsan e magulo, kaya ang tawag e palengke. Pero palengke na ang goal ay democracy, American-style baga.* [It's nice to have something like a *palengke* because at least, anyone is able to speak. It's like having a democracy. If you want to say something, you say it right away . . . that's why sometimes, it's a frenzy. But it's a *palengke* whose goal is democracy, American-style, as they say.]

The reference to "democracy, American-style" in this case is a not so subtle allusion to the America imagined by Filipinos long before they immigrated. Decades of formal colonialism and neocolonialism, exposure to a U.S. school system that privileged instruction in the English language over the local ones, extensive media exposure, and frequent exchanges between those who have gone to America and those who have stayed behind, created an America that was the "land of opportunity." My respondents frequently mentioned how their desire to access such wealth and power was a central impetus for coming over, even at the expense of risking hard-earned savings, starting over in a new place, leaving family members behind, and knowing that only a privileged few could afford the trip.

In their minds, this "land of opportunity" has also been the seat of democracy, where everyone is *"pantay-pantay"* [equal]. This premise was articulated many times in the meetings, especially when conflicts arose. In a disagreement over whether one delegate should be allowed to voice a dissenting opinion, an officer persuaded the audience to let her speak by reminding them that "in America, *pantay-pantay tayo* [we are all equal]." I gather that this notion includes other kinds of rights and privileges asserted by Filipinos in the United States, from freedom of speech to inclusive participation, tenets that they recognize as quintessentially American in their version of politics. Daisy Perez and others told me how corrupt and abusive politics could be in the Philippines, and how the rights of groups and individuals are not respected—surely one of the reasons why many shy away from politics of this sort, and why some leave the country altogether. In America, they said, "we have to be like the Americans because we are Americans already. We have to leave behind the bad things in the Philippines."

It is inappropriate, however, to simply accept these dichotomous comparisons without examining further the nuances and ambivalences associated with *palengke* politics. The appropriations from both Filipino and U.S. cultural and political contexts to produce something that I have termed "Filipino American-style politics" here are not neatly fused at all times. Respondents were quick to remind me that they are not merely "combining," and that "combinations" do not work ideally in all cases, even though most of them would agree that the basis for these actions lies in a shared cynicism about politics from both the Philippine and U.S. perspectives. Rey Torres, a former president of FACLA, commented:

> Yes, we borrow from everywhere . . . try to see which one can work at this time. Politics from the Philippines is dirty, but we also get something good from there . . . *'di ba 'yung palengke nga* [as in the *palengke*, right]? Democracy here can be good, so we borrow it too . . . but it (can be) dirty too. *'Yung mga Kano, malakas lang sa salita, pero sa gawa mahina. Malayo sa mga tinuturo nila sa eskuwela. 'Tangina nila.* [Those Americans, they are just

strong in words, but weak in deeds. Far from what they teach in schools. Those sons of bitches.] So, we practice how we want democracy to be practiced. *Kasi sa Kano, wala kang maasahan.* [Because from the Americans, you cannot rely on anything.]

This kind of democracy is indeed fraught with contradiction, even if it is viewed by many as emanating from a desired place. The experience of living in the United States, as shown earlier, has its promise, reward, and dark side. Rey Torres, like so many others, has learned to be wary about discrepancies between myth and reality and hesitates to elevate his new home to privileged heights, realizing the failure of this so-called land of opportunity to deliver what it upholds. The new country has afforded Filipino Americans opportunities to better their lives materially, but at the expense of being racialized, exploited, or treated unfairly. It is for these reasons that *palengke* politics reconfigures all its borrowings and appropriations in calculated ways and within the contexts of past and present conditions. We see such reconstitutions in the *palengke*s found in the United States in the ways they address "politicking" that are relevant, appropriate, and openly accessible to community members. At the same time, we recognize only traces of its prior and distanced existence somewhere else.

Yet, if *palengke* politics opens up possibilities of community organizing and building through a consensual determination of needs and goals, it also exposes itself to conflict. The atmosphere in the *palengke*s is often conducive to the possibility that communication will fail and that political activity will result in chaos or immobility. In the meetings I observed, there would be occasional points of contention in matters ranging from agenda decisions to the handling of finances, from election results to the wording of previous meetings' minutes. "Oh, we have a lot of in-fighting too," said one informant:

Mostly, it's personal, if you really think about it. You see all of that in newspapers. Someone wants to be a chairman . . . and then he loses . . . and then he accuses the winner [of] cheating. But the sad thing is that they all print the negative stuff most of the time. *Akala tuloy ng marami, puro away lang kami. Natu-turn off tuloy sila.* [Many people then think we're just full of bickering. They get turned off.] But it's not true. It's part of what we do. You have to accept that.

Battles for top positions have occurred not only in the big organizations like FACLA and COPAO, but also in the numerous smaller associations, prompting many to believe that the continuing increase in the number of new organizations is a result of the propensity for losing candidates to quit their old groups and form new ones (where they can, ideally, become the head). Yet, many are also willing to concede that such personal bickerings are inescapable parts of the political process. They only get magnified, perhaps as in mainstream and local media, because controversy, dissent, and images of disunity are presumed to be more interesting to readers and listeners. Said another respondent: "People like talking about us as crabs. You know what that means? *Mga talangka sa balde* [Crabs in a pail]. They all want to get to the top. But to get to the top, they step on one another." This crab metaphor is borrowed from the Philippines, which, as many also believe, is a site of "dirty" politics. "But it's like that in America *din* [too]. American politicians are also dirty," the respondent added.

If many are turned off by these kinds of conflict, many also opt to stay. Seemingly, those who choose to remain realize the importance of sticking to the stakes in Filipino American politics of this sort. A longtime FACLA member told me: "If not us, who will? We have to keep believing in this thing. Without these things [organizations], what will happen to us? What will our children tell us? That's why people like me spend extra hours here. I work too, you know. It's difficult but it's important." And people like these also press their comembers to do better. "The biggest thing in my mind," said another respondent, "is that we have to do things quicker. We need to move faster. We spend so much time socializing." As in the "Oriental" stores, politics among Filipino Americans is never without its *sosyalan* (socializing). Practiced as a way of negotiating through various social networks, *sosyalan* reduces the formality of organizational meetings (that some desire) to a more informal and relaxed communicative exchange that is, in turn, conducive to smoother or less stressful dialogue. Of course, *sosyalan* also might be practiced in excess and, therefore, might eventually lead to paralysis—something that officers try to minimize partly by differentiating the *sosyalan* practiced in the smaller associations from the *sosyalan* in the umbrella groups. According to a FACLA officer: "Socializing is really for the small town associations. They are more family-oriented . . . they do a lot of singing, dancing, eating in their meetings. That's okay. They are really families related to each other. But in FACLA, we are more for socializing on other levels. We do political contacts . . . business contacts. We also do cultural programs, but only on the side."

Additionally, those who have remained active assert that their commitment to these kinds of activities is a result of knowing that other people have paved the way, and that it is up to them to continue the work. In San Diego's COPAO, this has even meant protecting the community center in National City—their headquarters—from being moved to another place. During a time when the building's lessor was threatening to evict COPAO for nonpayment of rent, members refused to give in to suggestions that headquarters be relocated. In one heated gathering, a couple of members remarked:

> *Ano ito? Hindi tayo nakakapagbayad?* [What? We've not been able to pay?] Can you show us where our fees go? We don't want to move out. We like this place. It means a lot to us. We want to stay. Let's not move out.

> Yes! We have been here for a long time. *Marami ang naghirap para makarating tayo dito.* [Many people worked hard so we can be here.] Why give it up? Let's buy it! We should not give up. Many people will get mad. Especially those who worked here before. *Nakakahiya!* [It's a shame!]

Later, it was learned that funds were missing, causing one of the officers to resign even as he claimed that he was not responsible, or liable, for any lost monies. COPAO members were left to fight the eviction over the next months. After my fieldwork, I got the news that COPAO eventually moved out. Their new headquarters was still in National City, but in a smaller building. I asked the organization's secretary how things were, to which she replied:

> Oh, we try to adjust. We try to copy what we had before [in the other center] and we also improve on some. *Ganyan lang talaga. Ganyan kahit saan. Kahit anong association. Hindi lang mga Pilipino. Dito sa Amerika, ganyan ang nangyayari sa mga maliliit na grupo. Tayong mga Pinoy, sanay diyan. Pero dito rin sa Amerika, marami din tayong natututunan . . . marami tayong napapakinabangan dito.* [That's just how it goes. That's what happens every-

where. That's what happens to any kind of association. Not only to Filipinos. Here in America, that's what happens to small groups. We Pinoys
are used to that. But here in America too, we also learn a lot of things . . .
we make use of {or profit from} a lot of things here.]

In the appropriation of things American in these community formations, an important point could also be made about democracy and
its close relationship to civil society in the U.S. context. Alexis de Tocqueville wrote in 1848 about the Americans' unique inclination to
form political and social associations whose numbers were far greater
than that in most other countries at that time. Tocqueville saw these
associations as important parts of civil society in the ways they oper-
ated without state intervention and in their efforts at making democracy work, from managing the "despotic action of the majority" to
"pursuing in common the objects of common desire."[13] These observations resonate in the 1990s among these Filipino American organizations, something they have in common with Americans outside their
ethnic group, who have also formed associations of diverse interests.

Talking about COPAO's and FACLA's affinities with such historical antecedents is, however, qualitatively different from situating Filipino American community organizing within its present context. For
these people, it is not a matter of creating just any group or joining
just any association. Rather, it is participating in organizations whose
membership is solely or predominantly Filipino that makes a difference. Owing to their shared experiences and common agendas, these
Filipinos actively seek the company of their own kind so that acceptance and mutual interests are assured.[14] This kind of ethnic-based
organizing also allows for "doing politics" specific to the needs and
dispositions of the members, which in many ways challenges the pressures to conform to mainstream ways. Their experiences in other
local, statewide, and multiethnic political organizations, in which they
participate as minorities, have included unpleasant situations in which
they were either silenced or relegated to passive membership. Even
the histories of Filipino and panethnic organizations (such as Asian
American ones) reveal their very limited participation due to conflicts
of interests and anxieties about being pigeonholed under wider
rubrics.[15] With these Filipinos, as we have seen, much greater weight

is given to self-determined formations, hence, the appropriation of a version of democracy with a resistant edge.

There is a price to be paid for this kind of resistance, as many of my informants were quick to remind me. Mainstream kinds of politicking are themselves resistant to the kinds of change and accommodation demanded by marginal groups. "I don't think the big political parties want us," explains Roger Alano. "We try from time to time, but we never pass the 'little member' stage. And then it takes a lot of money too to run for office. How can we make it?" Further, although their exact numbers are difficult to obtain, many constituents are believed to have altogether given up hope in this strategy by refusing to engage in any of the organizations' activities. To those who have remained active, there is a glimmer of hope. A FACLA member told me: "We are the breeding grounds for future leaders. Sometime soon, we will get to big-time American politics too."

Indeed, the anxieties about the kind of assimilation (or resistance to it) I am describing here are certainly managed and localized via *palengke* politics. Politics, however, are not limited to the *palengke*. For beyond these spaces lies the arena of the beauty pageant, a forum that lends itself to extended political negotiation whose communicative registers rest on ideas about Filipino virtues.

Beauty Pageants

The Filipino Americans I interacted with never directly equated beauty pageants with politics. That is, beauty pageants are rarely if ever viewed as events that pertain to doing strictly political things. Yet our conversations reveal how closely tied the holding of pageants is to the kinds of *palengke* politics just described. "*Para ding palengke doon* [It's also like a *palengke* there]," remarked Wilma Galvan. "*Bago pa man ding ginaganap e pina-palengke nila 'yung coronation, mula sa pagbili ng ticket hanggang sa katapusan.*" [Even before it's held, they turn the coronation into a *palengke*, from the selling of tickets until the end.]

Here, I focus on beauty pageants that are held primarily to raise funds, similar to those found in towns and cities in the Philippines and those conducted by other ethnic groups in the United States.[16] In

Southern California, I saw in many instances that pageant organizers and participants always attended COPAO, FACLA, and other organizational meetings to sell tickets. Small and large social gatherings, whether induction ceremonies for new officers or annual reunions, consistently reserved a program spot for, say, the introduction of a beauty titlist or the presentation ("cat walk") of the "hometown pride" (a pageant winner bearing the name of a province, town, or city, as in Miss Batangas–USA or Miss Pride of USA Ilocandia); such gatherings were often emceed by a beauty queen herself. Organizational meetings also regularly discussed recent or future beauty pageants as part of their agendas. Hence, it may be the case that those I spoke with don't see beauty pageants as "doing politics," but perhaps they recognize and imagine a *specific* form of "doing politics" in the pageants coextensive with their "political" activities in the organizations.

I began to pay close attention to this notion upon examining the historical records of COPAO. According to several sources, the idea of forming COPAO as an umbrella organization actually originated at a beauty pageant that was held on 3 July 1971 at the El Cortez Hotel in San Diego. Three contestants surprised the audience by reading onstage the "antiestablishment manifestos" they had concealed in their clothes. In the middle of the question-and-answer portion of the pageant, they urged the community to focus on "issues of justice, poverty, the war in Vietnam (a national issue at that time), the plight of the Filipino American farm workers, and equality."[17] This occasion spurred the presidents of seventeen Filipino American organizations to form the President's Circle, which grew into COPAO as membership increased.

There is a good indication of such close links between pageant holding and some form of politics in past issues of Filipino American community newspapers. In the 1990s, the Filipinos I talked to understood the significance of beauty pageants in this context. Gloria Miranda, a FACLA officer, stated:

> *Iba talaga ang mga Pilipino. 'Yung mga beauty pageant natin . . . iba rin. Kita mo naman, nagmumula sa ganito ang unity natin. Kahit na akala mo e contest-contest lamang . . . aba, seryoso din ang mga ito.* [Filipinos are really different. Our beauty pageants . . . are also different. Just take a look, our

unity comes out of things like these. Even though you think it's just a contest . . . oh, these are also serious stuff.]

Beauty pageants, for Filipinos like Gloria Miranda, are sites of weightier issues than those in which women vie for such titles as Miss California, Miss Universe, and Miss International. In most of the pageants I witnessed, the audience was less preoccupied with who was physically the most beautiful, the most elegantly dressed, or the most talented than with the pageant as a venue for bringing people together, generating funds for organizational projects, and expressing particular political agendas. Hence, pageants such as these add a different dimension to community building.

Held primarily in community centers (or, occasionally, hotel ballrooms for much larger gatherings), beauty pageants open up spaces for practicing a kind of politics that is alert to history, to the syncretic appropriation of values and attributes from what are considered "Filipino" and "American" cultures, and to the pursuit of collective well-being. I call these spaces alternative sites because the events that occur in them and the meanings evoked by them go beyond what many of my respondents would say was the "usual thing" that happens in mainstream politics (in reference to the familiar ways they are excluded or marginalized) and mainstream beauty pageants. To these Filipino Americans, participation in the beauty pageants is connected to the strengthening of bonds of caring, commitment to common goals, and belonging to the realms of Filipino Americanness.

The coronation of beauty queens is an event many people look forward to. But long before the crowning, pageant organizers must determine the pageant's size and scope, depending on the number of people they anticipate will support it. Usually, pageants are organized to raise funds for a cause an organization supports. They are often held either on a one-time basis because of an immediate and unexpected concern (for example, for the victims of a volcanic eruption or flood in the Philippines) or on an annual basis with a different cause every year (for example, for scholarships for Filipino American students or funds for medical assistance for Filipino Americans in need). One or several causes are always mentioned along with the announcement of the pageant in flyers and newspaper ads. Mused one informant: "Our beauty contests are always for . . . different causes. Yes, we have a few of them that are really *pang-beauty* [for beauty] . . . but those only happen once or twice a year. The regular contests are those that are really for raising . . . donating money for different kinds of benefits . . . whether it's money needed for our projects here . . . or if it's money for the ones in the Philippines. It's always for a cause. People don't go if it's not for something."

The bulk of the work, however, comes with selling tickets, to which organizers and contestants themselves devote a lot of time and energy. A common experience, my respondents tell me, is getting accosted by these ticket sellers at social gatherings they attend. *"Diyos ko, kahit saan ka magpunta dito, laging may nagbebenta ng ticket para kay Miss ganyan o kay Misis ganito!"* [My God, everywhere you go here, there's someone selling tickets for Miss This or Mrs. That!], said Rose Sison. I have experienced this pressure too in many get-togethers of Filipino families, in school reunions, organizational meetings, and even in FACLA and COPAO House of Delegates sessions. In one COPAO postmeeting social, Violeta Ramos, an officer of one of the town-based organizations, came up to me and inquired: "Are you a member of any organization around here? Why don't you join ours? Are you from Cavite? Well . . . if not, what you can do is buy some tickets from me. *Sige na!* [Come on!] There's this beauty contest our group is having . . . or better . . . you should be one of our judges!" A refusal is hard to muster.

Selling tickets, according to many, is just like selling any other merchandise, except for the understanding between vendor and buyer that any profit made goes to a special cause. This is primarily the reason why the transaction is thought of as charity work, in which a vendor donates time and effort by selling tickets (characterized by many as "difficult work"), while a buyer donates cash to someone other than the seller. But what struck me as more interesting was the part in this kind of transaction played by an idiom of exchange specific to Filipinos. "Come on . . . this is for a good cause. *Makidamay ka naman! Iyang damay mo is all for our good*" [Be one with us! Your oneness is all for our good], Violeta Ramos told me. This notion of *damay*, a carry-over from the Philippines, is usually employed to mean commiseration, sympathy, or "condolence for another's misfortune."[18] "*Nakikiramay po* [My condolences]" is how one would use the word in talking to someone grieving because of a death. But in these cases, respondents use *damay* not really to condole with another but to be involved in a *damayan*—an activity or relationship of people helping other people.[19] Historian Reynaldo Ileto refers to this use of *damay*, that of "participation in another's work," in the context of nineteenth-century popular movements in the Philippines, but it is not difficult to find its echoes among Filipinos in twentieth-century America.[20] To *damay* is to enjoin another to participate in a cause; the result is having more people helping one another— "*Magdamayan tayo* [Let's help one another]," I overheard someone say. This ultimately reinforces a bond and creates a sense of oneness with the other *(pakikiramay)*. Because one is able to help, one is brought further into the other's domain. Hence, my translation of "*Makidamay ka naman*" into "Be one with us," as a stand-in for "participation in the work of another," casts *damay* as a mechanism for coconstructing and sustaining a community. "*Sino-sino pa ba naman ang magtutulungan kundi tayo-tayo rin?* [Who else would help us but us?]" Sison added. "*Ganyan talaga tayo, 'di ba?*" [We're really like that, isn't it true?]

If the practice of *damay* propels ticket sellers into communities of shared interests and forges bonds of oneness, holding the pageants offers visible recognition of the fruits of such labor. Said one organizer: "*Dito natin makikita 'yung mga nag-trabaho para sa mga contests na ito. Tayo rin naman ang nakikinabang. Tayo-tayo rin ang lumalabas na winners. Tulungan din, 'di ba?*" [Here, we see those who have worked for these contests. We're the ones who profit from these. We're the ones who come out as winners. It's helping one another, isn't it?] Against the spectacle of beauty titlists parading on stage, a strong sense of pride usually permeates the audience. Knowing that they have worked toward a goal and have accomplished it so that others may benefit is the source of a certain measure of joy, as is the knowledge that their work at the same time has made possible a community of Filipinos momentarily gathered together as one.

The occasion itself brings together sellers and buyers, organizers and contestants, and judges and spectators bearing witness to a product of shared labor. "*Siempre, we have our own manok.* [Of course, we

have our own contenders.] We cheer for them. We want them to
win!" says a ticket seller. Contestants were usually daughters of first-
generation immigrants, so one can say that the spaces of the beauty
pageants are feminized spaces, as opposed to the *palengkes*, which,
even though many of my respondents perceive them to be equally
accessible to both women and men, are often attended to by male
members and officers. "Yes, more women are [present] here," said the
ticket seller, "but both Filipinos and Filipinas participate in the background . . . and [as] audience. Sometimes, we have contests for boys
too . . . but only once in a while. Everyone tries to help."

Many pageants that I watched included swimsuit parades and question-and-answer segments; in these pageants, the number of contestants exceeded the number of titles available. For pageants in which
the number of contestants equaled the number of titles, certain segments were usually dispensed with in favor of a display of talent by
each of the contestants. I was a judge for several pageants in both Los
Angeles and San Diego, and it took me quite a while to figure out the
difference between these two kinds of pageants. At first, I seriously
assigned points for each of the competition portions for every pageant. Later on, I realized that, for some of them, I only needed to sit
and watch. "We tell you in the end who the winners are, the moment
we verify who sold the most tickets," Violeta Ramos told me once.
"These portions for talent and everything else . . . we have them there
for entertainment . . . to show the contestants' talents in singing this
Filipino song . . . or dancing this ethnic dance. But that's part of the
show. The important thing is that money was raised and the pageant
is successful. So just sit back and relax. *Diyos ko!* [My God!] We're all
winners anyway! We're all beautiful!"

Thus, before a contest, a few people have an idea of who will eventually win the titles at stake. Contestants who have also been engaged
in selling tickets might have some clue, but organizers make it a point
to keep the audience riveted. An immediate reaction may be that
these pageants are all staged or fixed. True, some of the winners are
determined before the pageants. But audiences are concerned less
about whether the winners are preselected or known beforehand
than about celebrating and socializing *(sosyalan)*; some pageants are

also called "coronation nights," suggesting that they are not always viewed as contests. People attend these events to signal their coming together as one, represented by a beauty titlist who allows them to feel pride in both a "beautiful" Filipino American woman and a job well done. Said one seller: "That's the time we see each other. It's like having fun while raising money!" In the weeks following the pageant, photos of the winners would be strewn over the front pages of the community newspapers, detailing their titles and the causes they have served.

For older Filipino Americans, coronation nights in the social halls would involve the crowning of a couple: Mr. and Mrs. FilAm Senior, or something to that effect. "They're [usually] *mag-asawa* [married] already," said one senior interviewee. "We crown them because they [contributed] the most . . . and then we ask them to parade . . . sit on the throne we made up here in the center . . . and then dance. It's nice. It's our way of awarding those that help us really good."

"This is something we are proud of," one contestant told me. "We reached out . . . and this title represents that." If you participated, she said, *"tulong mo na rin 'yan sa mga nangangailangan sa atin."* [It's also your way of helping those who are in need in our country.] People who have indeed participated realize the gains they are reaping in these events. But more important to them is the investment in bringing Filipino American communities together—in the process of helping each other to aid Filipinos in the United States and elsewhere, Filipinos are brought closer together. Another contest winner said: "I don't care much about the title for myself. The title refers to me . . . but it also means that I did my part in helping." *"Para na ring bayanihan* [It's just like *bayanihan* (a cooperative endeavor)]," noted Violeta Ramos: *"'Di ba ganyan sa Pilipinas? Ganyan din dito. Tayo-tayo na rin ang magtutulungan. Kita mo, kahit beauty contest e marami rin ang naeenganyong makisama at tumulong sa isa't isa."* [Isn't it like this in the Philippines? It's also like that here. We're the ones who can help each other. See, even if it's just a beauty contest, a lot of people are motivated to join with others and help one another.]

Both *bayanihan* and *damayan* ascribe the virtue of helping one another along similar lines. *Bayanihan*'s root word is *bayan*, which in

Tagalog means town, municipality, nation, home, or the public. To imagine *bayanihan*'s full force is to call into action these multiple referents, so "helping one another" in the spirit of *bayanihan* implies helping someone who comes from the same town or the same nation. In doing so, one is able to build stronger ties with the *bayan*, the people back home. And according to many, one ultimately helps in building the *bayan* in the United States, with Filipinos in the new country, by that very same practice.

I have also heard *bayanihan* mentioned along with its synonyms *tulungan* and *samahan* (COPAO supports projects called Operation *Samahan* and, as mentioned earlier, Operation *Tulungan*), and the implication has usually been an assurance of mutual aid and cooperative endeavor for the benefit of those here and in the Philippines. COPAO, FACLA, and the funds generated in the beauty pageants support projects targeting health care for seniors, drug abuse programs for the youth, legal services for civil rights cases, and trade and cultural shows. A significant portion of monies raised also benefits the poor, the needy, and the victims of calamities in the Philippines. Scholarships, donations for rebuilding and renovating schools, churches, and sanitation facilities, as well as seed money for small business enterprises are routed to the homeland on a regular basis. One local newspaper reporter told me:

> These contests raise . . . I would say, thousands of dollars each year . . . and I can be sure that they spend about half a million dollars every year for their social gatherings in various hotels, restaurants, and meeting halls . . . if you count the rest of Southern California–based Filipino American organizations. Meeting halls generate a lot of money, you know. Don't underestimate them . . . and don't underestimate the work of these people. They are serious about these things even if they look like they're just doing silly things in the centers.

"That's a lot of money," I said. He continued:

> Oh yes. Just count all these associations . . . the Cavite, Batangas, Laguna, Mindoro, Ilocos Norte, Cagayan [provinces in the Philippines] . . . et cetera associations. Then there are the U.S. place associations . . . San Diego, National City, Carson City, Cerritos, Norwalk . . . Filipino associations in these places . . . just count them. You also have the religious

organizations . . . the Knights of Columbus, the doctors, the engineers, the
dentists, the alumni people. If each of them, at least, hold a gathering and
a beauty contest each year . . . which most of them do . . . think of the
money involved there. Think of all the people who pitch in. They spend
. . . but they also generate money for things to take care of here . . . and
things to take care of there. They've been doing this for many years now.
They know nobody else will help them. They know that helping each
other has many results.

"A huge bulk of our money goes back to our other home," said
another beauty contest organizer. "We owe it to them." I asked,
"Well, what do you owe them?" "They're still part of us," she said.
"That's where many of us were born. That's where we draw our inspiration from . . . to work hard here, so that others like the ones back
home can also benefit. Well, we're here in America now. We also help
each other here. So, it's both helping here and there. We are part of
both worlds."

Filipino Americans find in these pageants social spaces that reflect
their tenuous positions as Filipinos who, in their eyes, are not fully
American (by virtue of their first-generation immigrant status) and not
fully Filipino anymore either (owing to their departure and distance
from the homeland). The orientation to the *bayan*, both in the context of activities in the United States and in reference to the homeland, is one anchor they hold onto to mitigate these tensions. Yet that
orientation is mired in conflict between, say, those who have chosen
to sever ties with the old country and those who insist on strengthening any connections they could shore up. Then there are those who
are not able to participate due to lack of time or money. And some
ventures fail to reach their goal for a variety of reasons: poor organization, lack of promotion, infighting among the organizers and participants, or unappealing causes that result in fewer tickets sold.

To those who are able to participate, the motivation, as mentioned
earlier, is predicated on the virtues of helping, often "because nobody
else will." To those who are successful in organizing such pageants,
beauty contests and coronation nights are the best possible means of
raising money and bringing disparate communities and individuals
together. "It works," said one organizer who used to be a beauty

titlist. "A lot of people participate . . . and it gets memorable because it means much more than raising money. It's for us. We are the ones who benefit."

Beauty pageants are also occasions for power negotiations. People like Violeta Ramos invest money and time to gain a foothold as leaders in the community. If their ventures succeed, they assume primary roles in community politics, and with their visibility assured, they are liable to command authority and respect from their presumed constituents. Holding pageants is, thus, fraught with politicking, as different personalities vie for positions of community influence, hoping that their *manok* or their daughter will win and enough money will be raised to fund projects. Some respondents have no qualms about describing these contests as *palengkes* in their own right. And when a *manok* wins, her sponsors win with her, as their names as individuals or members of an organization (including their causes) become identified with the beauty queen throughout her reign.

The stakes involved are not only influential positions, but what title holders represent. Locally, organizers revere beauty titlists to the extent that they embody the processes and effects of *bayanihan* and *damayan* of Filipinos in America. In their terms, "she's something to be proud of in our new home." More important, the appeal of beauty contests encompass the desire for recognition in the new place of settlement—in spite of all the pressures of living in a society that doesn't consider them as full members, they are able to accomplish something important to their lives in the United States. "It's not just winning," a contestant opined. "It's about achieving something . . . that we organized ourselves."

This also partly explains the propensity of many Filipino American organizations to give out achievement awards to their members or acquaintances, even outside their small groups. In some pageants, a portion of the agenda would be devoted to handing out trophies or medals to community leaders or those who have excelled in their professions. Even COPAO and FACLA occasionally host awards nights to recognize and acknowledge the merits and services of Filipino Americans "who have demonstrated excellence in their fields" and, in so doing, "have contributed to the upliftment of the [Filipino

American] community." "These are ways to announce to our community and the world that we are also achievers, even if many think that we are nobodies," said a FACLA member. "And it's not only about showing off. It's not only about someone being honored . . . for the sake of having someone there. It's about having someone good there so that others will see . . . and admire . . . and honor." The celebratory mood of these events is extended to moments of *sosyalan* after the ceremonies and speeches are over with. Ballroom dancing is always preferred to cap the night. Other postceremony activities are contests in *karaoke* singing and dancing, parlor games, and raffles. Usually, sons and daughters of members handle the sound arrangements, and portions of the program are devoted exclusively to their presentations of songs, dances, and other performances.

For beauty title holders, sharing the honor of being crowned with those being recognized for their achievement and hard work is thus imbued with the marks of success in America. Their image in the Philippines, however, is another matter, since more often than not, they are American born or assumed to be so by Filipinos back home. Usually, if enough money is raised, contest winners are sent to the Philippines to personally hand out donations raised in the United States. Town officials have been known to eagerly await these bearers of goodwill and treat them with lavishness as soon as they arrive. Some of the winners even take the opportunity to compete in beauty pageants in the islands as representatives of Filipinos in the States. The beauty titlist is a prized celebrity, for she not only shares with Filipinos back home some of the fruits of those who have labored in the "land of opportunity," she also personifies access to things American only a few Filipinos are able to gain. This is a primary reason why organizers carefully select whom to send home. For, as one contest judge said, "she [not only] represents us here, how we've been successful here . . . she also represents us there, how we have succeeded here too."

The representation of success in these instances is recognizably gendered, an issue that arose in some of my conversations with organizers, participants, and audience members. Most of the differences in opinion regarding whether these pageants are sexist or perpetuate an objectification of women lay along generational lines. First-generation Filipinos who organized and watched these contests viewed them as primarily held in the service of community interests, with women "merely" enacting certain roles. Filipino American beauty queens to them were women to be admired, respected, and emulated. Second-generation Filipinas who entered these pageants had mixed feelings about their participation, mostly expressed in terms of uneasiness and apprehension in being involved in something unfamiliar to them. Said one contestant:

> My parents were the ones who prodded me to do this. I was so embarrassed. I was scared too. I barely got through selling tickets ... and then the coronation night ... it was weird to me. Everyone was saying I was pretty. But I thought this was not about being pretty. At least, that's what they say. Thank God it ended quickly. Like, I wanted to get it over with. You know, this is something new to me. I've heard of these things before, but I never imagined myself being a contestant in them!

Some of them told me about feeling exploited as women, although they also said such pageants do have a redeeming value in the ways they support local and Philippine-based communities. As one of them said: "It's okay to join. You know that you're helping. And just as long as that's the first priority, I'm all for it."

In a general sense, these beauty pageants held in meeting halls and hotel ballrooms reflect both Filipino and American perceptions of geography, movement, and identity. Many of my interviewees observed that beauty pageants of this kind are appealing to Filipino Americans because back in the Philippines, they are extremely popular too. "It's like the Philippines being brought here. We Filipinos are very fond of them," Rose Sison told me. "Some say we got it from the Americans. But we have our own brand of it. *Kita mo nga dito* [If you notice, here], we don't really emphasize beauty ... beauty ... beauty ... it's really something much more than that." Two other organizers concurred:

> It's not only about American [standards]. Filipino standards [in the United States] are much more [than beauty]. Filipinas are beautiful because they have good hearts ... serve their people ... help each other. So, we mix them together. They mean so much more ... two worlds combined."

Well, we're beautiful already, *'di ba?* [isn't that so?] So what we do is we put this beauty into ... action. We have those pageants on TV ... Miss America ... Miss World ... we know that. But we copy them ... only in a small way. We put Filipino things in the center ... our talents ... and our community ... our projects into it. *Halo-halo tayo. Siempre, nasa Amerika tayo ... pero Pinoy pa rin, 'di ba?"* [We are mixed together. Of course, we are in America ... but we're also Pinoy, isn't that so?]

The spaces of the social halls are modified and appropriated to combine these two worlds. They become recognized as part of being Filipino in America as much as they are used to articulate the sense of being Filipino and American at the same time. "This place is ours," said one respondent, referring to a social hall in Cerritos. "It used to be this old warehouse. But we have converted it ... to become ... a Filipino room *'ika nga ... dito sa Amerika* [as they say ... here in America]." In Mira Mesa as well (a municipality in San Diego), a community center in the public park was named the Filipino American Senior Center—the result of a community project spearheaded by the town's older Filipino Americans. Numerous fundraising drives (including several beauty pageants) were held and assistance from the county offices solicited to make this center a reality. Said one senior citizen from there:

Meron tayong mga social halls sa Pilipinas, pero pang meeting-meeting lang ang mga iyon. Dito rin, may mga social halls pero 'yung mga puti, they just use them for meetings. Dito, ginagamit natin silang mga lugar para sa mga contest. Malayo ang pinanggalingan natin at saka ... marami na rin tayong mga mahihirap na karanasan dito. Pero tuloy pa rin tayo.... Ganyan tayong mga Pilipino dito sa Amerika. Nagugulat nga iyung iba. Tanong nila, ganiyan ba sa Pilipinas? Sabi ko ... hindi ... he-he-he ... ganyan ang mga Pilipino sa Amerika. [We have social halls in the Philippines, but they're only used for ordinary meetings. Here too, there are social halls, but the white people, they just use them for meetings. Here, we use them as places for our contests. We have traveled far and ... we have had difficult experiences here. But we go on. That's how we are—Filipino Americans—here. Others are really surprised. They ask, is that the way it is in the Philippines? I said ... no ... he-he-he ... that's the way Filipinos are in America.]

Indeed, we see how social halls exceed their perceived functions so that ultimately, they benefit the communities whose identities, desires, and needs are marked and pursued against pressures of immigration and marginality.

Both *palengke* politics and beauty pageants illustrate the nuances of a particular kind of politicking familiar to Filipino Americans in Southern California. They point to different ways of configuring how Filipino American immigrants meet their own needs within the constraints of their conditions and how they address these on their own terms. Navigating a series of borrowings and appropriations of things considered Filipino and applying them in America, these people find creative ways of circumscribing their distance from mainstream forms of politicking. At the same time, they attend to the potential of their own politics, which allow them some measure of unity, autonomy, and access. Practicing these versions of politics, as the *palengke* style shows, demands an alertness to both the benefits and limits of such syncretic forms. Delicately balanced between order and chaos, *palengke* politics have resulted in moments of equitable exchange, of community coconstruction and horizontal solidarity akin to a democratic public sphere.

Filipino Americans I have talked to, perhaps realizing how sharply their own politics differed from mainstream notions of it, have consistently directed my attention to alternative ways of imagining and handling community affairs. These are the politics that, to them, make possible an orientation to the homeland as a common point of origin and alliance (*"Pilipino tayong lahat"* [We are all Filipinos]), a source of virtues that can be appropriated (*"Ganyan tayo sa Pilipinas"* [We are like that in the Philippines]), and a beneficiary of charitable work. These are at the same time the kinds of politics oriented to the new settlements in the United States, with organizations and beauty pageants serving to mobilize Filipinos to address similar conditions and achieve common ends of representation, commitment, belonging, and recognition. To these people, such styles of politicking open up spaces for negotiating and articulating identities as Filipino Americans.

5

Homeland Memories and Media

Filipino Images and Imaginations in America

itting on one of the metal benches set outside a neighborhood "Oriental" store, I noticed a group of Filipino American *seniors* poring over the week's sampling of community dailies, cups of coffee and fresh-baked *pan de sal* close by. I approached them cautiously, not wanting to be a nuisance. My greeting, *"Kumusta ho kayo?"* [How are you doing?], and my grin seemed to help; although they exchanged puzzled looks among themselves, they returned my gestures with the customary smiles. I tried to start a conversation about the newspapers they were reading by asking, *"Ano na ba ho ang balita?"* [What news is there, sir?] to which one replied, *"Naku, marami. Baha na naman sa Pilipinas ... at namatay na pala si Chichay. Dito naman sa atin e tuloy pa rin ang kaso ng mga beterano."* [Oh, a lot. It's flooded again in the Philippines ... and Chichay (a popular Filipina comedienne) has died too. Here in our place, the court case of the (Filipino) war veterans is still going on.] The other readers nodded. I continued engaging them in small talk, asking if they gathered like this regularly. Their answers were almost affectionate: *"Alam mo, totoy...."* [You know, little boy....] In my inquisitveness, I wondered if they saw in me a *baguhan* (newcomer; one whom second- or third-generation Filipino Americans would call F.O.B., "fresh off the boat") who needed to know the ropes of immigrant life in America. One of them turned toward me and explained: *"Ganyan ang gawa namin halos araw-araw. Nagbabasa kami ng diyaryo. Aba, importante din ito . . . at masarap magbasa ng tungkol sa atin . . . habang nag-hihintay sa mga nagsho-shopping. Malayo nga ang Pilipinas . . . pero malapit din."* [We do this almost every day. We read the newspapers. Of course, this is also important . . . and it's a good feeling to read about us . . . while waiting for those who are shopping. The Philippines is really far . . . but it's also near.] Many minutes later, when the group was disbanding for the day, two of the men walked back toward the store to grab one more copy of each of the papers they just finished perusing. *"Para sa mga anak ko sa bahay* [For my children at home]," one of them said with a grin. *"Aba, libre naman ito a . . . at saka nagtatago din ako ng mga kopya."* [Well, it's free anyway . . . and I also keep copies.]

On another day, I visited the editorial office of the *Filipino Press* in National City, near San Diego. As I waited to interview its editor-in-chief, several of those milling about struck up conversations with me. I felt as if I knew them, or as if they already knew me and were just putting the pieces about me into place: *"Taga saan ka kamo? Anong apelyido mo? E 'di kilala mo siguro si . . . . Taga U.P. ka daw? E dapat makausap mo si . . . ."* [Where are you from again? What's your surname? Then, you probably know. . . . Someone said you're from U.P. (University of the Philippines)? Then, you must talk to. . . .] Then the editor snatched me away from them. *"Hoy! Sa akin gustong makipag-usap niyan!"* [Hey! I'm the one he wants to talk to!] In the one-room office, it was easy to get distracted. Journalists shared the limited space with columnists and beat reporters, who doubled as secretaries, typists, researchers, and receptionists. Typesetters and illustrators sat in front of shelves holding volumes of past issues and piles of paperwork. Filing cabinets overflowed. Phones rang intermittently. Telex machines buzzed constantly. Small groups of people continued to cram into the room, looking for Mr. This or Mrs. That, asking for a previous issue, wondering about an interview, delivering a press release, or complaining about a photo. Others stole a corner to whisper something to someone. The editor cleared folders away from a chair he offered to me: "Sit, sit. Don't mind them. This is how it is everyday here. *See, maliit nga itong opisina natin . . . pero atin 'to.* [See, our office may be small . . . but it's ours.] This paper is our own."

In many Filipino American commercial establishments in Southern California, one sees on display a wide selection of community newspapers, usually free for the taking. This is true, to some degree, for Filipino communities elsewhere in the United States and other countries. But with the exception of the San Francisco Bay Area, my informants tell me, no set of communities matches the number of local papers circulated in the counties and peripheries of Los Angeles and San Diego, owing primarily to the geographical distribution of Filipino immigrant settlements in North America. The ubiquitous newspapers occupy significant places not only in the sites where Filipino Americans meet, but also, as I wish to emphasize here, in sites where the narratives of Filipino American identity are imagined and imaged. Community newspapers comprise only one of the array of apparatuses that link individuals and range from families and kinship systems to religious ties and other social organizations. They are also one of the many media, like radio, television, and film, that operate as communication systems within and between societies. In this chapter, however, I focus on Filipino American community newspapers in Southern California as illustrations of a historically specific and localized avenue of community formation and expression. I suggest that they operate as alternative spaces for Filipino Americans who see themselves as active agents in the remembering, reconstruction, and representation of their collective identities.

For this study, I interacted with producers and readers of about nine community papers circulated in and around Los Angeles and San Diego counties. I say "about" because many publications appear, last for a few months, die out, then reappear once publishers regain control over resources. As local undertakings, these newspapers are susceptible to investor pressures, erratic markets, fluctuations in advertising and available human power, intemperate competition, and increasing costs of paper, supplies, and printing.[1] Nevertheless, most of the papers I looked at appeared weekly, with a combined circulation estimated at 350,000 Filipino Americans in Southern California—the largest group of Filipinos outside the Philippines.[2] I also examined the topics that appeared with regularity, the distribution and reception of these papers, and their significance for identity construction.

Advertising Filipino Americanness

Like most ethnic newspapers in the United States, Filipino American community newspapers exist in communities where there is a great demand or need to serve the interests of people of the same group.[3] Compared to mainstream papers, ethnic presses are small-scale, run with a minimal number of journalists, and—especially Filipino American papers— usually free of charge, with the costs of production and distribution shouldered by advertisers. The demand by members of an ethnic group for a newspaper of their own is not a new phenomenon. In 1922, sociologist Robert E. Park conducted a survey of immigrant presses to highlight their significant role in easing the transition of new arrivals settling permanently in the United States, both by preserving the languages, traditions, and values of their home countries, and by "assisting [their orientation] . . . in the American environment."[4] To some degree, Filipino American newspapers share this common ground with other immigrant presses of the past and present. But unlike many of the others, most Filipino papers are printed in English, owing to the facility of many of their readers in this language as a result of their U.S.-style education. This doesn't mean, however, that these papers are oriented solely toward "Americanization." Geared toward immigrant Filipinos as their primary readers, they encourage both retaining values that are "dear to Filipino hearts," as one editor told me, and acquiring "things American, like [formal] citizenship," as an advertisement for an immigrant law firm regularly asserted in the papers.

Advertisements in these papers render in their most visible forms the liminality of the immigrant experience and its assumed trajectory toward a more desirable state. Here, I refer primarily to large ads (some up to half a page) that promote the services of immigration attorneys in matters of naturalization/citizenship, labor certification, deportation defense, relative petitions, asylum applications, and change of status. With such statements as "Don't go to Immigration without us," these ads promise confidentiality and free initial consultation, beckoning those in transition to work out their legal status ("Green Cards For Your Family in Less Than a Year", "Solve All Your Immigration Problems Today") on their way to becoming "full-fledged Americans" and realizing "a bright future." Supplementing these ads are the columns penned by immigration lawyers detailing and explaining updates in immigration law, almost always in "frequently asked questions" format: How can I verify my work experience? How do I petition for a brother who is married? How much do I have to spend for filing a change of status from an H-1 visa to a permanent residency? According to several editors, these items offer free information tips, although only the basic answers are supplied. Usually, the catch is that every case is different, so columnists list the address and telephone number of their firm at the end of the piece "for further information."

That advertisements for immigration processing appear with great regularity and prominence in these papers assumes some things about the Filipino communities being addressed. Many Filipino Americans I interviewed noted the assumption of the general public that a good number of Filipinos are in the United States illegally or, at least, are in the process of working out their status from nonpermanent to permanent residency and, farther down the line, to naturalization. The local colloquial term for such Filipinos is "TNT," for "Tago Nang Tago," "always in hiding." TNTs are those who try to elude authorities, whether work supervisors or INS agents, by assuming aliases, falsifying documents, using fake work permits, or simply staying at home as household help. The range of options for TNTs is fairly wide, and their success at hiding their identities primarily rests on the discretion and secrecy of those who know of their status. In these communities, most attempts at questioning anyone else's status, whether TNT or not, are usually seen as improper (bastus) or, at the least, invasive (nakikialam). In one gathering I attended, for example, the host was especially miffed at another Filipino he was meeting for the first time, whose greeting included questions of whether the host's new wife had been in the United States for long (a coded question that assumes that, if one has been in the country for long, one would be "legal") or had just arrived recently (in his words, "à la mail order bride"), and whether she was a green-card holder or already a citizen. The host replied, audibly enough for everyone close by to hear, that "all of us are citizens here! *Bakit pa tayo magtatanungan? Baka INS ka?*" [Why should we ask each other? Are you an INS agent?] Of course, the host said these words with a smile on his face, as if he were returning joke for joke. But it conveyed his feeling about the guest's offensive behavior and insensitivity.

In this sense, the possession of legal immigration or citizenship documentation is highly important, but only to the degree it places its holders as "legitimate" or "authorized" members of the larger society. Indeed, it is seen as a requirement imposed by the state on its national citizenry.[5] So, to many respondents and others, having the proper papers means being able to freely circulate in the new place with the rest of the citizens of the nation and, thus, to enjoy the guarantees of "being an American," which include the right to work and the right to vote. Given the history of exclusion and disenfranchisement experienced by previous generations of Filipinos in the United States (because of "special status" or barriers to naturalization, for example) and the more contemporary calls for government crackdown on illegal immigration (which many Filipinos may be susceptible to), such guarantees are indeed crucial to a sense of belonging. The significance of legal status among those I talked to, however, extends only to matters concerning their relationship to non-Filipinos. Among themselves, authorized documentation is not a prerequisite for belonging, and asking about one's status is regarded as out of place, or even offensive, in conversations. As one respondent said:

Ke meron o walang papel, bakit pa tayo magtatanong? Basta Pilipino kung Pilipino. Papel lang iyan. Kung TNT, o e ano ngayon? Para bang marriage license. Papel din iyan. Hindi ka naman ibang tao talaga kung kasal ka na. Kaya yung mga nagtatanong kung TNT o hindi, kabastusan iyon. Ano ang pakialam nila kung legal ako kung hindi? Gobyerno lang naman ang mahilig diyan.

[Whether you have or don't have papers, why do we need to ask? Just say Filipino if one is Filipino. It's just a piece of paper. If one is TNT, well, so what? It's like a marriage license. It's also a piece of paper. You really don't turn into someone else once you're married. That's why those who ask about whether one is TNT or not, that's rude. Why should it be their business to know if one is legal or not? It's only the government who meddles in that]

Immigration ads are especially attuned to the sensitiveness of TNT issues. The letters "TNT" are never mentioned, but the status is alluded to in veiled terms: "We are the answer to your immigration agony.... *Kabayan, nababahala ka ba about your immigration problems? Handa kaming tumulong.* [Fellow countrymen and countrywomen, are you worried about your immigration problems? We are ready to help.] We give free consultation and guarantee honest and fast service." Beyond respecting customary practices and making sure that readers are not offended, these ads are cunning about attracting clients who feel more secure with secrecy. The ads hint at frightening possibilities: something that census data fail to enumerate, or something that INS agents fail to apprehend. So it is important that they promise honesty and confidentiality, since TNTs and others risk exposing themselves and their status to the public and the authorities once they avail themselves of the services advertised. TNTs also risk being duped by dishonest attorneys who cannot be brought before the law by an "illegal" subject.

TNTs hide their status but are not necessarily condemned to the fringes of the community. Many of my respondents said they can be found anywhere. They work in offices. They pay taxes. Visibility alone does not mark one's legal status, but there are tell-tale signs of illegality, such as not being able to leave the country or not voting. However protected by those in the know, TNTs are susceptible to being caught.[6] The newspaper ads indicate that some immigration law offices are very adept at maneuvering through the TNT's precariousness existence, aware of the profits that may lie with a market protected and fueled by stealth. They deploy a variety of rhetorical tactics to persuade those in hiding to "come out" so that their status may be "adjusted" and their worries "appeased."

Immigration law offices also advertise through radio and television, with local personalities and celebrities (e.g., artists, singers, actors from the Philippines) testifying to the "struggles" to attain "peace of mind" through the "generous services of [the] law offices." TNTs, as the acronym suggests, are like bombs waiting to explode. They are instruments of danger whose disarmament necessitates extreme caution and sensitivity.

One law office has gone as far as connecting and equating the risks, processes, and results of "adjustment of status" with "achieving independence," so that removing oneself from prisonlike constraints resembles the way citizens of a nation become independent of their colonizers.

> Happy Immigration Independence Day!!! From the law offices of. . . . This June 12, Filipinos around the world will celebrate with pride their national Independence Day. It is a day that they can reflect on the freedom that they struggled so long and hard to gain. No matter where a Filipino lives, or how many years that he or she has been away from home, a Filipino still maintains an undivided love and devotion to their home country, the Philippines.
>
> Unfortunately, many Filipinos cannot truly celebrate the freedom symbolized in their Independence Day. Because of their immigration status, they are like prisoners. They cannot travel back to their beautiful home country, because they are afraid they will not be able to return to the United States. They have been separated from their families, whom they have not seen in many years. Although Filipinos are highly educated and hardworking, they are forced to accept jobs far below their level of education and experience.
>
> Therefore, in celebrating Philippine Independence Day, it is time for you to declare your "Immigration Independence Day"—when you *finally* do something to solve your immigration problems, and be able to fully enjoy the life that this "Land of Opportunity" has to offer.
>
> Just as the heroes behind the Philippine Independence Day had to struggle, and did not give up, you must gather the strength and courage to do something to achieve the freedom and independence that you will enjoy, once you solve your immigration problems, and legalize your stay.
>
> At the law offices of . . . we understand Filipinos' dreams and fears, and we know how important your immigration situation is to you. We are committed to assisting you in solving your immigration problems, and believe you should be treated with the dignity and respect you deserve.[7]

This law firm's application of the tropes of freedom, struggle, and independence to immigration "situations" marks an interesting mix of analogies that has a particular currency among Filipino readers. June Twelfth is widely familiar to members of this community as Independence Day, and this day (or the weekend closest to it) has been celebrated mostly in local public gatherings, fiestas, or parades. Although the practice of celebrating Independence Day in these communities is fraught with ambivalence as to its significance in the U.S. context, the common understanding is that this day commemorates the Philippines' independence from Spanish rule. But, as in the advertisement, Independence Day also marks the beginning of massive immigration of Filipinos to the United States at the turn of the twentieth century—something that many Filipino Americans have no trouble remembering as central to the history of U.S.-Philippines relations. Because of the U.S. occupation of the archipelago that immediately succeeded Spanish domination, many of the current generation are hesitant to celebrate "independence." One interviewee remarked:

> *Ano ba itong independence day ... independence day? Kanino ba tayo naging independent? 'Di ba sinakop din tayo ng mga Amerikano? Kaya nga napapunta tayo dito. Tapos, minal-trato naman tayo. What's the ... thing about this independence day? Itigil na nga iyang mga iyan!* [What is this independence day ... independence day? Who were we independent from? Isn't it true that we were colonized by the Americans too? That's why we found ourselves here. And then, they maltreated us. What's the ... thing about this independence day? Let's put an end to these!]

Independence Day celebrations in the Filipino American communities I studied recognize freedom (from Spanish rule), yet simultaneously reveal the pain of colonization perpetuated by another power. This duality finds its way frequently into discussions at organizational meetings devoted to marking the day. Many articles and essays in the community newspapers also point to the celebration's debatable significance among "a people whose independence (from Spain and the United States) ... was never complete," as Ed Sumcad wrote in "Power Lurking in the Dark," in the *Mabuhay News* in May 1994. Some letters written to the papers have even recommended calling off any observance of the occasion, citing minimal Filipino American attendance as evidence that most of the community have no qualms about forgetting the event.

The immigration law firm's deployment of this event in its ad to create a sense of national familiarity and empathy among its target audience is successful only on this surface level. For down the line, where talk about independence is paired with "freedom ... [from] immigration problems," most of the rapport with the ad's readers disappear. I have had numerous discussions with readers about this ad, and many of them have expressed less than positive responses about it. Most said that, for one thing, the ad misrepresents and distorts the significance of "independence" in the context of Philippine history.

> *Hindi naman pareho iyon. Iba naman 'yung independence natin sa Pilipinas kaysa sa independence dito. Ano ang pinagsasasabi nila? Ang independence sa Spain e totoo nating kalayaan? At saka 'yung kalayaan sa Spain e kalayaan sa INS? 'Yang INS will be after us all our lives here. Ano iyan? Ano ang iniisip nila? Hindi? Para silang sira. Hindi kasi Pilipino iyan eh.* [It's not really the same. Our independence in the Philippines is really different from independence here. What are they talking about? Our independence from Spain is our true freedom? And also, our freedom from Spain is our freedom from the INS? The INS will be after us all our lives here. What is that? What do these people assume? Not so? They're like crazy. That's actually because (the advertisers are) not Filipino.]

Here, we see how the parallel with "independence" and "immigration" deployed by the advertiser fails to connect with its target audience, especially since many Filipinos assume that they are always potential targets of suspicion by the INS in so far as their "legality" is concerned. And this is so whether or not they possess legal documentation. Many think that other people's views of them are so attached to their being "foreigners" or "strangers" that "freedom from the INS" is just another myth.

My respondents voiced similar opinions about long-distance telephone service ads that use narratives of events in Philippine history while showing images of Jose Rizal, the national hero, and of battles fought by the Katipunan (the secret revolutionary society) against the Spaniards. Coming from corporate (AT&T) and "foreign" interests (assumed to be *hindi Pilipino* [not Filipino]"), these ads arouse suspicion because of their distorted or misappropriated rendition of history and their linking of it to profit making. *"Ang gusto lang ng mga iyan e pera."* [The only thing they want is money.][8]

Yet advertisements for immigration and telecommunications services, by their number and frequency, form the economic backbone of the local papers. Several publishers confirmed to me that revenues from these ads usually exceed $10,000 a month, enough to shoulder a good part of their publications' overhead costs. And for the marketing personnel of the companies that advertise in these newspapers, there is no better medium for pitching to the "ethnic markets." A local AT&T advertising and marketing staffer I talked to explained that her "bosses like these newspapers . . . because they target the customers we want . . . sometimes in their own language . . . and with . . . stuff familiar to them." I prodded her to tell me more about who designs the ads and how effective she thinks they are.

A, 'yung mga print ads at saka 'yung mga TV ads . . . nanggagaling iyan sa head office, sa New York ata. Siguro may mga Pilipino silang mga creative writers. Pero ewan ko lang . . . minsan mali rin. Sabi ng mga nagbabasa dito e ayaw daw nila 'yung mga ads namin. Kasi kung anu-ano na lang ang nilalagay . . . mga independence day dito, mga Katipunan doon. Oo nga, sometimes it doesn't make sense kung ano 'yung connection. . . . Dapat mas maingat sila. . . . At saka, tingnan mo rin iyang mga ads tungkol sa immigration. Maraming kuwarta iyan para sa diaryo, pero dapat maingat 'yung mga nagsusulat kasi baka kung ano na lang ang masabi nila. [Oh, those print ads and those TV ads . . . they come from the head office, in New York I think. Maybe they have creative writers who are Filipinos. But I really don't know . . . sometimes, they're also wrong. Many readers from here tell me they don't like our ads. Because they put different things . . . Independence Day here, Katipunan there. Well yes, sometimes it doesn't make sense what the connection is. They should be more careful. . . . And also, look at those ads about immigration. They bring lots of money for the newspapers, but the writers have to be careful because of what they say.]

Because immigration ads also bring into the open some hidden aspects of or wrong assumptions about Filipino life in America (e.g., immigration status or that everyone thinks of history the same way), they walk a fine line between making their readers laugh and making them appreciate their sensitivity and sincerity. This seems to be the reason that many such ads are written without much fuss (and without ambitious and ambivalent connections to Philippine history) and usually include the names of lawyers who are Filipino or of law firms that are Filipino owned, perhaps to help mitigate the anxiety of dealing with "those who cannot understand Filipino ways." Some law firms, however, make it a point to promote their attorneys who are not Filipino, to suggest that they can indeed be trusted since they have little interest in meddling in Filipino affairs and know the laws better (because they are "Americans"). (Some respondents said lawyers who are Filipino take cases "personally" and thus may jeopardize the outcome for their Filipino clients.)

The desire of TNTs to attain a condition of "legality" tends to be at odds with the relation of Filipinos to Americanness.[9] For despite the law firms' promises that authorized citizenship would entail "completeness," there remains among readers of their ads a strong suspicion that acceptance into the U.S. fold can never be fully guaranteed by a piece of paper. *"Kahit citizen ka* [Even if you are a citizen]," several readers mentioned, *"ang tingin sa iyo ng marami e iba ka . . . dayuhan ka. Hindi ka kasali."* [Many people still look at you as different (or other) . . . you're a foreigner (or outsider). You're not included.]"

Other ads suggest that the way to attain completeness is through material gain. This avenue to becoming American often requires saying yes to invitations to invest in property—ads announcing real estate "available at low cost" may occupy whole subsections of these papers. Readers are urged not only to purchase a house ("of one's own") but also to own automobiles, electronic appliances (primarily stereos and *karaoke* machines), and personal computers. These acquisitions are usually touted as rewards one can give oneself "for working hard in America." Many refer to these goods as *"katas ng 'Tate"*— "the juices of the States" (as in, the juices squeezed out of the U.S. economy), a variant of *"katas ng Saudi"* ("the juices of Saudi") invoked by Filipino contract workers in the Middle East.

Americanness is in this case defined in terms of assimilation by or inclusion in a culture of material consumption. Readers are very much aware of this pressure to "act like an American" by "buying like an American," as one told me, so that one can presumably be accepted. And advertisers key in to these assumed desires, aware that many of the papers' readers have disposable income on hand as professionals or service workers in the new place. "We know they have money to spend," said one real estate marketer. "And in America, it's spend, spend, spend. We take advantage of that." A Filipino reader agreed with this description of U.S. society, but expressed a critical view of such a culture of consumption:

> *Oo nga. Dito sa Amerika, kailangan bili ka nang bili. Kung wala kang utang, hindi ka Amerikano! Kuha din natin iyan sa mga Amerikano, a. Noong nasa Pilipinas ako, gusto ko, laging may ipon. Dito naman, nag-iipon para pambayad (sa mga binili). Kung hindi ka bumibili dito sa Amerika, ang tingin sa iyon ng mga tao, kawawa ka. Para bang trabaho ka nang trabaho, pero gusto nila, makikita 'yung mga resulta ng trabaho mo . . . sa mga gamit na binibili mo. Ang masama niyan, marami sa atin, ganyan ngayon.* [Oh yes. Here in America, it's always necessary that you buy and buy. If you don't have debts, you're not an American! See, we got that from the Americans. When I was in the Philippines, I always preferred to have savings. Here, instead, you save in order to pay (for the things you buy). If you don't buy here in America, people look at you with pity. It's like you work and work, but what they want is to see the results of your work . . . in the things you buy. Too bad many of us are like that now.]

Like the immigration lawyers' ads, these assume much about the transition of Filipino immigrants. The papers carry, for example, ads for quick printing of photos (for immigration dossiers), for driving lessons ("to learn the ropes of driving in America"), for pagers ("Be connected!"), portraits (to iconically represent success and the fact of families brought together again), airline tickets, tax preparation services, and cosmetic surgery and beautician services, as well as for Filipino restaurants and "Oriental" stores. These ads reveal the requirements of becoming full Americans prescribed by U.S. society, even while they occasionally hold onto some notion of Filipinoness—for instance, *"tangkilikin natin ang sariling atin"* [let's patronize our very own], and "experience home cooking . . . just like home." As two Filipina readers said:

> *Ang daming kailangang gawin dito sa Amerika! Kailangang magpaganda. Kailangang matutong magmaneho . . . pero siyempre, hinahanap din natin*

paminsan-minsan 'yung mga bagay na galing sa atin. Mabibili lang ang mga iyon sa mga Oriental store. Ako nga, ang gusto kong nag-aayos ng buhok ko e Pilipino pa rin. [There are so many things one needs to do here in America! One needs to look beautiful. One needs to learn how to drive . . . but of course, we also look occasionally for the things that come from our country. You can only buy them at the Oriental stores. In my case, I even prefer to have my hair done by Filipinos.]

Wow, ang patriotic mo naman. Sabagay, kahit nandito na tayo sa Amerika, gusto natin 'yung mga pamilyar sa atin. Aba, first class din ang mga iyon. [Wow, you're really so patriotic. But then again, even if we're here in America, we want those things which are familiar to us. Well, they're also first class.]

Tailored to immigrant readers via their ethnic immigrant coding, these ads bridge the gap between what one doesn't have (yet) and what one needs to have in the new place. These include specific products and services for those with newly acquired disposable incomes and recently achieved social or citizenship status. Most ads either use the Tagalog/Taglish language or Filipinize their products or services to attract those seen as being in states of transition. But readers are quite cautious, recognizing the dangers of material wealth in America, so that being in "transition" carries some degree of tension.

Kung wala kang pera, e di wala kang mabibili. Ang hirap dito, akala nang marami, ang dami nating pera. 'Yung mga suwerte siguro. Pero 'yang mga pagka-materyoso, dapat lang we need to be careful. . . . Marami na akong nakitang nasira diyan. Kasi ang mga Amerikano, ganoon. Mga gastador. [If you don't have money, well, you can't buy anything. The trouble here is that many think we have a lot of money. Those who are lucky, perhaps. But being materialistic . . . we really need to be really careful. I've seen many people destroyed by it. It's because Americans are like that. Spendthrifts.] We don't need to be like them.

Marami sa atin gastador na rin. Kasi marami sa atin, akala e ganoon para maging Amerikano. You know, you're in America . . . ano pa ang gagawin mo? Kapag hindi ka gumagasta, are you less [of an] American and more [of a] Filipino? Hindi naman dapat ganoon. [A lot of us are spendthrifts too. It's because many of us think it's the way to be an American. You know, you're in America . . . what else do you do? If you don't spend, are you less American and more Filipino? It shouldn't necessarily be that way.]

Ads that employ Taglish in their copy are primarily those that promote communication and transportation services. These include phone companies advertising for overseas phone services, airlines, cargo, and dollar remittance businesses. The power and appeal of these ads lie in their addressing the persistent liminality of the Filipino American immigrant experience—the desire to keep the lines humming between (at least) two homes, and the need to prevent even the semblance that ties have been severed, often across wide geographical distances. "We keep families together," one Sprint ad announced in the *California Examiner* of November 23–29, 1994. And in Taglish, playing on the lyrics of a popular Filipino ballad to generate more appeal and familiarity, the ad continued:

> *Saan ka man naroroon . . . ngayon, puede nang tawagan silang lahat . . . kahit ilan at saan man naroroon. Only Sprint Worldwide gives you unlimited savings sa lahat ng long distance bills ninyo forever . . . anywhere, any number, any day, any time.* [Wherever you are . . . now, you can call them all . . . no matter how many and wherever they are. Only Sprint Worldwide gives you unlimited savings in all of your long distance bills forever . . . anywhere, any number, any day, any time.]

AT&T's full-page ads (like this one in the *Philippine News,* August 31–September 6, 1994) compete with Sprint's by quoting a popular Filipina theater, movie, and recording artist (both in the Philippines and in the United States), Lea Salonga, in Taglish:

> *Ang galing ng musical arrangement! Lahat-lahat, dinig ko. Para na rin akong nandiyan sa Maynila!* [The musical arrangement is very good! I can hear everything. It's as if I'm there in Manila!] 7 out of 10 people who call the Philippines prefer the sound quality of AT&T TrueVoice Service. Lea can hear her music in the Philippines as if she's right in the studio. Just like Lea, you too can hear the melody of the real sounds of the Philippines. *Ang malambing na boses ni Nanay, halakhak ni Tatay, at iba pang matatamis na tunog na nagpapangiti ng inyong puso.* [The endearing voice of Mother, the laughter of Father, and many other sweet tunes that will put a smile in your heart.] That's what At&T TrueVoice Service is all about. It gives you sound quality that is so clear, crisp and true-to-life, it makes you forget the miles between you and your loved ones. You feel like you're right there beside them, close enough to hear what their hearts are saying. *Malinaw ang resulta.* [The results are clear.] AT&T.

Your True Voice. *Ang Tunay na Tinig.* [The Sound that is Real.] AT&T.
Your True Voice.

Readers have found such ads to be most appealing in the ways they
depict their disconnection from the Philippines and their wishes to
reconnect, electronically at least. Here is the possibility of connecting to the homeland in the most literal sense: "as if I'm there." So
the ad presents the product and the service as recognizing the distance that separates Filipinos here and Filipinos elsewhere and also
as the circuits that mediate and mitigate this distance. Altogether,
these commodities may be said to mimic, as much as sell to, the experience of immigration among their prospective consumers—the anxieties of separation and displacement may be recalled but simultaneously contained (at a price).

AT&T also promotes discounted overseas calls with the assistance
of Tagalog-speaking telephone operators. These are lucrative enter
prises for the company, and perhaps equally so for those who facilitate remittances or money transfers. One ad boasted: "Your remittance dollar supports more than just your family. It supports a nation.
[Avail yourself of] the fastest way to send money to the Philippines!"
Indeed, it has been estimated that Filipinos in the United States wire
as much as $1 billion annually, making them one of the most lucra-
tive sources of capital flow into the Philippines.[10]

Other ads offer employment, particularly in the health care industries in California ("English-speaking nurses," specified one ad), as
well as specialized, short-term courses in various skills and professions.
There are numerous ads for tickets for concerts, hotel services, casi-
nos, psychic services, and credit reconstruction. Yet it is not so much
that these ads "introduce" immigrants to new products and services.
Readers have been exposed to them even before their arrival in the
United States or through other mainstream media. They have seen
ads that are gender coded (e.g., those that appeal to Western notions
of beauty) and class coded (e.g., those that are targeted to lower- or
higher-class consumers). The difference is that these ads direct their
attention to their specific needs. Good examples are ads for driving
lessons. To many immigrants, driving in the new country or, more significantly, in Southern California is markedly different from driving

in the Philippines.[11] Certain road regulations, as well as a number of traffic signs and protocols, may not be that familiar. Driving in Southern California is also perceived by many as a necessity, rather than a luxury, primarily because of the area's limited public transportation facilities. These are the reasons that such ads communicate with a sense of urgency, as if time is about to run out on their readers. "The time to act is now," urges one ad for driving instruction. Or, as one auto insurance ad proclaimed: "Be secure now . . . or be sorry later." To the newly arrived and to those who have been here for a long while but have not driven, it makes sense to learn how to drive as soon as possible in order to "get to places." One respondent said: *"Ganyan ang buhay ng mga baguhan dito . . . laging nagmamadali. Baka mahuli sa biyahe. Kailangang matuto kaagad magmaneho. Kailangang may insurance kaagad."* [That's how life is for those who just came in . . . always in a hurry. They might miss the boat. One needs quickly to learn to drive. One immediately needs insurance.]

The sheer number of these ads in the community papers affirms the significant presence of companies that capitalize on this immigrant market. To be sure, newspaper publishers rely heavily on these space buyers to sustain their businesses by guaranteeing advertisers a specific market reach for their messages. "Your passport to greater ad market value," touted a promotional announcement of one of the papers. But as I have been discussing, there are several ways of comprehending the value of these ads that directly appeal to the Filipino American communities I studied. First, these ads may be necessities for the publishers, who rely on them for the income they generate. Because all of these newspapers are free of charge, and only a very small amount of revenue comes from home-delivered subscriptions, publishers depend on advertisers to survive. This dependence, however, does not exactly amount to advertisers controlling the content of the papers. Several publishers told me that, generally, advertisers keep a hands-off stance when it comes to what else a newspaper contains, and only in infrequent cases has there been any intrusion. Ads that look like feature columns, articles, or news items are too thinly disguised to be mistaken for them.

Second, advertisers take advantage not only of the extensive reach of the newspapers in the communities they target but, more importantly, of the particular constructions of Filipino American identities in the goods and services they sell, so that they manage to speak and vend directly to their potential buyers. But as we have seen, the ways in which the ads address their markets as immigrants in need of formal documentation and as potential buyers who want to join a consumer-oriented culture also produce skepticism on the part of their readers. "Legal status" and ownership of property are not central to their lives, and, despite the pressure to conform, many have been quick to consider these matters unimportant to or distanced from what they think as "Filipino."

Third, advertisements in the papers capitalize on the readers' propensity to connect with the homeland, as they evoke the bridging of distances via communication technology. Many readers have found appealing the ways the ads speak to their condition of separation and to their desire for reconnection. To those who can afford the services, communication technology is then a constitutive mechanism for defining identities.

But more significant than the advertisements are the ways in which Filipino Americans use the local papers to forge communities of belonging among their readers and producers. Crucial to this activity are the recognition of a shared history of mainstream media exclusion and the deployment of alternative practices of cultural exchange that bring together memories of the homeland and narratives of contemporary conditions in the new place.

"At Home ... in a Paper of One's Own"

Park's 1922 survey of immigrant presses stressed that newspapers of this sort function to facilitate the transition of newly arrived populations into the culture of their host settlements.[12] We saw this at work specifically in the nature and frequency of advertisements that target Filipino American readers whose statuses as citizens and consumers are in transition. In varying characters and intensities, there is a good chance that newspapers put out by other ethnic groups in the United States have similar emphases. I have seen this to be true among Russian American, Armenian American, Vietnamese American, and Spanish-language

papers in and around Los Angeles and San Diego Counties. But to
stop at merely identifying what Filipino American presses share with
their counterparts in other ethnic communities masks the historical
specifics of the conditions in which these newspapers exist and thrive—
specifics that reveal experiences of racialization different from those
faced by whites and other groups of color in the United States. Editors, journalists, and readers consistently reminded me of how "different" their papers were from the others, "because others don't know how
it is to be a Filipino in America." One reporter told me, "Other newspapers [that] cover us . . . if at all . . . miss [out] on what we really are.
We're called this and that . . . like blacks or Asians or Hispanics. Maybe
we're all the same, but we're also different." Here, we see how Park's
assessments, in the long run, obliterate important differences across
immigrant presses that helped determine not only their survival but, to
a great extent, their nature and emphasis.

Indeed, if one looks closely at Park's study, the implicit criterion
Park uses in evaluating the "success" of immigrant presses is their
ability to be integrated into the commercial and cultural landscape
of the United States—a landscape in which appeals to the "univer-
sal" are desired, "foreignness" is erased, and differences with the
mainstream society (e.g., divergent political views) are suppressed.
Little wonder that Park's lists as successful immigrant presses those
put out by white ethnic groups whose desire to assimilate runs parallel to the presumed preference of the state to have all of its immigrant populations conform to the dominant culture.[13] Disregarding
the differential treatment of immigrant groups on the basis of their
color, Park's study misses out on the interplay of race relations that
confront different racial and ethnic groups when they publish community papers.[14]

To understand the effect of such differences, one can refer to the
vibrant press that Filipino American communities of the 1900s to the
1950s built and sustained against the climate of exclusion and the bru-
talities of nativism, something that Park's survey almost completely
overlooks (save for one entry). Unlike some immigrant presses of its
time (a number of white ethnics also used the press to document and
clamor against racism), these Filipino American papers sought to

expose the bigotry and hatred specially directed at Filipino farm workers and laborers. They informed their readers of a critical and creative mass of Filipino workers fighting for equality, dignity, and access to civil society. They were determined to clarify what "special" relationships the Philippines had with the United States when the designation of U.S. territory/colony did not reconcile with Filipino ineligibility for citizenship in America.[15] This is a history that contemporary Filipino Americans inherit once they settle in their new country, a ground they find in common not with other ethnic groups, but with Filipinos of previous generations.[16]

Beyond their group, the Filipino American press shares a lineage of resistance with black, Latino/Chicano, and other Asian media to racial subordination. The connections between racial domination by a group and the effect of the dissemination of its ideology in media and popular culture in all sectors of society are difficult to overemphasize in this context. Media historian Jane Rhodes contends that, in the United States, "racial identity has been and continues to be . . . a crucial factor in determining who can produce popular culture and what messages are created."[17] For groups relegated to the margins and lower rungs of the racial hierarchy, this has meant a sustained struggle to gain a foothold in mainstream and corporate-controlled media channels, to oppose and challenge dehumanizing stereotypes, and to seek alternative avenues for self-determination and representation.[18]

Cast against such historical and contemporary settings, it is apparent that the impetus for publishing and reading a paper "of one's own" from a Filipino American perspective is more than fulfillment of a need. Readers of the *Los Angeles Asian Journal, TM Weekly Herald, Mabuhay Times, and The Filipino Press*, among others, take pride in the abundance and regularity of these papers despite the perceived marginality of their ethnic group. "It's amazing to see that we can do it even though many others think that we are nobodies," said one Filipino American. Among editors and publishers, some of whom had previously worked in mainstream newspaper offices, such pride is most articulated in being able to do something worthwhile for the community beyond what the larger publishing system compels them to do:

regard their audience as discrete interest groups and treat them merely as potential consumers. A Filipino American journalist told me:

> Of course, my publisher wants to make money too. But, really, there are no viable information media at the moment for Filipinos. Our newspaper wants to do that service. Think about it, there's nothing much about Filipinos, or much less even the Philippines, in the big papers. In the *San Diego Union-Tribune*, I found three clippings about Filipinos, two of them about Filipino youth gangs in San Diego. If it's not too little reporting, it's distorted reporting. What else can you trust to read about your own other than someone who wrote it for you?

In a conversation with two editors of local papers in Los Angeles, I asked about the kinds of coverage that people like them would consider limited or "distorted."

> Oh, you know, we have lots of activities here ... like our fund drives that benefit Filipinos here and other people too. We raise thousands of dollars for these health projects ... and I haven't seen any paper here in Los Angeles or Ventura Counties cover that. *Hijo*, have you seen any of your papers in San Diego do that? Or, what about politics? I don't see these papers talking anything about Filipinos for office. Do you? How do we know about them if we don't read the locals?

> And then, our problems too. I saw one report in the [Los Angeles] *Times* yata [I think] about teenage suicide. That's a big problem, but it was this tiny tiny back-page thing. And because of that, everybody is scared of us. *Tapos* [And then], I invite these big reporters from the big papers to come for our Pinoy Night {an awards night for Filipino American achievers in Los Angeles} and nobody comes. *Puro* [Too many] songs and dances ... if there is any coverage ... *ang konti pa nga* [it's very little]. That's Pinoy, all right, but that's not only us. We also get on the biggies when the criminal is Pinoy ... or when the illegal alien is Pinoy. So that's how many people see us. We are much more than this. We also do a lot for California. We are engaged in many things ... welfare, politics, economy.... That's why we have to report our own in our own papers.

The alternative appeal of such community newspapers among Filipino Americans also goes farther than simply providing a separate space for gathering information not covered by the mainstream press. Many readers inform me of how much it means to them to feel "at home" in a place they considered their new home but where they are still regarded as guests by most people around them. "I am a citizen of this country now . . . supposed to be not a foreigner anymore, even though many think I am. *Akala nila hindi ako Amerikano din* [They think I'm not an American too]," one earlier generation Filipino American reader told me, "but that doesn't mean I've forgotten where I came from." Reading about Filipinos, whether from California, other parts of the States, the Philippines, or elsewhere, helps these respondents deal with a strong sense of disconnectedness or displacement brought about by immigration and separation. Another reader confirms: "Reading these [newspapers] makes me feel at home here . . . the new home . . . but there is still that other home. *Nakakamiss nga.* [I really miss it.] It's so far away and I feel like I'm in this other world . . . that is hard to connect [with] many times. It's hard to adjust. So I have this habit now of trying to adjust by doing it . . . like . . . I don't forget the [other] country even if it's far already." In a world of greater transience and impersonal arrangements, these Filipinos use the community press to reconnect with each other, not so much to bring the pieces back to their original whole, but to reconstruct what used to be and still are discrete aspects of their lives into different forms and products through particular constructions of memory. As I show later, such an activity would include forging a special connection (political, emotional, and financial) with people in the Philippines as expressed through the reportage on politicians, celebrities, and calamity victims, as well as a nostalgic recollection of the homeland through selected depictions of its scenic spots. The newspapers also serve as vehicles for the collective sense making of their conditions and experiences in their new homeland.

Usually displayed in racks outside Filipino stores, restaurants, and video rental outlets, these community papers are picked up by the patrons of these establishments. According to several publishers, their readership is primarily composed of newly arrived immigrants (those who came after 1965). Earlier generation and younger generation Filipinos (who have their own papers) also read the papers, but with less frequency. The number of readers who subscribe regularly for home or office deliveries is not that high, compared to the publishers' estimates of readers who pick up the papers at the stores. This may be due to the money involved in paying for delivery (instead of picking up a paper free) and the erratic production of most of the papers, which may not be delivered as expected. Still, home delivery does appeal to those who do not frequent the stores as much. Filipino American residences do not cluster together as much as those of other groups (especially in Los Angeles County), but many Filipinos are familiar with the location of commercial establishments that cater specifically to Filipinos in the area.

The primary language of most of the papers I saw was English. Reporters and editors told me that they know that their readers have adequate facility with the language, owing to their exposure principally to educational institutions in the Philippines that used English as the main language of instruction. However, like the advertisements, some sections are written in Tagalog, while some are in Taglish, and a few are in other Philippine languages and dialects. Several older columnists write in Tagalog, especially when their focus is Philippine history, language, or culture. Movie-gossip feature pieces are also occasionally in Taglish. English is reserved for "hard" news, the other languages for the "soft" or informal sections of the papers.

Outside some commercial establishments, like the neighborhood "Oriental" store or the Filipino-owned donut shop in the San Diego suburb of Mira Mesa that I frequented, Filipinos regularly and informally convened to engage in small talk around issues usually covered by the community papers. Said one frequent participant:

> *Nagkakila-kilala kami dito kasi pare-pareho kaming nagbabasa ng diyaryo ba. Napansin namin e pare-pareho din 'yung mga binabasa namin. Pare-pareho din kaming umiinom ng kape't kumakain ng donut. Kaya hayun, ngitian muna, tapos nagkakilala't nagkakuwentuhan. E ano pa ba naman ang mapapagusapan namin kundi 'yung mga binabasa namin dito . . . tungkol ba sa atin.* [We met each other here because we were all reading the newspapers, you know. We noticed that we were reading the same things. We were all drinking coffee and eating donuts too. That's why, there you go, we smiled at each other first, then we met and shared stories with each other. Eh, what else could we talk about if not those (stories) we've been reading here . . . about us, you see.]

I then asked, "What sustains your group to meet like this regularly?" "Well," he said, *"sinu-sino pa ba ang magkakaintindihan tungkol sa atin*

kundi tayo-tayo na rin. Tayo din naman ang may interes dito, 'di ba?"
[Well, who else could understand us and our homeland if not us?
We're the ones who have an interest here, true?]

It is no surprise, then, that the front pages of these papers cover
political, economic, and social events and issues that emanate both
from the former homeland and the new settlements, symbolized
most clearly by the Philippine and U.S. flags in most of the papers'
banners. Even the names of many papers refer to both the Philippines or Filipinos and to Los Angeles, San Diego, California, or the
United States. At the time I was doing my fieldwork, news about
national and regional elections as well as calamities in the Philippines shared headlines with local political races and community
organizational activities Filipinos in Southern California participated in. Readers are especially keen on keeping track of the state
of political affairs and the status of political actors in the Philippines
(*"mga kabahayan din iyan"* [they are also our compatriots]) to gauge
changes taking place in the homeland and how these changes affect
the country's standing in national and international arenas. And
news about the frequent natural calamities that strike the Philippines also trigger concern for those they have left behind. Said one
reader: "Of course we care about them, even if they are very far
away. We want to know what's happening so that we [can] know if
they need any help from us. Some of us [even] go home if the emer-
gencies are too big."

Articles about Filipino dignitaries and celebrities visiting California appeared along with those that reported on Filipino Americans
visiting the Philippines for business prospects or to make donations.
Celebrities have a way of strengthening social and economic networks because of readers' perception of them as role models or "people with importance," according to another reader. There were also
items about Filipinos who have died in the United States or in the
Philippines, and of Filipino victims or perpetrators of crime in the
United States. Knowing what was happening in at least two worlds
brought into public discourse evidence of attachments to them both.
"Malayo na ang nalakbay ko [I've traveled far already]," mused another
Filipino reader, "but I always want to be reminded about my former

home. It matters in understanding myself here." "Why and how does it matter?" I asked. She replied:

> Well, it keeps me awake . . . it makes me think of myself as someone who is from somewhere. Many of us . . . forget . . . *kung saan tayo galing . . . at kung sino ba tayo dito . . . mga Pinoy sa Amerika. Pero kapag nagbabasa kami ᴨᴜ ᴅᴵᴠᴵ ᴊᴏᴵ ᴘᴀᴠᴀᴠᴠ ᴊ ᴄᴜᴍᴀᴦᴀᴀᴨ ba ang pakiramdam ko . . . kasi pamilyar at saka nakikipag-usap sa atin. Parang ᴅᴵᴨᴜᴵ ᴵᴜᴵᴏᴊ ᴵᴜᴊᴜ ᴨᴀᴵᴀᴵᴀᴦᴵᴦᴵ ᴵᴵ ᴵᴵᴵᴵ ᴵᴵᴵ [where* we came from . . . and who we are here . . . Filipinos in America. When we read the newspapers, we get this comfortable feeling . . . because they're familiar and they speak to us. It's then like we're not put aside.]

Many others said that this refusal to forget ties to one's former home runs counter to the pressures to conform to what they see as American-style values and interests—something that many are told have a strong presence in their lives by non-Filipino employers, teachers, or friends, who encourage them to shed their original culture. In the same breath, however, these people were quick to alert me of the false promises of the "melting pot" ideology. Conformity, to their minds, has not resulted in their full acceptance as Americans and their true equality with others, and it is precisely their reluctance to fully assimilate that animates their media activities. This is especially visible in letters to the editor and commentaries that speak of conflicts about life in the United States. Examples of titles are: "Being Hyphenated Americans," "What Do We Do When We are Discriminated [Against] at Work?" and "Violations of Our Rights." One opinion-piece writer related her hesitation at giving up her culture at the expense of becoming "American" by noting that, "although we may be very familiar with the American way of life and will probably assimilate to many of its values, there is that indelible flame in our hearts of still being a Filipino."[19]

The papers' orientation to the Philippines serves as both a source and a sign of the ethnic rootedness central to Filipino American identities. This is apparent not only in the frequency of articles referring to events in the Philippines and regular pieces (usually pitched to the younger readers) detailing "lessons" in Philippine history and language (*"Ang Sariling Wika"* [Our Own Language]), but also in the regular coverage of activities of Filipino movie celebrities. Editors told me their audience always look forward to reading gossip about the movie industry back home. These bits of information connect readers to a popular culture they are familiar with, constantly reminding them of personalities they identify with and keeping them abreast of movies that might end up in the local Filipino video stores. "They like to know what's happening to their movie idols . . . their latest films . . . who got married to whom, and who has passed away," one reporter said. Or, as one movie scribe put it, "They want to know the juicy details . . . the ones who do *bomba* [appear in the nude] . . . *mga naglaladlad ng kapa . . . mga call boy and call girl. Kung sino 'yung mga hiniwalayan at sinu-sino 'yung mga mahihiwalay. Ay tsismis . . . kahit saan, sumusunod ang tao!*" [those who come out of the closet . . . call boys and call girls. Those who have sought separation from their spouses and those who will be separated soon. Ay, gossip . . . people follow it anywhere!]

Many feature articles concern popular tourist spots in the Philippines. The same reporter continued: "We also write pieces on our scenic spots, with photos. They're all beautiful . . . it's nice to show them." Like movie celebrity gossip, stories about places and people left behind mitigate anxieties of distance and displacement. Places in the homeland are often rendered as pure, natural, and paradiselike, in articles with titles like "Villa Escudero: Quezon's Hidden Treasure," "Breathless in Boracay," "Iloilo: The Awakening of a Sleeping Beauty," and "Cebu Remains the Queen City of the South." Most readers delighted in such depictions. "That's how we want to remember the Philippines," said one. Against the harsh conditions of settling on foreign soil and encountering unexpected circumstances, these remembrances act as coping mechanisms—yet another way of momentarily suspending the ordeals of immigrant life. These same readers are also cognizant of the other faces of their changing homeland. Said one: "But, of course, we know that it's very different now too . . . what with pollution, poverty, volcanic eruption, and all that."

As articulated in the newspapers, there are multiple, sometimes competing, narratives of life for a Filipino in the United States. Many of those I interviewed spoke of fantasizing about this "land of milk and honey" prior to coming over. Fueled by Hollywood movies and American-style education, their dreams featured better lives in places they assumed would afford them greater opportunities. Only upon arrival did many of them realize the false promises of democracy and equality, for even those who were able to "make it" saw themselves relegated to "second-class citizenship." In many letters to the editor, commentaries, and news articles, accounts of racism, marginality, exclusion, and misunderstandings between Filipinos and the larger society reveal these contradictions. A lot of space in the papers I saw was given to exposing and challenging blatant forms of racism and sexism, such as those reflected in the words of talk-radio host Howard Stern ("They eat their young over there"), of a character in the television sitcom *Frasier* ("For that amount of money, I could get myself a mail-order bride from the Philippines"), and of superintendents of Filipina nurses who ordered them not to speak Tagalog at work. Other articles prompted discussions on the civil rights violations of Proposition 187, on government attempts at policing the borders, and on immigrant bashing in general. They expressed the deleterious effects of these actions on the Filipino American communities, showing how vulnerable they are (and have been) to the violence and unfair treatment that other groups of color face in U.S. society. Opinion pieces tried to make sense of these unexpected and unfamiliar situations, the dark side of the American dream. Said one journalist:

> It can get to be insane here. We have to bring [these incidents] out in the open. Our newspapers make us talk about these dirty things. But we have to put them out so that many will know and many will fight [against these] for each other. There are lots of stupid and dirty things here ... discrimination and violence to us as Filipinos. We don't have to hide them. It's our right to bring them out.

Another asserted:

> Many people who live in the Philippines don't really know how living here is. It's hard for them to understand too because they only see America on TV and movies ... and everything [seems] to be so clean and nice. We too arrive here not really knowing, you know ... but then we hear of these things and we experience them too ... sometimes outright .... sometimes in hiding. That's why we need to report them and expose them in the papers so that others here who think we are okay or whatever ... can see that we experience these things too.

Narratives of Filipino life in America also extend inward to more local affairs. In most of these papers, a great deal of coverage is reserved for reporting and announcing activities of a myriad of social organizations Filipinos in Southern California have established. From hometown and provincial associations to alumni, trade, and religious clubs, these Filipino American groups find in their community papers the channels to convey their multilevel alliances. These conduits of collective belonging aid in reconstructing identities and redefining agendas. A reporter told me how valuable the papers are for the associations in making their members regard themselves not merely as Filipinos from the Philippines but Filipinos who are also Caviteños, Pampangos, Ateneans, lawyers, and Methodists—reflective of the heterogeneity of a population that shares desires and goals of support and alliance across boundaries. These are the Filipinos who have also become American, and Filipinos who care about each other. Articles regularly reported meetings and fundraisers aimed at benefiting common causes, including donations to calamity victims in the Philippines, scholarships to those in need on both sides of the ocean, and financial as well as volunteer assistance to local community projects for senior citizens, free medical aid, voter registration, political organizing, and cultural events. These causes receive attention in varying degrees, depending on the immediacy of the situation. Health assistance, for example, was covered in great detail during the two winter seasons I did my fieldwork, when free flu shots especially for the senior community were most needed. And voter registration drives as well as political organizing for Filipino American candidates for the school board and other local offices received much space in the papers before elections.

Those who have run for local office, both Filipino and non-Filipino, know the importance of these community papers in making the public aware of their agendas. According to one columnist:

For the record, *Mabuhay News* played a major role in . . . candidates' exposure. In addition to printing the candidates' press releases, like what some of the newspapers did, *Mabuhay News* carried out personal interviews. The most effective publicity of *Mabuhay News* complementing its interviews, according to impartial observers, were the state-of-the-art featuring of political analyses covering the candidates' strength and positive qualities deemed important to serve the interest of the community once they are elected to office.... From [a] candidate's perspective, miscalculating the role of the Filipino-American press may prove fatal.... Knowing how to play these local media ... which can reach into the grassroots levels of politics ... oftentimes ensures winning.

In these ways, newspaper editors and reporters privilege the creation and maintenance of community ties and support systems over the commercial interests one would expect of mainstream papers. Even though susceptible to the forces of capital (owing to their reliance on advertising to sustain the papers), these local weeklies attempt to evade total absorption into the system of profit-driven entrepreneurship through active participation in networks of caring. "We don't make money out of these announcements and political analysis," commented a publisher:

> We simply put them there because we want to serve our readers. Ads only provide us the money. But the rest [of the paper] is really for the community that we care for. If I want to make money, I will not survive in this business. I can make money elsewhere. But here, *tulong ko na lang sa kapwa Pinoy* [it's my way of helping Pinoys like me].

It would be erroneous, however, to paint these community newspapers as sites of simplistic consensus. Like other ethnic groups, Filipino Americans do not speak with one voice all the time, and their interests and agendas occasionally conflict. A Filipino American reader who used to be a reporter told me:

> Oh yes, we have our own quarrels too. *Siyempre, meron ding awayan.* [Of course, there are also arguments.] But I think these newspapers make us talk to each other so that we have dialogue ... instead of not talking at all. We learn many things when we give each other a chance. And also, we make our own ideas known to others who are far away and those who never participate ... but may want to.

News items often detail recent quarrels of local Filipinos involved in organizational politics in which name calling (in its most biting forms) would be highlighted. "It gets to be really ... *sakit ng ulo* [a headache]," said a reporter:

We get accused of siding with someone ... putting the other down ...
like we're biased or something. But it's hard to be ... not biased ...
because some of them are your friends ... some of them, you don't like.
You try to do the best you can. Many times, these people barge into our
offices and scare all of us! They want to file suits ... la, la, la ... and
then they threaten us ... and then they scream and say they want to see
another [report] that will take all the lies back. But I don't think they
are lies. They are just personality conflicts.

Here, we see how the local papers are important to readers whose
reputations are perceived to be put at risk when they get covered,
owing to the presumed wide readership of the papers and their potential influence. The value of the presses to this community is, then,
underscored by the image of such papers as influential or powerful
within the communities, to the extent that the contestation of these
media spaces can occasionally be fierce.

On the editorial and opinion pages, various viewpoints on issues
that affect Filipino Americans are more freely explored and chal-
lenged—serving as alternative spaces for those whose views may not
be regularly deemed as "objective" or "balanced." "We are more
open to opinions in other pages of the papers," said a publisher:

You know, we still want to put out news that looks like news ... the ones
which are fair ... objective ... the ones which look at different sides. Now,
if people want their opinion on something ... or there are some who want
to say something that will side with one issue ... we can allow that in these
other pages. We try not to censor, you know. We try to be a free press.
In the Philippines, when I was young, that was it. Then, it was censored.
But now, it's free again. We want to have that freedom here too. It's America here. 'Di ba [Isn't it true], we're free here?

Analyses of local political activities identify intergroup cleavages and
campaign errors, and the working out of such differences. Comparisons
and connections are sometimes made with politics in the Philippines,
yet another remnant of Filipino American journalism of the 1900s, and,
especially, of the 1960s, 1970s, and 1980s. Many reporters I talked to
remarked that the generation of exiles who wrote in the Filipino American community papers against the Marcos dictatorship were "fearless"
in expressing their political convictions and unambiguous in forging the

presumed "natural" connection of Filipino and Filipino American lives. "It was many years ago," said an editor to me:

> Times may be different . . . Marcos is out already. But we still see some of that [kind of] journalism now. Of course, we think that that journalism was better, because it was so active and . . . [filled with] a lot of force. As an editor, I try to bring out that . . . power. It really made people active in politics, you know. We can use that today too. They are good models for the younger reporters.

The reach of these community newspapers goes beyond political, generational, and ethnic lines. Profiles of community leaders and achievers provide models of a variety of ways in which people can participate in political and social activities in conventional or alternative forms. Articles on community activists and activities offer insights on running for public office, pursuing different causes, and managing small-scale events. Many write-ups also tackle issues that include and affect second- and third-generation Filipino Americans. From stories about political/cultural awareness and achievements of the youth to the adverse effects of gang involvement and troubling suicide rates, these papers also attempt to reach younger Filipino Americans in the communities they serve. Said one second-generation reader:

> At first, I was not really interested in reading these newspapers. But as I got older and more conscious of my roots, I gradually came to see them as important . . . and necessary in understanding who I am, where my parents came from . . . our many cultures, the things we share, and where we are going too. These newspapers are also important to us, so I read them often now.

Some of these younger members of the population have already made their mark in the communities as active supporters and organizers of various endeavors. A few of them have been staff members or regular contributors to the papers and, recently, have also established their own San Diego monthly, *Kalayaan*. Appealing to younger readers, *Kalayaan* uses more state-of-the-art graphics and features articles that focus on their interests. For example, the first issue was devoted to "reclaiming" Filipino American history, which other local Filipino American papers would have already covered. In other issues,

the paper put out stories on "Pinoy rap," young poets, and the deleterious impact of drug abuse and gang violence on teenage life.

There have also been attempts by several Filipino American newspaper publishers to extend their readership to other Asian and Pacific
American communities in their areas—groups that Filipino Americans feel affinity with on the basis of their shared geographical origins and parallel immigration history (i.e., of racial exclusion or discrimination). Papers like *Pacific Asian Times* and *Asian World* in San
Diego County attest to the increasing importance, for members of
these groups, of expanding their efforts to combine energies toward
common goals. Perhaps they realize the opportunities that may be
seized by forming panethnic coalitions to work for common interests. Subsections and advertisements in Thai, Chinese, and Vietnamese reveal more and stronger communication links among what
used to be disparate minority population groups. Said one Filipino
American reporter who worked for the *Asian World:*

> I find that we Asians have a lot in common. Well, we Filipinos are seen
> as Asians, right? And so, I . . . believe that . . . we can work together if we
> realize that we have problems that are similar. It's hard sometimes because
> we have different languages. You know, we have really different . . . cul-
> tures . . . most of the time. But I think it's worth trying. We even hold
> workshops together. So we see that we also share things a lot. Our news-
> paper wants to keep these . . . connections . . . you know, make them
> stronger for all of us.

Some of these newspapers have also joined, or have themselves
established, other media ventures targeting the same market. One of
the more popular community papers has invested in closed-circuit
radio broadcasting under the banner of "Radio Manila." Like its
print counterpart, Radio Manila's roster of programming includes
news from and about the Philippines, immigration updates, and
movie "controversies." Recently, it has expanded to the Philippines
as well (part of a corporate relationship with Manila's Radio Veritas)
to "enable Filipinos in the Philippines to listen to the top news events
in America and the Filipino community in the United States, and,
on the other hand, for Filipinos in America to learn about the latest
news in the Philippines," according to its ad. This same newspaper

publisher also established business ties with FILSAT, a company that
sells twenty-four-hour Filipino programming (movies, TV dramas,
sitcoms, MTVs, etc., all produced in the Philippines) via satellite
signals received by home television customers with a satellite dish and
decoder. Their sales records to date reveal close to a thousand (and
growing) subscribers eager for cultural products from the Philippines and local sites outside Southern California (e.g., news and
entertainment programs produced in the Bay Area and Chicago).

Video tapes of movies, television shows, and concerts from the
Philippines comprise yet another set of nodes of communication
among these Filipino Americans. Although not directly tied financially to the local newspapers, distributors of these tapes offer their
wares in spaces next to the community papers (which advertise them
too). The popularity of these videos (most in Tagalog) attests to the
propensity of many Filipino Americans to keep connected with the
homeland. I have also witnessed a growing inclination among some
younger generation Filipino Americans to purchase or rent videos or
audio cassettes that feature the musical talents of Philippine-based
rap/pop artists.

A more recent development is the creation and maintenance of Filipino discussion groups on the Internet. One group that includes
subscribers/lurkers from Southern California is the Palaris Net,
started by Filipinos in the Bay Area. In this case, a "virtual" community of Filipinos in the United States and elsewhere (including
Australia, Singapore, Japan, and Italy) is made possible through an
electronic medium that knows no geographical bounds and that
promises, therefore, to use a space that is not place-specific. Messages
originate from and are retrieved in several places. To those who are
able to obtain access to such a network, this means, among other
things, the participation in dialogues, in instantaneous and simulta-
neous ways, on various issues that are of interest to participants. In
these ways, the definitions of "Filipinoness" (much less of "Filipino
Americanness") become more multifaceted as they are multispaced.

Astounded by the proliferation of media available to Filipino American communities in Southern California and elsewhere, journalists I
have talked to also observe that conditions have changed in many

ways because of the initial work in community presses by Filipino immigrants before them. Commented one older newspaperman:

> I think that one of the main reasons why we have so much media things today is that we are experiencing the benefits and advantages . . . of those who have sacrificed before. You know, back in the old days . . . and many of you were not here yet then . . . we already had a lot of these newspapers already. Now, we are continuing their job. There are different readers . . . new readers . . . but the tradition is that these newspapers kept the Pinoys before alive and with each other. Now, we're doing the same *banana* [a local expression that means 'the same thing']. We like these papers because they keep us together now. Even if we live far apart from each other . . . we can talk . . . and know about one another because we have these newspapers.

Among the many media available, local newspapers, for these communities, are still the most widely used. Local papers to many readers and publishers are the most accessible because they are free and "could be found anywhere you see a Filipino store." And these papers, as the preceding quote suggests, speak to the communities they address and strengthen their ties with each other to become not only tools for communicating but crucial components of what it means to be a Filipino in these communities.

Important to consider here, as well, is that these papers do not necessarily follow the assimilative framework dictated by the larger society. "We're not really trying to be like the big papers," added the senior journalist:

> We do not want to be like them. Because to be like them, we will [then] leave out . . . all that is dear to us . . . everything that makes us Filipinos and Americans with a Filipino touch, *'ika nga* [as they say]. Now, do you understand that? Okay . . . it makes a big difference, you know. What we want is for the big papers to be like us. You know, papers that care about people . . . not just for money. We want them to have us in the big papers . . . the national papers too! Many different angles . . . many different roles . . . for many different people. And be sensitive to who they are . . . where they come from . . . and what they really are . . . not those stereotypes. I hope they listen to us . . . look at what we do. We care for the community . . . and it shows in our newspapers.

Knowing too well the pitfalls of cultural integration on a group level, these Filipino Americans are indeed cynical about media integration as well. Two avid readers of the papers told me:

Oh . . . ayoko ngang maging katulad niyang malalaking diyaryo itong mga diaryo natin. Mahirap na. [I don't want our papers to be like the big newspapers. It's risky.] I don't think the [large] newspapers are really interested in us. If they have stories about us . . . all they are only interested [in] is to bring these stereotypes of us to their readers. They're not interested in hearing us . . . and having us heard by them and other people. They don't care. I love our papers. I hope they stay that way.

Well, you think it's enough that we see our faces in the big papers. But I think it's not about "enough." It's not even about just having Filipinos in the papers. Some Filipinos do work there already. And they can be so not Filipino, you know. Well, that's what their jobs require too . . . to act like all of them there. I think it's about having our own say in what we want to do. In the [big] newspapers, I think we will just be quiet. They will say . . . okay, we covered your group already. That's it for now. Next will be next year. So, we really don't want that. I think what many Filipinos want is to have . . . dignity . . . so that all these other people will listen and not make fun of them. We want them to listen to us. They should see what we are doing so they can change . . . not always us. They should learn from Pinoys."

And one of the Filipino American pioneer newspaper publishers reminded me that to think of them as "assimilating" into mainstream journalism would be to misunderstand the role and significance of the papers to those who put them out and those who read them.

Think of it this way, *hijo*. We have these papers because no one wants us out there. These [mainstream] newspapers don't even care about us. So we have these newspapers in our communities. See? It is our own. It is us speaking to us. We have these small and dirty offices . . . we have small budgets . . . we have reporters and writers who do double or triple jobs. Why are we in this business? We sacrifice because we care. A lot of us have already given up . . . close the shop . . . because there's no money. Not because there are no more readers . . . or no more people to care about. We know there are Filipinos out there who need these newspapers. It's their habit already. So we go on. It's something we can call that is made by our own . . . and for our own people.

Many Filipino Americans see community newspapers as rich and vibrant sources of empowerment. They use them to communicate among themselves and with others in a multitude of ways to define who they are, where they are from, and what interests and positions they could share in their present community. These conduits open up possibilities of agency despite exclusion. "What is most important to remember here," a Filipino American reporter remarked, "is that we can call this paper ours. We hire our own, we print the stories we want to print, we make our own rules. We can't count on others to do this for us. Here, at the least, we are able to speak." This is an activity that many would brush off as separatist or isolationist, given Southern California's history and present conditions regarding interethnic and interracial relations. But in the minds of Filipino Americans who write and read about themselves and their larger world in these newspapers, it is a kind of self-determination that might change the world around them—a kind of participation that for now won't be allowed space in the mainstream press, but that later may be emulated by a more multivocal local and even national press.

What matters to these groups in a most fundamental way is the question of who can belong to this nation, and on what terms. Battles for limited resources and employment spaces are usually fought against the backdrops of citizenship and belonging, of who has rights and who does not. For these people, it is not a matter of coexisting or of having a space relegated to a few of them, but of having voices and being heard. It is a matter of understanding their histories and realities, how they are different from others and what they have in common with others. Ultimately, it is a matter of belonging and participating as full citizens in the nation that is America. In view of mainstream media exclusion, these newspapers serve as alternative sites for meaningful and empowering constructions of Filipino American communities.

Conclusion
Re-marking Locations

"Pilipino ka?" "Hindi. Amerikano. Amerikanong Pilipino.
Bakit? Ikaw, Pilipino ka ba?" [Are You Filipino? No. I'm an
American. An American who is Filipino. Why? How about
you, are you Filipino?]

—Exchange between Filipino Americans from San Diego

A mong Filipino American communities in Southern California, there is a dated but popular joke that goes like this:
every time someone asks an oldtimer, "Are you Filipino?"
the answer would usually be "No, I'm not Filipino, I'm
Ilokano." Or "No, I'm Bisaya."[1] The joke is that both Ilo-
cano and Visayan refer to Filipino ethnic/geographical
groups. A more recent variant of this question-and-answer
joke circulates in conversations among Filipinos and
between Filipinos and non-Filipinos: "Are you Filipino?"
"No, I'm not Filipino," or "No, I'm not Filipino *anymore.*
I'm an American who is Filipino." Delivered completely in
Tagalog—*"Pilipino ka? Hindi. Amerikano. Amerikanong
Pinoy. Bakit? Ikaw, Pilipino ka ba?"* [Are You Filipino? No.
I'm an American. An American who is Pinoy. Why? How
about you, are you Filipino?]—the joke combines a denial

of one's Filipinoness (but uttered in fluent Tagalog, so expressing one's Filipinoness at the same time) and an affirmation of qualified belonging to the category "American."

I have heard these lines mentioned particularly by second- and third-generation Filipinos, and also by first-generation immigrants who have gained formal citizenship or another form of status (e.g., legal) after several years of settlement, and who, therefore, have presumably acquired some currency in attempting to "pass," as some would say. But in the context of my fieldwork on Filipino Americans, I suggest that "passing" cannot be reduced simply to its denotative meaning of "trying to be something one is not." Rather, I suggest that this kind of "passing" is evocative of a state in which one is able to consider oneself as something one is *supposed to be*, despite the wishes or denials of others.

Taking these jokes seriously, then, has been one way to look beneath the surfaces of conversations and social practices.[2] In this concluding chapter, I discuss the logic and trajectories of such jokes as I retrace the arguments and themes of this book. As I have examined the public activities of shopping, politicking, socializing, and communicating that Filipino Americans carry out among themselves and with others, I have also explored the nuances of identity construction within the historical contexts they operate in, the contemporary situations they live in, and, most importantly, the local and place/space-specific tenors of their engagement with themselves and with the rest of society. As I have been arguing, one fundamentally understands these discourses and practices as motivated by a necessity—according to Filipino Americans—to respond to and resist historical and institutional experiences of racialization and exclusion, as well as by a desire to claim a "space" within the construct "American" on their own terms. Hence, the unstated object of the jokes about whether or not one is Filipino is precisely to respond forcefully to the question of who can be called American, and, on what terms. Spoken in a sarcastic or mocking tone yet delivered with humor, the retort "I'm an American . . . an American who is Filipino" signals to its listener a recognition of belonging that should not have been questioned in the first place. That is why the statement comes off as a joke.

Central to this book is the question of what constitutes Filipino American identities in Southern California. On the basis of fieldwork narratives, conversations, and observations of practices engaged in by Filipinos in commercial establishments, community centers, and media channels, I have contended that ethnic identity constructions are rooted in specific references to locations and constitute some particular set of positions. Such references to locations are geographic, historical, cultural, and political.

Location and (Anti)Assimilation

I have used the term "locations" in this book to analyze what constitutes "ethnicity" from the perspectives of Filipino Americans as subjects of history and contemporary reality. "To locate" means to determine or to specify a position of something with regard to something else.[3] An emphasis on locating pushed sociologists in the United States in the 1920s and 1930s to document and assess the position of ethnic groups along a continuum of adaptation to society.[4] The main objects of their study were groups considered "foreign" who were immigrating to America. Measuring the immigrants' adaptability to society presumed that they started out in the new country as strangers who in time became full-fledged Americans as they learned the ropes. That meant shedding their original language, customs, traditions, and values to transform themselves into American English-speaking, God-fearing, democracy-oriented citizens. The term for this process was "assimilation," and it was further specified that *all* immigrant groups undergo such a transformation in varying degrees.[5] Social scientists were then likely to pinpoint on the assimilation grid which groups adapted at what pace and with which mechanisms.

Sociologists Michael Omi and Howard Winant note that these initial attempts to carve out a sociology of ethnicity came in response to a predominant view that held that racial differences across groups of people were biologically determined.[6] That is, an individual's race genetically predisposes one to possess characteristics that last a lifetime. This notion supplied its adherents with a scientific basis for defining racial inferiority and (white) superiority. Challenges to this way of thinking came via the Chicago school of sociology, which repositioned race as but one of the many components of ethnic identity. At first, race, now coded as "descent," was still held as a biological determinant among other determinants in the list of ethnic identifiers. But later, this school of thought built its case primarily on the composition of a group's *cultural* or social attributes. Such attributes included (former or original) nationality, religion, language, customs, and traditions that people carried with them to the new country.[7]

This emphasis on culture helped shape these sociologists' determination to pinpoint which cultural elements of a group enabled it to assimilate in America. This trajectory toward assimilation was deemed not only inevitable[8] but also desirable for all the groups and for the United States in general.[9] Assimilation, to them, led to social and economic mobility and increased political participation.[10] The same social scientists found ethnic dispositions and associations to be temporary.[11] Sociologist Robert E. Park specified patterns of assimilation in groups by projecting their behavior on a series of stages in a cycle that invariably proceeded from contact to competition, to accommodation, to assimilation.[12]

To the degree that assimilation and its variants, acculturation and integration, sought to explain the differing ability of immigrant groups to "fit into" society politically, economically, and socially, sociologists were criticized for the apparent political agendas (rather than "objective" observations of the "real" world) that defined their enterprise. Their perspective was rejected as too limited and too strictly defined, ignoring the effect of immigrant groups on society to focus only on society's effect on the immigrants.[13] Constituted as a one-way process, their assimilation theory also did not take into consideration that ethnic groups may enter society in different stages (if one were to use Park's cycle), or skip some parts of this progression, or even aim for little or no assimilation at all. Moreover, it was proferred that the assimilation theory privileged the mainstream culture by defining it as the only avenue of adaptation open to immigrants; this placed too much of the burden to change on the "minorities," not recognizing that the dominant society may also play a role (or even change) in the process of adaptation.[14] Politically, it seemed expedient to relegate the blame for a group's inability to assimilate on their culture's lack, rather than on the larger society's reluctance to accept them.

In spite of the criticism, from the 1940s until the 1960s the assimilationist emphasis gained ground via the theory of cultural pluralism, which was resurrected from the earlier writings of Horace Kallen.[15] Kallen and his later followers broke with the overt racist ranking of groups that resulted from comparative studies across ethnicities.[16] The cultural pluralists viewed ethnic groups as distinct and different but equal; they emphasized sensitivity to the uniqueness and diversity among people.

With the Civil Rights movement in the 1960s, cultural pluralism gained a more significant hold in studies of ethnicity, as groups previously ignored or marginalized demanded to be heard. The thrust of the scholarship during this period (and up to the present, to some degree) was to document ethnic groups' contributions to society, and in the process to elaborate on the resiliency and determination of their cultures to flourish despite marginalization.[17] Ethnicity again came to the fore, along with its accompaniments—race, culture, language, and nationality—in order to acknowledge and lend density to a multiethnic view of the United States: "out of many, one." For a moment, it seemed as though cultural pluralism rested on solid ground. It confounded the assimilationist tendency to ignore the margin's impact on dominant culture with a pluralist kaleidoscope of cultures.[18]

Yet, the very same movement, along with its repercussions in the Chicano (Latino), Asian American, Native American, and feminist alignments, triggered debates on the nature of subjectivity and group dynamics in America. Ethnicity was perceived to be a too weak and insufficient construct to account for the various oppressions and marginalizations of individuals and groups defined according to race, class status, and sexuality. Numerous scholars demanded a reorientation of the ideological underpinnings of the social sciences, questioning and expanding the breadth and depth of their work. Of great interest, particularly with regard to ethnic studies scholars, was the critique of the racialized foundations of U.S. society that determined the life chances of and consequences to people of color. One of the results of the scholars' demands was the institutionalizing of various ethnic studies departments in academia; these produced studies on previously marginalized groups and their comparative or unique experiences, along with their histories and collective struggles for power.[19] This movement has meant the resurgence of critiques against racism, internal colonialism, assimilationist perspectives, sexism, and conservative nationalism.

Various strains of the cultural pluralist view still dominate much of the contemporary scholarship regarding U.S. ethnicity; the *Harvard Encyclopedia* is an example (see Chapter 1). "Multiculturalism" has also been used recently as a code word for diversity and sensitivity to cultural differences among ethnic groups.[20]

Locating Filipino Americans thus entails recognizing them as members of an ethnic group who are dialectically historically positioned by others, and who position themselves in locations that allow them to critique U.S. society. Filipino American identities constantly and consistently trace their articulation and circulation between homeland and settlement sites; in the contexts of U.S.-Philippine relationships of colonialism, neocolonialism, and labor recruitment; and in the interplay of economic, political, and social forces that define belonging and citizenship. By "positioning themselves," I mean the critical stances taken by Filipino Americans against their historical and contemporary racialization in the United States, full assimilation into U.S. mainstream society, and exclusion from membership in the political and cultural realms of U.S. citizenship. Such stances have produced alternative sites for the practices of community building that critically appropriate elements from the homeland and from the new places of settlement—making possible an active engagement in the transformation of their lives as Filipinos and Filipinas in the United States.

These kinds of articulations of Filipino Americanness resonate with what Stuart Hall calls constructions of identity "that come from some place, some history, and some cultural tradition that are, at the same time, perpetually in dialogue with selves and with others."[21] Understood as a process, identity constructions in these settings reveal patterns of claiming spaces as practices of forging communality, shifting boundaries of ethnic formations, and constant negotiation between structural forces and active agents. Filipino Americans respond to the conditions they face in their new country and the changes they see in their environment, as much as they produce opportunities for the transformation of their lives wherever and however they can.

Ethnic Positions

Primarily, Filipino American ethnic "positionality" critically interrogates relationships to the homeland and to historical and contemporary racial politics in the United States. In the jokes, for example, we can recognize that connections to regional politics from the homeland are being rearticulated in the new place. Indeed, the one-liners about not being Filipino, but Ilokano or Bisaya, can also be considered serious statements about what it means for the respondents to be identified as Filipinos in America. Posed not really to learn whether the person is more Filipino or less Filipino than one had in mind, the joke's question offers a way in which a Filipino in the United States can be defined from a position of both similarity and difference. The questioner is relatively sure that the person being asked came from the Philippines or has roots from the same homeland, but the questioner also learns about the particularity of that Filipinoness; in this instance, the particularity of regional identity in the Philippines.

What we see here is the desire to resist homogenization, specifically in the U.S. context. One of my respondents said: "Oh, of course, you're never asked in the Philippines if you're Filipino. And if the question of where you're from is asked, I oftentimes think that what they're really asking is Are you Tagalog? From which part of Manila? ... To which I respond with pride, 'No, I'm not from Manila. I'm an Ilokano.'"

This answer strikes me as particularly interesting because, for someone born and raised in Manila, there is this mostly unnamed and unacknowledged privileging of Tagalogs as the Philippines' center and representative of Filipinoness—a privileging that, in this case, is flatly resisted. Carried over to the United States, such resistance gains currency and potency as Filipinos—even in or in spite of the joke context—verbalize resistance to homogenization not only in the Philippine context (being lumped into one rubric known as Filipino) but in the United States (being lumped into one category known as Filipino American).

So, beyond their reflection of hometown cultural pride, I read these statements as meaningful gestures of making known what is excluded, even at the risk of sounding exclusionary. That is why the responses are delivered with a smile, like a joke. Because underneath these gestures, Filipinos know that it was not the Tagalogs who made up most of the first waves of Filipino immigration, but the Ilokanos and the Visayans who became Filipino Americans once they crossed the border. These gestures reveal a strong sense of regional citizenship that is historically rooted in the homeland and is now surfacing in the new settlement—in the stores, the social halls, and the community newspapers—as part of the process of negotiating not only Filipinoness but, even more, Filipino Americanness. Applied to this heterogeneous composition in the United States, Filipinos also see themselves as multigenerational, as having different class and social statuses, and as men and women.

Additionally—regarding the statement "No I'm not Filipino, I'm an American who is also Filipino"—one can see how a denial of Filipinoness on the surface is also an insistent claim of inclusion in the category American. Here is yet another important instance of resisting homogenization, this time of what is called or what can be called "American." Again, one can consider a long history of marginalization and invisibility as a context or position from which such an utterance might be made (a history the questioner is expected to know), and from which the category "American" is forcefully interrogated.

Arthur Schlesinger provides an example of this surviving context in one of his lobs against ethnic resurgence. He remarks that the "eruption" of the "cult" of ethnicity in multiculturalist and politically correct discourse should be seen as a threat that seeks to disunite America because of its "separatist tendencies [whose] . . . result can only be the fragmentation, resegregation and tribalization of American life."[22] He appears to contend that any deployment of ethnic difference runs counter to the American ideal and practice of forging one culture out of many—the founding image of the nation. Schlesinger cites the words of eighteenth-century French observer Hector St. John de Crevecoeur, responding to the question, What is America: "[where] individuals of all nations are melted into a new race of men." If America's past and present success in mitigating ethnic and racial conflict is to be secured for the future, Schlesinger argues, then it is imperative that it "hold itself together."[23]

One way to understand Schlesinger's position, as well as those that parallel his, is to examine it in the context of nationalism. Benedict Anderson, a foremost historian of nationalism, claims that it is a product of modernity, in that capitalism, print technology, and "the fatality of linguistic diversity" in the eighteenth century united people to imagine themselves a community based on "deep, horizontal comradeship."[24] He says that notions of a "homogeneous empty time" gave certain cultural forms, such as the novel and the newspaper, the capacity to imagine the simultaneity of the nation among their readers. Ernest Gellner, another historian, concurs, adding:

> All this—mobility, communication, size due to refinement of [labor] specialization—imposed on the industrial order by its thirst for affluence and growth, obliged its social units to be large and yet culturally homogeneous. The maintenance of this kind of inescapably high (because literate) culture [required] protection by a state, a centralized order-enforcing agency or rather group of agencies, capable of garnering and deploying the resources which are needed both to sustain a high culture, and to ensure its diffusion through an entire population, an achievement inconceivable and not attempted in the pre-industrial world.[25]

These changes, according to Anderson, merge with, and are sustained by, the idea of a "community" or nation with which a powerful connection to a motherland (*patria*), the site of one's birth and perhaps death is forged. Gellner's term for this is "national sentiment."[26] Bear in mind, however, that these connections between land and nation arise out of specific conditions in history, and not out of a "natural" predisposition. It is state apparatuses, like educational systems that designate the use and dissemination of a dominant language, that prescribe and legitimate these connections as natural and unchangeable.[27] Nations and nationalisms are, therefore, political and social constructions.

These histories of the birth of the modern nation and the modern state might tempt one to observe how Schlesinger's words resonate with the demands of the nation-state formed centuries ago on the basis of homogenization of previously discrete individuals, on their unified attachment to a homeland, and on a teleology of progress—the march from a preindustrial, premodern time and space to an industrial, modern society.[28] I am making a historical leap here not to gloss over the complexities of colonialism, migration, and globalization, among others, that surely differentiated and amplified various forms of nationalism, but only to point out some of nationalism's persistent forces over time. Schlesinger's insistence on "one nation, among many," as a founding tenet of U.S. society to which we ought to adhere is so congruent with Anderson's and Gellner's findings (of homogeneity and unity of national sentiment) that it is difficult to miss their historical continuities.

Yet Schlesinger's America is not Gellner's preindustrial Europe. Anderson notes that the sustained growth of capitalism, particularly the advances in transportation and communication technologies, has transformed nations and nationalisms. Increased migration from the peripheries of advanced nations to their cores, for example, has brought "inequalities and misery . . . 'closer' to privilege and wealth than ever before in human history."[29] And, perhaps more relevant for Schlesinger, "notions of nationality (in the classical sense, tied to political participation and territorial loyalty) have tended to become ethnicized."[30]

Ethnicization has many faces, one of which is the ethnic nationalism I described earlier. In the United States, however, owing to its history of multiethnic peopling, ethnicization takes on particular forms and trajectories. And it commands particular forms of resistance—from calls to restrict immigration and get rid of affirmative action programs to refusal to institutionalize multiethnic curricula.[31] To be sure, Schlesinger's critique of ethnicity rests on the argument that ethnicization leads to the "tribalization" of America. This critique echoes those that condemn ethnic resurgence elsewhere—

mostly labeled "ethnic cleansing"—for its insistence on resurrecting
the marker "tribe" in the struggle for power.[32] To these critics, "tribe"
is a premodern category, an example of "atavistic forces which civilization, in the form of the centralized state, has struggled to expunge
or contain."[33]

But, as David Lloyd points out, it is precisely our ideological and
political notions about nations and nationalisms that need to be chal-
lenged. For instance, these views fundamentally favor only one construct of "nation": that which can be realized only through the submergence of irrational, tribal, and heterogeneous identities in favor
of a homogeneous one—thus creating a "unified" nation. In this view,
"nationalisms" are only valid if they subscribe to the attainment (or
capture) of a nation-state in that one form. Nation-states can then be
justified in using violence (to suppress differences, for example) in
the name of that single construct of the "nation." Schlesinger provides
no room in his rhetoric for challenging these constructions. For him,
America is unquestionably and unchangeably one nation. It has an
American culture (in the singular), and any effort to include diversity
as an additional element has to be contained in "the quest for unifying ideals and a common culture."[34]

Thus a Filipino American's claim to Americanness can, on one
hand, be read as a strategy of denying Filipinoness in favor of inclusion or incorporation into U.S. society. Surface renunciations of Filipinoness are acts that many Filipinos would initially interpret as
betraying one's homeland. As one Filipino American gay man told
me, these are "things that are only said by *pretty . . . pretty* people"—
"pretty" being the code word for "pretentious." Or, as a Filipino
American newspaper publisher said to me:

> There's a lot of plastic people lurking around here. They fake their accents,
> bleach their skin, have their noses and asses fixed . . . boob jobs too and
> penile enlargements. Here, look at my secretary . . . she's got blonde hair
> and colored contacts. *Filipina iyan.* [She's Filipina.] They're so silly. But I
> can see through them. Those brown skins can never hide from me.

Here, we see the desire to belong to mainstream (white) culture
expressed by imitating what is perceived to be the "American" look.

But, as the editor asserts, looks are never enough, because we "can see through them." So Filipinos' perception of such imitation and their understanding that others recognize their color regardless of how much they try to look like "the rest" produce a critical awareness of the limits of "trying to belong." In many instances, the outright denunciation of imitation has resulted in fiery exchanges. Many Filipino Americans in the stores, the social halls (especially where beauty pageants are held), and the newspapers insist on looking critically at things perceived to be Filipino or American.

On the other hand, such attempts at belonging can be understood as not synonymous with assimilation. As one second-generation informant said to me: "I have a lot of pride in my Filipino background. Heck, my parents are both Filipino. But I was born here, and I have all the right to be called a part of this country. For others to keep on insisting that I am Filipino more often sounds like I'm not American to me. I'm an American too."

What we also hear being articulated is a notion of citizenship that demands adjustment on the part of the dominant group, not the other way around—that is, not what assimilation demands, not what immigrants or nonwhites need to conform to in order to be included in the American rubric. Instead, here is an attempt to subvert or reconstruct what "American" means, one that recognizes the nation's diverse population and its varying, but related, histories, goals, and powers.

Parts of my project have addressed the continued reshaping of identities and re-marking of locations of Filipino Americans, brought about by changes in their world and their circumstances. We have seen how larger "Asian" markets are rapidly encroaching on the spaces of the smaller "Oriental" stores, and how such local businesses are attempting to survive by, for instance, expanding their client reach and vending products and services that target other Asian Americans and Latinas/os. And some newspapers and other media channels (including electronic or cyberspace) devote spaces that allow communication not only among Filipinos in America, but between Filipino Americans and other Asian Americans, and between Filipinos in the United States and those in other parts of the world. Many of my respondents are actively engaged in building coalitions and associations among

people of color in Southern California and in other parts of the United
States, recognizing how their lives are intertwined as racialized subjects and creating alliances against common conditions of marginality and exclusion. In this sense, the construction of Filipino Americanness is a process that, at certain critical moments, includes the
development of parallel relationships, support networks, and communities of interest with other racialized groups in the United States.

I am reminded of one Filipino American interviewee who said that
"we cannot be forever treated like guests in the house ... in America
... because as guests, we'll never be able to move furniture around."
For, however much all these statements challenge and negotiate the
meanings and identities of Filipinoness, a lot of wrangling and questioning concerns the other side—the side of the category "American."
I believe that, especially for Filipinos in the diaspora and in America
in particular, negotiations about identity in relation to ethnicity are
fought, although unequally, on the grounds of both Filipinoness and
Americanness. Here we are reminded that the process of group identification, which we know is never absolutely stable, is subject to the
play of history and the play of difference between selves and others.[35]
In these cases, the play of difference asserts itself from the perspective
of Filipino Americans as a productive and transformative affirmation
in the face of denial.

The "Spaces" of Filipino Americanness

The renewed interest in studies of space within the social science disciplines, particularly in anthropology, sociology, and social geography, arose by way of criticisms against treating space as a given or
naturally assumed component of social relations.[36] Traditional scholars, this criticism went, have a tendency to sidestep the important
notion of space by regarding it as an unproblematic designation that
houses bounded communities (such as societies, cities, nations, or
regions) and contains distinct cultures. Classical Marxism, writes one
critic, held history (time) as a major player in world dynamics, while
space was relegated to the sidelines, mostly as a receptacle of change
rather than a constitutive element of it.[37] In anthropology, scholars

were disposed to think of the world as a collection of countries divided by discontinuous borders, in their work on groups of people who are moored in place.[38]

These perspectives created and sustained the notion that we can simply affix people to their place, for example, when we refer to the "Filipino society" or an "American culture." Space, in this view, becomes merely a "neutral grid" on which we can assign fixed patterns and points of "cultural difference, historical memory, and societal organization."[39] To the critics, it was imperative that space (or cultures attached to space) be treated as a moveable category.[40] For instance, many people cross borders on such a regular basis to work elsewhere that their notions of residence cannot be pinned down to one site anymore. And when people settle in a new place, they take their culture (in complicated ways) with them to the new locale.

While it may seem that these questions regarding the naturalized association of culture with place were congruent with the contemporary realities of heightened movement of people across the globe, the impetus for space theorizing also had its ideological and political bases. First, it was claimed that when scholars assume a natural division of cultures and nations, they mask the imperialist logic behind the description, enumeration, and hierarchical ranking of various groups of people. Unquestioned descriptors and boundaries in charts, maps, and reports tend to mimic the work of the colonial bureaucrats who surveyed their possessions at the time of conquest. We need to ask why and how these descriptors of people and places were produced and with what effect, rather than to assume their a priori existence.[41]

Second, traditional approaches to space necessarily, but incorrectly, assume autonomous, static cultures and independent nations, even though much empirical evidence can be found regarding the varying interconnections between cultures and nations in the past and the present. The critics propose, instead, that cultures affect each other at points of contact in multidimensional ways, without predictable results.[42] The impact of colonization and present-day cultural imperialism in various contexts, for instance, can be explored beyond the usual observation that "all victims were/are duped." People and the political, social, and economic relationships they operate in can then be viewed not strictly as reflections of power from "above" but as forms of power themselves. As sites of power, spaces are treated as fundamentally political and therefore open to varying expressions of agency.

Third and most important, the new adherents of space studies reevaluate the deeper assumptions and tools of social science by questioning not only their intimate linkages with colonialism (internal and external), subjugation, and patriarchy, but also their participation in legitimating dominant forms of knowledge through their representations.[43] For example, the preoccupation with exotic, untouched cultures assumes to an extent the superiority of the observer's culture as the basis of comparison—exotic versus civilized, untouched versus advanced. What is needed, the new space theorists say, is the rigorous problematizing of categories and descriptors that legitimate hierarchies and essentialisms, as well as attentiveness to the ways in which cultures, places, and identities bear the marks of relationships of power.[44]

Recent encouragement of space studies comes from transnational studies. In the preface of the premier issue of the journal *Diaspora*, Khachig Tololyan describes this emergent field, which focuses on the ways by which nations and peoples are variously constituted by migrations, interdependencies, and communication links. Calling for contributions especially from postcolonial scholars, Tololyan remarks that "the vision of a homogeneous nation is now being replaced by a vision of the world as a 'space' continually reshaped by forces—cultural, political, technological, demographic, and above all economic—whose varying intersections in real estate constitute every 'place' as a heterogeneous and disequilibriated site of production, appropriation, and consumption, of negotiated identity and affect."[45]

Indeed, as I have remarked earlier, the globalizing effects of late capitalism have decentered and transformed identities as much as they have contributed to the reconfiguring of "places" and the ways we understand them.[46] I anchor my study of Filipino American spaces to these notions.

The spaces of the "Oriental" stores, the social halls, and the media channels may seem bounded geographically. But as I have treated them in this work, these spaces are themselves parts of ethnic identity construction among Filipino Americans, and they are interrelated with other spaces. On one level, these are spaces that bear the set of markers imposed on those who occupy them. These markers include their identities as ethnic, racial, gendered, and national in so far as they are received externally, that is, markers that are assigned by those outside of their group. On another level, these are the spaces that mark the cultural symbols and negotiations they do with themselves and with others regarding their identities as Filipino Americans. These spaces are used to express such identity negotiations. They also become part of Filipino American identities themselves. For instance, Filipino "Oriental" stores are not only spaces where Filipino Americans shop. They have also become important sites of social interaction—places where Filipino Americans see each other to talk about issues that affect them and ideas that matter to them. "Oriental" stores, from the outside are racialized spaces, imagined by others as places where you buy Asian goods and see Asian people shop. But to Filipino Americans, these "Oriental" stores are not Orientalizing in any derogatory way (when characterizing Asians, for example, as dirty, exotic, wily). Along with the other adjacent spaces—barber shops, beauty salons, and video stores—"Oriental" stores are spaces where they reconstitute their identities as productive and multilayered, and in active conversation with those who might render them otherwise as Orientals. In consequence, they reconfigure the spaces of the "Oriental" stores, as such stores become part of their sense of who they are.

Space, as I use the construct in this study, therefore attains critical importance as a site where constructions and reconfigurations of identities become possible or are denied.[47] On one hand, space is an arena in which negotiations regarding the meanings and practices of identities are imagined and enacted. On the other, a form of reterritorialized space itself constitutes identity articulation, as it brings about experiences of dislocation, nostalgia, and resettlement by immigration and even offers possibilities for community and agency. This is where space, in relation to identity and ethnicity, becomes politicized.

Principally, "locating" Filipino Americans for this project rested on the question Who is Filipino American? It is important to consider the diversities and divisions within these people—they are of different ages, sexes, classes, and occupations. They come from different places in the Philippines, have diverse backgrounds, profess to varying political loyalties and affiliations, and reside in different locations in the United States. But they also have things in common. They come from the same homeland or are descended from people who come from it. Often, they have organized and mobilized, by themselves and with other groups, against antiunion employers and policymakers engaged in educational, economic, and social welfare discriminatory practices. And most Filipinos who live in Southern California patronize the same stores, socialize and organize together in community centers, and use the same media resources.

In mapping and explaining each site of this fieldwork as a space of specific practices, I have focused on the processes by which Filipino American ethnic identities are configured and recreated, owing to the communities' shared historical and contemporary realities. These sites disclose distinctive dimensions and flavors of the Filipino American experience in at least three ways. One is the past and continuing racialization of Filipinos in the United States. The persistence of discrimination, for example, shapes Filipino American consciousness of their shared circumstances and helps to mute the generational and class differences in the communities. A second is a diaspora consciousness wherein memories, practices, and values are shaped by real and imagined notions of the "homeland" and the adopted country. And a third is the syncretic nature of Filipino American "culture" that principally finds expression in places that are created—the "Oriental" stores, social halls, and community newspapers—and linguistic practices (e.g., Taglish) that are employed in the adopted country.

The richness and complexity of such spatial expressions reveal how Filipinos in the United States can be viewed as active agents engaged in defining themselves against those that seek to render them invisible, and in transforming themselves in a place that continues to exclude them and treat them as marginal. Through and within the spaces of "Oriental" stores, we see actors reconfiguring what it means to shop, to socialize, to be with and in one's own. In the social halls, the cultures of politics Filipino Americans practice reveal their anchors to community interests and their resistance to mainstream "politicking." And in the spaces of community media, we discern the workings of identity negotiations through the intertwined and, oftentimes, competing positions of being Filipino, Filipino American, Asian American, and American. Filipinos who are in America negotiate identities, as these social cartographies reveal, on the unequal terrain of both Filipinoness and Americanness. What matters is how Filipino Americans situate themselves within these boundaries, from positions grounded in where one is from, as much as in where one is and where one wants to be.

Notes

Introduction

Epigraph: The quotation in the epigraph is from a personal interview I conducted between 1992 and 1995. Almost all of my interviews were conducted primarily in Tagalog mixed with some English (the local term is *Taglish*). The translations here and throughout the book are my own, unless otherwise noted.

1. For the population estimate: Leon F. Bouvier and Anthony J. Agresta, "The Future Asian Population of the United States," in *Pacific Bridges: The New Immigration from Asia and the Pacific Islands,* edited by James T. Fawcett and Benjamin V. Cariño (Staten Island, N.Y.: Center for Migration Studies, 1987), 285–301.

2. Apparently, the figures may be even higher than reported, for many believe that the number of undocumented Filipino aliens may be significantly large. See Dwight L. Johnson, Michael J. Levin, and Edna L. Paisano, *We, the Asian and Pacific Islander Americans* (Washington, D.C.: GPO, 1988); Jonathan Y. Okamura, "The Filipino American Diaspora: Sites of Space, Time, and Ethnicity," in *Privileging Positions: The Sites of Asian American Studies,* edited by Gary Y. Okihiro, Marilyn Alquizola, Dorothy Fujita Rony, and J. Scott Wong (Pullman, Wash.: Washington State Univ. Press, 1995), 387–400; Edna L. Paisano, Deborah L. Carroll, June H. Cowles, Kimberly A. Debarros, Ann J. Robinson, and Kenya N. Miles, *We, the American Asians* (Washington, D.C.: GPO, 1993); and U.S. Bureau of the Census, *1990 Census of Population and Housing Summary* (Washington, D.C.: GPO, 1992).

3. The charge of "invisibility," as I discuss in Chapter 2, is broad and complex. It has been frequently attributed to the so-called historical amnesia pertaining to U.S. imperialism in Asia and the far-reaching consequences of racism in the United States that have rendered Filipinos and their histories as insignificant, minor, or unnecessary—all this, despite Filipinos' long presence in the United States and their crucial participation in U.S. nation building. See, for example, the works of Oscar V. Campomanes, "The Institutional Invisibility of American Imperialism, the Philippines, and Filipino Americans" (paper pre-

sented at the Annual Meeting of the Association for Asian Studies, Los Angeles, Calif.), 25 March 1993; Fred Cordova, *Filipinos: Forgotten Asian Americans* (Dubuque, Iowa: Kendall/Hunt, 1983); Martin F. Manalansan IV, "Searching for Community: Filipino Gay Men in New York City," *Amerasia* 20, No. 1 (1994): 59–73; Jesse Quinsaat, ed., *Letters in Exile: An Introductory Reader on the History of Pilipinos in America* (Los Angeles: Asian American Studies Center, University of California, Los Angeles, 1976); and E. San Juan Jr., "Mapping the Boundaries: The Filipino Writer in the U.S.A.," *Journal of Ethnic Studies* 19, No. 1 (Spring 1991): 117–131.

4. Systematic state classification has a long history. In reference to Asian Americans, see Ronald Takaki's historical overview in *Iron Cages: Race and Culture in Nineteenth Century America* (New York: Knopf, 1979) and Juanita Tamayo Lott's discussion of census categorization in *Asian Americans: From Racial Category to Multiple Identities* (Walnut Creek, Calif.: Altamira, 1998). Lott notes that, historically, "classifications reflected a class-stratified, racially hierarchical system of access to resources that was monitored by White men in power" (19). However, I must concede that there have been exceptions, as in many statistical reports for educational access, labor force participation, and crime occurrence in states like California and Washington, which take a separate count of Filipinos. The point being made here is that lumping Filipinos together with other groups, such as Asian Americans, in both formal and informal categorizations is still frequent.

5. For an argument about the diversity of Asian American histories, cultures, and politics, see Lisa Lowe's "Heterogeneity, Hybridity, Multiplicity: Marking Asian American Differences," *Diaspora* 1, No. 1 (Spring 1991): 24–44. For astute analyses of Filipino American historical and contemporary subjectivities, see Oscar V. Campomanes's "The New Empire's Forgetful and Forgotten Citizens: Unrepresentability and Unassimilability in Filipino American Postcolonialities," *Critical Mass* 2, No. 2 (Spring 1995): 145–200; and Yen Le Espiritu's *Filipino American Lives* (Philadelphia: Temple Univ. Press, 1995).

6. Akhil Gupta and James Ferguson, "Beyond 'Culture': Space, Identity, and the Politics of Difference," *Cultural Anthropology* 7, No. 1 (February 1992): 6–23.

7. Benedict Anderson, *Imagined Communities: Reflections on the Origin and Spread of Nationalism* (New York: Verso, 1983).

8. Gupta and Ferguson, "Beyond 'Culture'," 6–9. I write "reterritorialized," because space here takes on meanings outside of its topographical attributes and is thus apprehended and experienced differently.

9. I opt not to engage in the debates over "Filipino/a" and "Pilipino/a," following the mainstream usage of "Filipino" to refer to the people and "Pilipino" to refer to the language. There are those who insist on the use of "Pilipino" for both people and language, as an expression of indigenous or traditional language usage in the Philippines.

10. These were data supplied to me voluntarily by those I interviewed. Recognizing the tensions involved, I refrained from asking for any information about citizenship status. For more on this issue, see Chapter 5.

11. For an analogous argument with respect to Asian Americans and other people of color in the United States, see chapter 1 of Lisa Lowe's *Immigrant Acts: On Asian American Cultural Politics* (Durham, N.C.: Duke Univ. Press, 1996).

12. A discussion of the dynamics of opposition and contestation can be found in George Lipsitz, *A Life in the Struggle: Ivory Perry and the Culture of Opposition* (Philadelphia: Temple Univ. Press, 1988).

13. I do not wish to imply that confessional ethnographies are "bad." Certain agendas and contexts are appropriate to this ethnographic style. I am more concerned about the deleterious consequences of prioritizing and centering my presence in the field in this study. See John Van Maanen, *Tales of the Field: On Writing Ethnography* (Chicago: Univ. of Chicago Press, 1988).

14. See Brad Bagasao, "Asian American No More," *LA Weekly* 1, No. 12 (1989): 43. For a discussion of Asian American panethnic movements, refer to Yen Le Espiritu, *Asian American Panethnicity: Bridging Institutions and Identities* (Philadelphia: Temple Univ. Press, 1992).

Chapter One

Epigraph: Igorot and Mangyan, referred to in the chapter epigraph, are indigenous groups in the Philippines.

1. William Petersen, "Concepts of Ethnicity," in *Harvard Encyclopedia of American Ethnic Groups*, edited by Stephan Thernstrom (Cambridge: Harvard Univ. Press, 1980), 234.

2. I develop this dichotomy based on a review of the anthropological scholarship on ethnicity in the traditional social sciences: G. Carter Bentley, "Ethnicity and Practice," *Comparative Studies in Society and History* 29, No. 1 (January 1987): 24–55. Also refer to Bentley's "Theoretical Perspectives on Ethnicity and Nationality," *Sage Race Relations Abstracts* 8, No. 2 (1983): 1–53. A similar but abbreviated work that focuses on ethnicity in the U.S. context is Kathleen Neils Conzen, David A. Gerber, Ewa Morawska, George E. Pozzetta, and Rudolph J. Vecoli, "The Invention of Ethnicity: A Perspective from the U.S.A.," *Journal of American Ethnic History* 24, No. 105 (March 1992): 3–41.

3. Bentley, "Ethnicity and Practice," 26.

4. Ibid., 25. For a substantial discussion of cultural symbols and practices that undergird ethnic identity, see Mary C. Waters, *Ethnic Options: Choosing Identities in America* (Berkeley: Univ. of California Press, 1990), chap. 5.

5. The struggles are rationally determined because of their internal logic: group interests are threatened, so "practical goals" need to be pursued to manage or contain these threats. Bentley, "Ethnicity and Practice," 25. Also refer to

Michael Hechter, "The Political Economy of Ethnic Change," *American Journal of Sociology* 79, No. 5 (March 1974): 1151–1178.

6. One of the foremost proponents of the primordialist approach in anthropology is Clifford Geertz. See his "The Integrative Revolution: Primordial Sentiments and Civil Politics in the New States," in *Old Societies and New States*, edited by Clifford Geertz (New York: Free Press, 1963), 105–157, and *The Interpretation of Cultures* (New York: Basic Books, 1973). Bentley mentions Immanuel Wallerstein as one of the instrumentalists' leading advocates. See Wallerstein's "Ethnicity and National Integration," *Cahiers d'études africaines* 1, No. 3 (1960): 129–139. Nathan Glazer and Daniel Patrick Moynihan add the descriptor "situational" in their analysis of "interest group" ethnicity, to downplay culture and highlight political-economic structure. See their *Beyond the Melting Pot: The Negroes, Puerto Ricans, Jews, Italians, and Irish of New York City*, 2d. ed. (Cambridge, Mass.: MIT Press, 1970).

7. See Fred Matthews, "Paradigm Changes in Interpretations of Ethnicity, 1930–1980: From Process to Structure," in *American Immigrants and Their Generations: Studies and Commentaries on the Hansen Thesis after Fifty Years*, edited by Peter Kivisto and Dag Blanck (Urbana: Univ. of Illinois Press, 1990), 170–171.

8. For primordialists, the bonds of ethnicity are likely to fade with each succeeding generation. For example, studies of ethnic groups in the United States indicate that primordial attachments decline in significance among immigrants and that the generations beyond the first turn into assimilated native-born people. See, for example, Herbert J. Gans, "Symbolic Ethnicity: The Future of Ethnic Groups and Cultures in America," in *On the Making of Americans: Essays in Honor of David Reisman*, edited by Herbert J. Gans, Nathan Glazer, Joseph R. Gusfield, and Christopher Jencks (Philadelphia: Univ. of Pennsylvania Press, 1979), 193–220. For instrumentalists, mobilization on behalf of ethnic interests may wane or increase depending on the nature and degree of competition among groups over time and space. See, for example, Joseph Rothschild, *Ethnopolitics: A Conceptual Framework* (New York: Columbia Univ. Press, 1981).

9. Yen Le Espiritu, "The Intersection of Race, Ethnicity, and Class: The Multiple Identities of Second-Generation Filipinos," *Identities* 1, No. 2 (1994): 17.

10. Ibid., 5.

11. A concise overview of the departures from previous frameworks, as well as the continuities across these orientations in ethnohistorical and sociological studies of ethnic groups, can be found in Peter Kivisto, "The Transplanted Then and Now: The Reorientation of Immigration Studies from the Chicago School to the New Social History," *Ethnic and Racial Studies* 13 (1990): 455–481.

12. David Harvey, *The Condition of Postmodernity* (Oxford: Basil Blackwell, 1989), 240. Also see Frederic Jameson, "Postmodernism, or the Cultural Logic of Late Capitalism," *New Left Review* 146 (1984): 53–92.

13. Stuart Hall, "The Question of Cultural Identity," in *Modernity: An Introduction to Modern Societies*, edited by Stuart Hall, David Held, Don Hubert, and Kenneth Thompson (Cambridge: Blackwell, 1996), 619.

14. For a sustained analysis of identity's destabilization, refer to Smith, "Postmodernism, Urban Ethnography." An instance of globalization's consequences for a particular ethnic/racial identity is found in Michael Kearney, "The Effects of Transnational Culture, Economy, and Migration on Mixtec Identity in Oaxacalifornia," in *The Bubbling Cauldron: Race, Ethnicity, and the Urban Crisis*, edited by Michael Peter Smith and Joe R. Feagin (Minneapolis: Univ. of Minnesota Press, 1995), 226–243.

15. See, for instance, the works of Micaela di Leonardo, *The Varieties of Ethnic Experience: Kinship, Class, and Gender among California Italian-Americans* (Ithaca: Cornell Univ. Press, 1984); Michael P. Smith, Bernadette Tarallo, and George Kagiwada, "Colouring California: New Asian Immigrant Households, Social Networks, and the Local State," *International Journal of Urban and Regional Research* 15 (1991): 250–268; and Claire Dwyer, "Constructions of Muslim Identity and the Contesting of Power: The Debate over Muslim Schools in the United Kingdom," in *Constructions of Race, Place, and Nation*, edited by Peter Jackson and Jan Penrose (Minneapolis: Univ. of Minnesota Press, 1994), 143–159. Certain works have also reanalyzed depictions of previous generations of ethnic groups by detailing the complexities of their experiences with new data viewed from alternative perspectives. See, as examples, Franca Iacovetta, *Such Hardworking People: Italian Immigrants in Postwar Toronto* (Montreal: McGill-Queen's Univ. Press, 1992), and April R. Schultz, *Ethnicity on Parade: Inventing the Norwegian American through Celebration* (Amherst: Univ. of Massachusetts, 1994).

16. See the collection of articles in Michael Peter Smith and Joe R. Feagin, eds., *The Bubbling Cauldron: Race, Ethnicity, and the Urban Crisis* (Minneapolis: Univ. of Minnesota Press, 1995). I appropriate the term "postmodern" in this case not to suggest an isolated, random, or independent logic behind ethnic group identification but to highlight a processual, relational, historical, and transformative register to such an identification. For a critique of postmodernity in relation to ethnic writing and ethnography, see E. San Juan Jr., *Racial Formations/Critical Transformations* (Atlantic Highlands, N.J.: Humanities Press, 1992), chap. 4.

17. Thernstrom, *Harvard Encyclopedia of American Ethnic Groups*, vi.

18. Ibid., vii.

19. On the notion of the "local" in Philippine history and relationships of power, see Vicente L. Rafael, *Contracting Colonialism: Translation and Christian Conversion in Tagalog Society under Early Spanish Rule* (Ithaca: Cornell Univ. Press, 1988), 16–22.

20. Smith, "Postmodernism, Urban Ethnography," 497.

21. Michael Ignatieff, *Blood and Belonging: Journeys into the New Nationalism* (New York: Farrar, Straus, and Giroux, 1993).

22. James A. Banks, *Teaching Strategies for Ethnic Studies*, 4th ed. (Boston: Allyn and Bacon, 1987), 7–8. For a study of an Asian American community in this light, see Min Zhou, *Chinatown: The Socioeconomic Potential of an Urban Enclave* (Philadephia: Temple Univ. Press, 1992).

23. Pozzetta, "Concepts of Ethnicity," 239; John Bodnar, *The Transplanted: A History of Immigrants in Urban America* (Bloomington: Indiana Univ. Press, 1985).

24. Paul Gilroy, "Cultural Studies and Ethnic Absolutism," in *Cultural Studies*, edited by Lawrence Grossberg, Cary Nelson, and Paula Treichler (New York: Routledge, 1992), 187–198.

25. Michael Peter Smith and Joe R. Feagin, "Putting 'Race' in Its Place," in *The Bubbling Cauldron: Race, Ethnicity, and the Urban Crisis*, edited by Michael Peter Smith and Joe R. Feagin (Minneapolis: Univ. of Minnesota Press, 1995), 12–17.

26. Arthur Schlesinger, "The Cult of Ethnicity, Good and Bad," *Time*, 8 July 1991, 27. Variations of such criticisms of multiculturalism also appear in Schlesinger's collection of essays, *The Disuniting of America: Reflections on a Multicultural Society* (Knoxville: Whittle Books, 1991).

27. I do not, however, condone interethnic violence as a means of advocating ethnic "rights" and claims in the name of territorial supremacy and legitimacy. My intent here is to illustrate the usual construction of these forms of nationalism as antimodern and irrational.

28. David Lloyd, "Nationalisms against the State: Towards a Critique of the Anti-Nationalist Prejudice," in *Reexamining and Renewing Philippine Progressive Vision*, edited by John Gershman and Walden Bello (Quezon City, Phil.: Forum for Philippine Alternatives, 1993), 216. I have benefited tremendously from Lloyd's critical review of the literature on nationalism.

29. A critique of this argument can be found in Elizabeth Ellsworth, "I Pledge Allegiance," in *Race, Identity, and Representation in Education*, edited by Cameron McCarthy and Warren Crichlow (New York: Routledge, 1993), 201–219.

30. E. San Juan Jr., "Configuring the Filipino Diaspora in the United States," *Diaspora* 3, No. 2 (Fall 1994): 117.

31. Cornel West, "The New Cultural Politics of Difference," in *Out There: Marginalization and Contemporary Cultures*, edited by Russell Ferguson, Martha Gever, Trinh T. Minh-ha, and Cornel West (Cambridge: MIT Press, 1990), 19–36.

32. Sarah Banet-Weiser, "Crowning Identities: Performing Nationalism, Femininity, and Race in U.S. Beauty Pageants," (Ph.D. diss., Univ. of California, San Diego, 1995), 18.

33. This is not to say that the management of inequalities is always in the direction of exploitation and of its official maintenance. There have been attempts at combating racial discrimination, for example, through state-sponsored civil rights initiatives. Ronald Takaki, however, would contend that such is the case in the de jure sense; that is, racial discrimination is prohibited by law. But in the de facto sense, he says, racism still exists. Hence, the practice of inequalities in this case appears to be resolved legally but not necessarily eradicated socially. Ronald Takaki, "Reflections on Racial Patterns in America," *Affirmative Discrimination: Ethnic Inequality and Public Policy* (New York: Basic Books, 1988), 34–35.

34. The principal representative of this literature is Carlos Bulosan and his novel *America Is in the Heart* (Seattle: Univ. of Washington Press, [1946] 1973).

35. Martin F. Manalansan IV would add sexual preference, as in, "Are you gay?" He argues that gayness has a particular inflection far different from the Filipino signifier *"bakla,"* in "Speaking of AIDS: Language and the Filipino 'Gay' Experience in America," in *Discrepant Histories: Translocal Essays on Filipino Cultures*, edited by Vicente L. Rafael (Philadelphia: Temple Univ. Press, 1995), 193–220.

36. I appropriate this term, which Judith Butler uses in the context of gender performance that "troubles" the routine and expected practices of social behavior by failing to "repeat" acts that meet the expectations of social convention: "[The] abiding gendered self [is] structured by repeated acts that seek to approximate the ideal of a substantial ground of identity, but which, in their occasional discontinuity, reveal the temporal and contingent groundlessness of this 'ground.' The possibilities of gender transformation are to be found precisely in the arbitrary relation between such acts, in the possibility of a failure to repeat, a de-formity, or a parodic repetition that exposes the phantasmatic effect of abiding identity as a politically tenuous construction." *Gender Trouble: Feminism and the Subversion of Identity* (New York: Routledge, 1990), 141.

37. On Philippine nationalism, refer to Benedict Anderson, "Hard to Imagine: A Puzzle in the History of Philippine Nationalism," in *Cultures and Texts: Representations of Philippine Society*, edited by Raul Pertierra and Eduardo F. Ugarte (Quezon City, Phil.: Univ. of the Philippines Press, 1994); Renato Constantino, with the collaboration of Letizia R. Constantino, *The Philippines: A Past Revisited* (Quezon City, Phil.: Tala Publishing, 1975); Reynaldo Ileto, *Pasyon and Revolution: Popular Movements in the Philippines, 1840–1910* (Quezon City, Phil.: Ateneo de Manila Univ. Press, 1979); and Rafael, *Contracting Colonialism*. Anderson remarks, for instance ("Hard to Imagine," 94–95), that at the time the Philippines' national hero Jose Rizal was writing, "political, cultural, and social changes were making problematic the older hierarchy. Not less important to bear in mind is the fact that the word filipino/a was then just beginning a momentous transformation. For most people in the country—which everyone called Filipinas or Las

Filipinas—up to the end of the nineteenth century, the word was principally a synonym of 'criollo,' or pure blooded Spaniard born in the archipelago, and it was always spelled, Spanish-style, with a small 'f.' But it was also, almost imperceptibly, starting to be claimed by upwardly mobile Spanish and Chinese mestizos [or persons of mixed descent], in periodic alliance with the traditional 'filipino' creoles in political opposition to the 'peninsulares' [or Spaniards born in Spain] controlling the colonial army, administration, and ecclesiastical high command. After 1900 . . . it quickly acquired a primary political meaning, referring to all the sons and daughters of the country, no matter what their 'racial' origins. And it went upper case."

38. Arnold Molina Azurin, *Reinventing the Filipino: Sense of Being and Becoming* (Quezon City, Phil.: Univ. of the Philippines Press, 1995), esp. 11–79.

39. Yen Le Espiritu, *Asian American Panethnicity: Bridging Institutions and Identities* (Philadelphia: Temple Univ. Press, 1992), 79–80, 102–109; and Linda Trinh Vo, "Paths to Empowerment: Panethnic Mobilization in San Diego's Asian American Community" (Ph.D. diss., Univ. of California, San Diego, 1995), 110–117. I do not mean to suggest that Filipino Americans are always anti-panethnic. Ethnic coalitions have been instrumental in forwarding causes that Filipino Americans found they had in common with other groups. I share Espiritu's and Vo's optimism about panethnicity as a crucial arena for contesting racism at present and in the future.

40. For an illuminating discussion of "resistance," see James C. Scott, *Weapons of the Weak* (New Haven: Yale Univ. Press, 1985), esp. 289–303.

Chapter Two

1. Fred Cordova, *Filipinos: Forgotten Asian Americans* (Dubuque, Iowa: Kendall/ Hunt, 1983), 114.

2. For this chapter, I relied heavily on these works regarding Filipino immigration to the United States: Lorraine Jacobs Crouchett, *Filipinos in California: From the Days of the Galleons to the Present* (El Cerrito, Calif.: Downey Place, 1982); Yen Le Espiritu, "Introduction: Filipino Settlements in the United States," in *Filipino American Lives* (Philadelphia: Temple Univ. Press, 1995), 1–36; and Antonio J. A. Pido, *The Pilipinos in America: Macro/Micro Dimensions of Immigration and Integration* (New York: Center for Migration Studies, 1986).

3. Colonization looms large in many studies of population movements that look at "world systems" paradigms as they are tied to cross-national relationships of political and economic subordination. On Asian movement to the United States, see, for example, Lucie Cheng and Edna Bonacich, *Labor Immigration under Capitalism: Asian Workers in the United States before World War II* (Berkeley: Univ. of California Press, 1984).

4. The forced service, mostly of men, was a central feature of the "polo" labor system instituted during the Spanish colonial period as an important component of the empire's economy. See O. D. Corpuz, *The Philippines* (Englewood Cliffs, N.J.: Prentice-Hall, 1965), 27–28; and Crouchett, *Filipinos in California*, esp. 5–17. On native seamen who remained in California, Crouchett cites Austin Craig and Conrado Benitez, *Philippine Progress to 1898* (Manila: Philippine Educational Co., 1916), 23.

5. The year 1763 marks the first instance of recorded Filipino settlement in North America, at St. Malo's Bay in Louisiana. However, the first recorded Filipino arrival on the continent is dated in 1587, in Morro Bay, California, by San Luis Obispo. See Marina E. Espina, *Filipinos in Louisiana* (New Orleans: Laborde, 1988), 5–7.

6. U.S. colonization was resisted strongly by Filipino revolutionaries fighting for independence from any external rule. See Teodoro Agoncillo and Milagros Guerrero, *History of the Filipino People*, 7th ed. (Quezon City, Phil.: Garcia, 1987), esp. chap. 13; James H. Blount, *American Occupation of the Philippines, 1898/1912* (rpt. by Manila: Solar Publishing, 1991 [1913]), esp. chaps. 9, 15, and 16; and Crouchett, *Filipinos in California*, 21–25.

7. I use the term "interventions" to denote differential U.S. control of these territories. For example, Cuba was considered "freed," even though the United States still exercised the right to intervene in Cuban affairs when it desired to do so. See Blount, *American Occupation of the Philippines*, chap. 2; George S. Boutwell, "Free America, Free Cuba, Free Philippines," in *The Philippines Reader*, edited by Daniel B. Schirmer and Stephen Rosskamm Shalom (Boston: South End, 1987 [1901]), 52–55; and James A. LeRoy, *The Americans in the Philippines: A History of the Conquest and First Years of Occupation* (Boston: Houghton Mifflin, 1914), 350–360.

8. For an elaboration, see the articles in Daniel B. Schirmer and Stephen Rosskamm Shalom, eds., *The Philippines Reader* (Boston: South End, 1987), esp. chap. 2.

9. Walter L. Williams, "United States Indian Policy and the Debate over Philippine Annexation: Implications for the Origins of American Imperialism," *Journal of American History* 66, No. 4 (March 1980): 827–828, citing correspondence of U.S. enlisted men in the Philippines that appeared in the 1900 *Congressional Record*.

10. The most often cited texts for such views include the speeches and writings of President William McKinley, Vice President Theodore Roosevelt, and Secretary of War Elihu Root. See ibid., 810–825. A parallel happening was the regeneration of the "frontier myth" in the U.S. imperial project, in which "Asians become figurative Apaches and the Philippines becomes a symbolic equivalent of Boone's Kentucky or Houston's Texas." For Roosevelt, however, "the democratic concepts [of 'liberty' and 'consent of the governed'] are irrelevant to the

Filipinos because their racial gifts and state of development preclude their making civilized use of them." Richard Slotkin, *Gunfighter Nation: The Myth of the Frontier in Twentieth-Century America* (New York: Harper Collins, 1992), 53.

11. The relationship between imperialism and racialization has a long history, which I abbreviate here. Williams and Slotkin write about Native American subjugation in intimate connection with U.S. expansionism that predicated and sustained the arguments in favor of the colonization of the Philippines. I have found Williams's ideas useful in explaining the provenance of Filipino racialization in the United States. The Filipino presence in the United States later produced racial analogies with Chinese and Japanese. I do not mean to imply that Filipino racialization in the United States was a simple extension of the racism perpetuated against all people of color who were already settled in America and its territories. Although institutional and ideological racism were in partnership with the principles of white supremacy, which always positioned white European American groups at the top of the social-political hierarchy, they produced discrete and varying statuses for different groups at different times. For a discussion of this phenomenon in California history, see Tomas Almaguer, *Racial Fault Lines: The Historical Origins of White Supremacy in California* (Berkeley: Univ. of California Press, 1994). Filipinos were, thus, seen initially as similar to Native Americans and other Asians, but not quite like them, because Filipinos had brown skin, had Spanish-sounding surnames, were Christian, and later, could speak English. Because of these, I am inclined to think that Filipino racialization, then and now, eludes traditional categorization by race and, as a result, is always subject to misattribution or goes unrecognized.

12. Renato Constantino, *The Filipinos in the Philippines and Other Essays* (Quezon City, Phil.: Malaya Books, 1966), 39–65; and Pido, *The Pilipinos in America*, 49–50.

13. It should be noted, however, that the principal aim of the public school system was to pacify strong pockets of the Filipino population who were adamantly resistant to U.S. colonization. The rest of the country was deemed susceptible to anti-American sentiments, and, as an extension of the colonial government's manifest destiny, the teaching of American values and precepts was used as an instrument to win over people to the side of the so-called benevolent state. It is in this sense that subjugation was synonymous with Americanization, as "Filipinos had to be trained as citizens of the American colony." Constantino, *The Filipinos in the Philippines*, 45. For a study of "benevolent" colonialism, see Vicente L. Rafael's "White Love: Surveillance and Nationalist Resistance in the U.S. Colonization of the Philippines," in *Cultures of United States Imperialism*, ed. Amy Kaplan and Donald E. Pease (Durham: Duke Univ. Press, 1993), 185–218.

14. I am in agreement on this point with Oscar V. Campomanes: "The consequences of this inaugural moment of U.S.-Philippine relations for latter-day

U.S. Filipinos are manifold and extend to their politics or forms of recognition and emergence." See "The New Empire's Forgetful and Forgotten Citizens: Unrepresentability and Unassimilability in Filipino-American Postcolonialities," *Critical Mass* 2, No. 2 (Spring 1995): 145. Also refer to Pido, *The Pilipinos in America*, 48–62, and E. San Juan Jr., "Configuring the Filipino Diaspora in the United States," *Diaspora* 3, No. 2 (Fall 1994): 117–134.

15. Cordova, *Filipinos*, chap. 5; Carey McWilliams, *Brothers under the Skin* (Boston: Little, Brown, 1964), 200–230.

16. Some of them were also known as "fountain-pen boys," who were "liked as students and prized as houseboys . . . being grateful wards of the American government." McWilliams, *Brothers under the Skin*, 324.

17. Cordova, *Filipinos*, 124–129; Barbara M. Posadas and Ronald K. Guyotte, "Unintentional Immigrants: Chicago's Filipino Foreign Students Become Settlers, 1900–1941," *Journal of American Ethnic History* 9 (Spring 1990): 40.

18. Many could not return home because of lack of funds and fear of being called "failures." Posadas and Guyotte, "Unintentional Immigrants," 26–48.

19. Espiritu, "Introduction," 4.

20. Barbara M. Posadas, "At a Crossroad: Filipino American History and the Old-Timers' Generation," *Amerasia* 13, No. 1 (1986–1987): 86, citing her interview with Honesto P. Llanes, Chicago, Illinois, 15 August 1979.

21. I use the appellations "America" and the "United States" in this section to mean the U.S. mainland and its territories outside of the Philippine archipelago. Since the Philippines was effectively a U.S. colony from 1898 to 1946, immigration of Filipinos to other parts of the States ought to be considered "internal" during this period, and "external" beyond it.

The economic explanations for Filipino migration are well documented, especially in studies of individual decisions to migrate based on comprehensive interviews, and in those that have analyzed structural forces that propel emigration. According to one review of the scholarship in this area: "Migration was perceived primarily as an economic opportunity to be taken advantage of by individuals and the state. This has remained a central theme in the body of research on Philippine labor migration, and even studies without an explicitly economic framework usually include the maximization of economic returns relative to costs as one important factor in the examination." Joyce Yukawa, *Migration from the Philippines, 1975–1996: An Annotated Bibliography* (Quezon City, Phil.: Scalabrini Migration Center, 1996), 9.

22. Pido, in *The Pilipinos in America*, 118, notes that the labor shortage was also a result of the abolition of slavery, the expansion of the U.S. frontier beyond the West, and the exclusion of Asian immigrants in 1882 (Chinese), 1908 (Japanese), 1917 (Asians, including people from India), and 1924. Also refer to David M. Reimers, *Still the Golden Door: The Third World Comes to America*, 2d ed. (New York: Columbia Univ. Press, 1992), 4–10.

23. For firsthand accounts of Filipinos from this generation, see Roberto V. Vallanca, *Pinoy: The First Wave* (San Francisco: Strawberry Hill, 1977). Most of those who came from the Ilocos provinces in the Philippines were known as *sakadas* (the local term for farmer), while those in the Alaskan canneries were known later as Alaskeros. Cordova, *Filipinos,* chap. 3.

24. Espiritu, "Introduction," 7. Also refer to Ronald Takaki, *Strangers from a Different Shore: A History of Asian Americans* (New York: Little, Brown, 1989), 315–354.

25. These acts excluded Japanese, Chinese, and other Asian immigrants, except Filipinos, who were considered U.S. nationals. Reimers, *Still the Golden Door,* 4–6.

26. Bruno Lasker, *Filipino Immigration to Continental United States and to Hawaii* (New York: Arno, 1969 [1931]), 347–353; Miriam Sharma, "Pinoy in Paradise: Environment and Adaptation of Pilipinos in Hawaii, 1906–1946," *Amerasia* 7, No. 2 (1980): 97.

27. Lasker, *Filipino Immigration,* 167; Sucheng Chan, *Asian Americans: An Interpretive History* (Boston: Twayne, 1991), 17–18.

28. Chan, *Asian Americans,* 39–40; Cordova, *Filipinos,* chap. 3; Crouchett, *Filipinos in California,* 31–37; and Takaki, *Strangers from a Different Shore,* 318–322.

29. H. Brett Melendy, *Asians in America: Filipinos, Koreans, and East Indians* (Boston: Twayne, 1977), 40.

30. Cordova, *Filipinos,* 22–72; Pido, *The Pilipinos in America,* 48–52.

31. The restrictions were based on the Naturalization Act of 1790, which allowed for the naturalization of "free white aliens" only. Crouchett, *Filipinos in California,* 34. Also see Ronald Takaki's "Reflections on Racial Patterns in America: An Historical Perspective," *Ethnicity and Public Policy 1* (1982): 1–23, for a more thorough elaboration of U.S. racism and the law.

32. Crouchett, *Filipinos in California,* 34.

33. Williams, "United States Indian Policy," 816–817.

34. The comparison with Asians, particularly Chinese and Japanese workers, fueled a lot of strong sentiment regarding Filipino exclusion, again because of Filipinos' special status. Like other Asians, Filipinos were considered a part of the "mongrel stream" that could not be assimilated. But unlike other Asians, their immigration could not be curtailed because they were technically U.S. nationals. See Alexander Saxton, *The Indispensable Enemy: Labor and the Anti-Chinese Movement in California* (Berkeley: Univ. of California Press, 1971); Robert A. Divine, *American Immigration Policy* (New Haven: Yale Univ. Press, 1957); and Bill Ong Hing, *Making and Remaking Asian America through Immigration Policy, 1850–1990* (Stanford: Stanford Univ. Press, 1993), 30–31. I have also benefited immensely from Lisa Lowe's insights on the relationships between Asian immigration and Asian American citizenship and racialization. See her *Immigrant Acts: On Asian American Cultural Politics* (Durham: Duke Univ. Press, 1996).

35. Those who attempted to improve their lives through education experienced discrimination after graduation. For example, those who studied law were not allowed to take the bar exams. Vallanca, *Pinoy,* 28.

36. One recorded legal case with regard to antimiscegenation was *Salvador Roldan v. California* in 1933. Roldan argued that under the Antimiscegenation Law of 1880, the intermarriage of white and Mongolian races was prohibited, and that he was of "Malay" race, not "Mongolian." He won the case and married a Caucasian. After the court ruling, the state legislature added the "Malay" race to the prohibited categories. See Takaki, *Strangers from a Different Shore,* 330.

37. I thank Oscar Campomanes for pointing out to me the parallel significance and inconsistencies of the *Plessy v. Ferguson* ruling of 1898 for Filipino/U.S. nationals in the mainland, Hawaii, and Alaska from 1903 until 1934.

38. Takaki, *Strangers from a Different Shore,* 339–343.

39. Crouchett, *Filipinos in California,* 39.

40. On this accommodation, see Posadas, "At a Crossroad," 87.

41. Cordova, *Filipinos,* 73–81; Jesse Quinsaat, ed., *Letters in Exile: An Introductory Reader on the History of Pilipinos in America* (Los Angeles: UCLA Asian American Studies Center, 1976); and Sonia Emily Wallovits, *The Filipinos in California* (San Francisco: R and E Research Associates, 1972 [1966]), chap. 6.

42. Crouchett, *Filipinos in California,* 40–44; Howard De Witt, *Anti-Filipino Movements in California: A History, Bibliography, and Study Guide* (San Francisco: R and E Research Associates, 1976).

43. Some worked as movie extras, chauffeurs, and prizefighters (boxers). See Benicio Catapusan, *The Filipino Occupational and Recreational Activities in Los Angeles* (San Francisco: R and E Research Associates, 1975 [1934]), chaps. 3 and 5.

44. Benicio Catapusan, *The Social Adjustment of Filipinos in the United States* (rpt. by San Francisco: R & E Research Associates, 1972 [1940]), chap. 4.

45. Espiritu, "Introduction," 14–16; Melendy, *Asians in America,* 90–96.

46. Hing, *Making and Remaking Asian America,* 37.

47. Research documents this phenomenon as analogous to that of other Asian Americans. See Chan, *Asian Americans,* 45—61; Espiritu, "Introduction," 10–11.

48. Catapusan, *Filipino Occupational and Recreational Activities,* chaps. 7 and 8; Vallanca, *Pinoy,* 50–53.

49. Takaki, *Strangers from a Different Shore,* 341–342.

50. See Carlos Bulosan, *America Is in the Heart: A Personal History* (Seattle: Univ. of Washington Press, 1973 [1943]); and Manuel Buaken, *I Have Lived with the American People* (Caldwell, Idaho: Caxton Printers, 1948).

51. Emory S. Bogardus, "Filipino Americans," in *One America,* 3d ed., edited by Francis J. Brown and Joseph S. Roucek (New York: Prentice-Hall, 1952), 361–373; Catapusan, *Filipino Occupational and Recreational Activities,* chap. 4; and Melendy, *Asians in America,* chap. 6.

52. The limit was increased to 100 per year in 1946 as part of a concession to the Philippines, which had assisted the United States during World War II. Reimers, *Still the Golden Door,* 15–16.

53. Crouchett, *Filipinos in California,* 40, citing Hyung-Chan Kim and Cynthia G. Mejia, *The Filipinos in Ameria, 1898–1974: A Chronology and Fact Book* (New York: Oceana Publications, 1976), 81.

54. Crouchett, *Filipinos in California,* 45–59; Espiritu, "Introduction," 17–18; and Takaki, *Strangers from a Different Shore,* 357–363.

55. The principal causes of increased immigration during this time were the War Brides Act (1945), which allowed the Filipino spouses and dependents of U.S. servicemen and Filipino enlistees to enter the United States, and the McCarran-Walter Act (1952), which permitted spouses and dependents of naturalized Filipino Americans to enter beyond the quota of 100 per year. Reimers, *Still the Golden Door,* 21–22, 25–28.

56. Crouchett, *Filipinos in California,* 62.

57. Espiritu, "Introduction," 17–18.

58. Hing, *Making and Remaking Asian America,* 36–38, 65; and Pido, *The Pilipinos in America,* 65–66.

59. Wallovits, *The Filipinos in California,* chap. 7.

60. California Department of Industrial Relations, *Californians of Japanese, Chinese, and Filipino Ancestry* (San Francisco: Department of Industrial Relations, 1965), 12–14.

61. The quote is from an issue of the *Congressional Record* cited by Reimers, *Still the Golden Door,* 19. It specifically referred to the Judd Bill, which formed the basis for the McCarran-Walter Act. The bill stipulated the retention of the provisions of the National Origins Act of 1924, which restricted immigration to 2 percent of the population figures of the 1890 U.S. census. This census records most immigrants as coming from Northern and Western Europe, people who were mostly considered racially white and, therefore, preferable.

62. Hing, *Making and Remaking Asian America,* 40; Reimers, *Still the Golden Door,* chap. 3.

63. Chan, *Asian Americans,* 145–147; Reimers, *Still the Golden Door,* 92–99.

64. This nativist trend would reach its height in the 1980s. See Roger Daniels, *Coming to America: A History of Immigration and Ethnicity in American Life* (New York: Harper Collins, 1990), 388–391.

65. Ibid., chap. 13; Reimers, *Still the Golden Door,* chap. 3.

66. A more comprehensive study of these shifts, with reference to Los Angeles, can be found in the collection of articles in Paul Ong, Edna Bonacich, and Lucie Cheng, eds., *The New Asian Immigration in Los Angeles and Global Restructuring* (Philadelphia: Temple Univ. Press, 1994).

67. Crouchett, *Filipinos in California,* 67.

68. It also helped that schooling in the Philippines continued to be patterned after U.S. education. As Crouchett notes, "No other Asian immigrant group—indeed, very few other immigrants from any nation—came with a prior knowledge of the English language." Ibid.

69. The Philippines has been the major source of foreign-trained nurses in the United States. Paul Ong and Tania Azores, "The Migration and Incorporation of Filipino Nurses," in *The New Asian Immigration in Los Angeles and Global Restructuring*, edited by Paul Ong, Edna Bonacich, and Lucie Cheng (Philadelphia: Temple Univ. Press, 1994), 164–195.

70. Fred Arnold, Urmil Minocha, and James T. Fawcett, "The Changing Face of Asian Immigration to the United States," in *Pacific Bridges: The New Immigration from Asia and the Pacific Islands*, edited by James T. Fawcett and Benjamin V. Cariño (Staten Island, N.Y.: Center for Migration Studies, 1987), 111–114.

71. Reimers, *Still the Golden Door*, chap. 8.

72. Toward the later part of this period, Filipinos relied heavily on family reunification for immigration because of the stricter rules imposed for professional/skilled worker entry. See Hing, *Making and Remaking Asian America*, 89.

73. See John M. Liu, Paul M. Ong, and Carolyn Rosenstein, "Dual Chain Migration: Post-1965 Filipino Immigration to the United States," *International Migration Review* 25, No. 3 (Fall 1991): 487–513.

74. Chan, *Asian Americans*, 170; Daniels, *Coming to America*, 356–360; Bok-Lim C. Kim, *The Asian Americans: Changing Patterns, Changing Needs* (Montclair, N.J.: Association of Korean Christian Scholars in North America, 1978), 150–156; and Pido, *The Pilipinos in America*, 77.

75. Pido, *The Pilipinos in America*, 53–56.

76. Espiritu, "Introduction," 19.

77. Chan, *Asian Americans*, 149–150.

78. Hing, *Making and Remaking Asian America*, 92.

79. Espiritu, "Introduction," 20.

80. See Yukawa, *Migration from the Philippines*, 1–7. James A. Tyner, in "The Social Construction of Gendered Migration from the Philippines" (*Asian and Pacific Migration Journal* 3, No. 4 [1994]: 589–617), offers insights on the precarious placement of Filipinas in overseas contract work. On the marketing of Filipina "mail-order brides" in the 1980s and the 1990s, refer to Roland B. Tolentino, "Bodies, Letters, Catalogs: Filipinas in Transnational Space," *Social Text*, Vol. 14, No. 3 (Fall 1996): 49–76.

81. Edita A. Tan, "Labor Emigration and the Accumulation and Transfer of Human Capital," *Asian and Pacific Migration Journal* 2, No. 3 (1993): 304–305.

82. On the problematic success of the program, see Manolo I. Abella, "Labor Mobility, Trade, and Structural Change: The Philippine Experience," *Asian and Pacific Migration Journal* 2, No. 3 (1993): 249–250.

83. Madge Bello and Vincent Reyes, "Filipino Americans and the Marcos Overthrow: The Transformation of Political Consciousness," *Amerasia* 13, No. 1 (1986–87): 73–83. Also refer to the excerpts from the statements issued by a coalition of Filipino and Filipino American activists against U.S. support for the Marcos administration in Schirmer and Shalom, *The Philippines Reader,* 267–271.

84. The village was named after Paulo Agbayani, a Filipino labor leader. Crouchett, *Filipinos in California,* 76–00, Royal F. Morales, *Makibaka, The Filipino American Struggle* (Los Angeles: Mountainview, 1974), chap. 2.

85. A more thorough treatment of Filipino farm labor history can be found in Craig Scharlin and Lilia V. Villanueva, *Philip Vera Cruz: A Personal History of Filipino Immigrants and the Farmworkers Movement* (Los Angeles: UCLA Labor Center, Institute of Industrial Relations, and the UCLA Asian American Studies Center, 1992).

86. U.S. Bureau of the Census, *1970 Census of Population and Housing Summary* (Washington, D.C.: GPO, 1972), and *1990 Census of Population and Housing Summary* (Washington, D.C.: GPO, 1992); Dwight L. Johnson, Michael J. Levin, and Edna L. Paisano, *We, the Asian and Pacific Islander Americans* (Washington D.C., GPO, 1988); and Dwight L. Johnson, Michael J. Levin, and Edna L. Paisano, *We the American Asians* (Washington, D.C.: GPO, 1993). Apparently, the figures may be even higher than reported, since many believe that the number of Filipino undocumented aliens, including temporary visitors who overstay their visas, is significantly large.

87. Pido, *The Pilipinos in America,* 114–115.

88. For an important overview of issues surrounding Filipino labor migration, refer to Joyce Yukawa, "Introduction: Trends, Issues, and Research on Philippine Labor Migration," in *Migration from the Philippines, 1975–1996: An Annotated Bibliography* (Quezon City, Phil.: Scalabrini Migration Center, 1996), 1–35. Also note the insightful discussions of the phenomena of transnationalism and diaspora among Filipinos in Jonathan Y. Okamura, *Imagining the Filipino American Diaspora: Transnational Relations, Identities, and Communities* (New York: Garland, 1998).

89. James O. Allen and Eugene Turner, *The Ethnic Quilt: Population Diversity in Southern California* (Northridge, Calif.: Center for Geographical Studies, California State University, Northridge, 1997), pp. 129–148.

90. Crouchett, *Filipinos in California,* 72; Ong and Azores, "Migration and Incorporation of Filipino Nurses," 177–79. In New Jersey and New York, for example, Philippine-educated or practicing dentists are required to attend and finish at least two more years of U.S. dental school even before they take the boards for licensing.

91. In 1977, Filipinos, along with other groups under the auspices of the United Farm Workers of America, pressed for the repeal of legislation so that by the following year, "any medical graduate who had actually practiced medicine or

surgery for a period of not less than 15 years in a foreign country or other state of the United States would be required to pass only that portion of the written examination relating to clinical competence and clinical science." Crouchett, *Filipinos in California*, 78. Also see Takaki, *Strangers from a Different Shore*, 434–436.

92. Morales, *Makibaka*, chap. 4; Pido, *The Pilipinos in America*, 120–124. In Chapter 3, I probe the significance of racial categorization in relation to *Orientalization* with respect to Filipino Americans. For a discussion of the issues associated with referring to Filipino Americans as Asian Americans among Filipinos who are gays, see Martin F. Manalansan IV, "Searching for Community: Filipino Gay Men in New York City, *Amerasia* 20, No. 1 (1994): 59–73.

93. UCLA Asian American Studies Center, *National Asian Pacific American Political Roster and Resource Guide*, 6th ed. (Los Angeles: UCLA Asian American Studies Center, 1995).

94. Harold Brackman and Steven Erie, "Beyond 'Politics by Other Means'?: Empowerment Strategies for Los Angeles' Asian Pacific Community," in *The Bubbling Cauldron: Race, Ethnicity, and the Urban Crisis*, edited by Michael Peter Smith and Joel R. Feagin (Minneapolis: Univ. of Minnesota Press, 1995), 282. Also see Don T. Nakanishi, "The Next Swing Vote? Asian Pacific Americans and California Politics," *Racial and Ethnic Politics in California*, edited by Bryan O. Jackson and Michael B. Preston (Berkeley: Univ. of California at Berkeley, Institute of Governmental Studies, 1991), 25–54.

95. Smith and Feagin, "Beyond Politics," 282–303.

96. For the 1984 figures, see ibid., 284. The 1990 U.S. census estimates that 64.4 percent of Filipinos are foreign born and only 53.8 percent of them are naturalized. Johnson et al., *We the American Asians*, 8. Also refer to Pido, *The Pilipinos in America*, 107–111.

97. Moreover, there is a strong perception among Filipino Americans that full participation in the U.S. body politic may require full assimilation (i.e., selling out): the acceptance of the "cultural dominance of the majority on the latter's terms." Some of them also question whether political participation is a viable means of empowerment. I discuss these issues in Chapter 4. Pido, *The Pilipinos in America*, 101.

98. Ibid., 96–102. For discussions of issues that concern Filipino Americans and Asian Americans as a whole, refer to U.S. Commission on Civil Rights, *Civil Rights Issues Facing Asian Americans in the 1990s* (Washington, D.C.: U.S. Commission on Civil Rights, 1992.

99. First Lady Hillary Clinton recently referred to such a Filipino presence in the United States labor pool. In a speech addressed to Filipinos at a meeting of the members of the Asia Pacific Economic Exchange (APEC) held Manila in November 1996, she remarked that she knows Filipinos personally—several of them as members of the White House service staff (Filipino Americans from the armed forces) and one of them as the First Couple's personal physician.

100. The numbers cited reflect the aggregate Filipino population in the United States, not just the post-1965 arrivals. Johnson et al., *We the American Asians*, 4–9.

101. Others refer to this marginalization as a form of structural "nonintegration." See Wayne A. Cornelius, "The 'New' Immigration and the Politics of Cultural Diversity in the United States and Japan," *Asian and Pacific Migration Journal* 2, No. 4 (1993): 439–450.

102. On invisibility at academic institutions, refer to the remarkable insights in Oscar V. Campomanes, "The Institutional Invisibility of American Imperialism, the Philippines, and Filipino Americans" (paper presented at the Annual Meeting of the Association of Asian Studies, Los Angeles, Calif.), 25 March 1993. Sucheng Chan also notes that "to this day, very little information about the Philippine-American War" can be found in U.S. textbooks, in Chan, *Asian Americans*, 17.

103. I say this with regard to the increasing number of Filipinos being naturalized, according to INS figures cited in Pido, *The Pilipinos in America*, 109.

104. Espiritu, "Introduction," 22–26; Pido, *The Pilipinos in America*, 105–107.

105. For a study of these space-specific linkages, see Jonathan Y. Okamura, "The Filipino American Dispora: Sites of Space, Time, and Ethnicity," in *Privileging Positions: The Sites of Asian American Studies*, edited by Gary Y. Okihiro, Marilyn Alquizola, Dorothy Fujita Rony, and K. Scott Wong (Pullman: Washington State Univ. Press, 1995), 387–400.

106. U.S. Bureau of the Census, *1990 Census*.

Chapter Three

1. My count of such "Filipino American stores" is eighty-six for L.A., and twenty-eight for San Diego, based on both observation and entries in the 1992–1993 Southern California Filipino American Phonebook. No official count of such stores is available, although my figures closely match those compiled by the Filipino American Storeowners Association in 1990; this organization has since disbanded (phone interview, Ronaldo Salamat, 15 October 1992.) Nevertheless, small retail businesses like these are significant, especially when considered in light of ethnic enclave and economic niche formation in the United States. According to the U.S. Census Bureau, businesses owned by Asian Americans and Pacific Islanders as of 1987 were the largest among minority-owned businesses in terms of average annual receipts, with receipts per firm of $93,221 in 1987, compared to an average of $64,131 for minority-owned businesses overall. A huge majority of these firms are located in California. Of the 18,471 California firms listed as Filipino owned, 7,059 were in the Los Angeles–Long Beach area, while 1,819 were in San Diego. In both locations, retail trading placed second highest (next to services) in number of firms by industry group.

(U.S. Bureau of the Census, Economics and Statistics Administration, U.S. Dept. of Commerce, "Survey of Minority-Owned Business Enterprises," U.S. Bureau of the Census, June 1991.

2. Ten respondents were not sure.

3. Edward Said, *Orientalism* (New York: Vintage Books, 1978), 31–110.

4. For a more contemporary rendition of this argument, with particular reference to Asian Americans, see Lisa Lowe, "Heterogeneity, Hybridity, Multiplicity: Marking Asian American Differences," *Diaspora* 1, No. 1 (Spring 1991): 24–44.

5. U.S. Bureau of the Census, *Federal Population Censuses*, National Archives Microfilm Publications, Washington, D. C., n.d.; Elena S. H. Yu, "Filipino Migration and Community Organizations in the United States," *California Sociologist* 3, No. 2 (Summer 1980): 76–80; and Juanita Tamayo Lott, *Asian Americans: From Racial Category to Multiple Identities* (Walnut Creek, Calif.: Altamira Press, 1998), 35–38. I say "certain agencies" because some national and state censuses did account for Filipinos as a separate group during the period, particularly when counting the number of migrant laborers who entered the United States during the 1920s. See Chapter 2.

6. The quote is from radio personality Howard Stern, whose comments about Filipinos were aired in his nationally syndicated talk show in September 1992, eventually resulting in protests and threats of legal action by Filipino American groups. Stern's next comment, "and I think they eat their young over there," mentioned in the context of alleged cheating by Filipino youth in the Little League World Series, provoked even greater reaction (see Cherie M. Querol-Moreno, "Radio Slur vs. Filipinos Draws Angry Reactions," *Los Angeles Philippine News*, 14–20 October 1992, p. 1). I view this recent occasion of Filipino "bashing" as emblematic of and consistent with other Orientalized representations of Filipinos perpetuated by popular media. In Hollywood movies (*Back to Bataan*, RKO, 1945, and *An American Guerilla in the Philippines*, TCF, 1950, among others) and television shows (as in certain episodes of "Wild, Wild West," "Streets of San Francisco," and "Hawaii Five-O"), Filipinos, along with Chinese and Japanese, have been depicted as barbaric, lazy, unprofessional, stupid, or callous. See an extended discussion of Orientalism in Robert G. Lee, *Orientals: Asian Americans in Popular Culture* (Philadelphia: Temple Univ. Press, 1999). Frequently, the descriptions included the notion that Filipinos eat dogs, something that Filipino American writer Jessica Hagedorn would wittingly deploy in her novel *Dogeaters* (New York: Pantheon, 1990). That Filipinos look and behave like monkeys is another racist notion that until recently was caricatured by some L.A.-based artists (and censored); see James Rainey, "Banner of Roasting Dog at City Hall Art Exhibit Is Removed," *Los Angeles Times*, 25 May 1993). For another diatribe against Orientalist stereotypes in a more direct, encompassing, and deconstructive fashion, refer to David Henry Hwang's play *M. Butterfly* (New York: Plume, 1988).

7. For example, Ivan Light, *Ethnic Enterprise in America* (Berkeley: Univ. of California Press, 1972), and Ivan Light and Edna Bonacich, *Immigrant Enterprises: Koreans in Los Angeles* (Berkeley: Univ. of California Press, 1988).

8. Refer to Chapter 1 for a more sustained discussion of ethnicity and identity.

9. This brings to mind Marx's treatise on commodity values and their relationship to labor. Marx asserts that the value of a commodity has objective existence, determined by the quantity of human labor that produced it and by its relationships with other elements of production and distribution. The difference lies in the value we assign to it. However, as we see here, *beyond* human labor, other "qualities" of products are used to determine their value. Marx would probably refer to this as fetishization of commodities, where labor-power value disappears when money is introduced into the exchange. I believe that among these shoppers, labor-power value actually becomes more salient as the perceived value of the goods takes on a different, more inclusive, character. However, I do not wish to deny the notion that the labor perceived here is not mythologized and abstracted from its real conditions. I deal with this later in the discussion of nostalgia. See Karl Marx, *Capital*, vol. 1 of *The Marx-Engels Reader*, 2d ed., edited by Robert C. Tucker (New York: Norton, 1978).

10. For a more thorough discussion of the history of the *sari-sari* store in the Philippine context, see Edgar Wickberg, *The Chinese in Philippine Life, 1850–1898* (New Haven: Yale Univ. Press, 1965), 45–123.

11. Susan Stewart, *On Longing: Narratives of the Miniature, the Gigantic, the Souvenir, the Collection* (Baltimore: Johns Hopkins Univ. Press, 1984), 43–58.

12. Hamid Naficy, "The Poetics and Practice of Iranian Nostalgia in Exile," *Diaspora* 1, No. 3 (1991): 298.

13. See Vicente L. Rafael's "Taglish, or the Phantom Power of the Lingua Franca," *Public Culture* 8, No. 1 (1995): 101–126, for an elaboration of this point.

14. I give the literal translation of *"tusok-tusok da fish balls"* only for syntactic clarity. The expression originated with female college students in Manila who buy deep-fried fish balls (a local delicacy also found in U.S. "Oriental" stores) hawked by street vendors.

15. City of San Diego Planning Department, "A Decent Home for Every San Diegan," in *San Diego's Industry, 1969–1980: A Planning Analysis* (San Diego, Calif.: San Diego Planning Department, 1971), 24–25. Other valuable references that discuss racial zoning are Mike Davis, *City of Quartz* (New York: Vintage, 1992), and John R. Logan and Harvey L. Molotch, *Urban Fortunes: The Political Economy of Space* (Berkeley: Univ. of California Press, 1978).

16. See Victor Gruen and Larry Smith, *Shopping Towns USA* (New York: Reinhold, 1970), for the history of shopping centers and malls in Southern California.

17. Ibid., 15–25. Other references include: City of Los Angeles Planning Department, "Commercial Element: Background Study," Los Angeles, City

Administration Office, January 1972; Philip Langdon, *Orange Roofs, Golden Arches* (London: Michael Joseph, 1986); and Susan Strasser, *Satisfaction Guaranteed: The Making of the American Mass Market* (New York: Pantheon, 1989).

18. These points apply particularly to Korean grocers in the inner cities of places like Los Angeles and New York. See Illsoo Kim's "The Koreans: Small Business in an Urban Frontier," in *New Immigrants in New York*, edited by Nancy Foner (New York: Columbia Univ. Press, 1987), 219–242.

19. This is not to imply that there are no cross-racial dynamics in the stores. It seems to me that a reluctance to talk about racial tensions signals a deeper anxiety about the costs of engaging in ethnic-based commerce, which is a subject that could be explored in another study.

20. A discussion of the concepts of "pedagogy" and "performance" can be found in Homi K. Bhabha, "Dissemination: Time, Narrative, and the Margins of the Modern Nation," in *Nation and Narration* ed. Homi Bhabha (London: Routledge, 1991), 291—322.

21. Salman Rushdie, *Imaginary Homelands* (London: Granta, 1991).

22. Henry Louis Gates Jr., "Hybridity Happens: Black Brit Bricolage Brings the Noise," *Voice Literary Supplement*, October 1992, pp. 26–27. For criticisms of Asian American representations in popular culture, see Dorinne Kondo, "M. Butterfly: Orientalism, Gender, and a Critique of Essentialist Identity," *Cultural Critique* 16 (Fall 1990): 5–29; and Lowe, "Heterogeneity, Hybridity, Multiplicity," 24–44.

23. Judith Butler, *Gender Trouble: Feminism and the Subversion of Identity* (New York: Routledge, 1990), 17–25.

24. See Naficy, "Poetics and Practice of Iranian Nostalgia," for an ethnic group–specific discussion of this point. Also refer to Michael Kammen's insightful discussion of nostalgia in *Mystic Chords of Memory: The Transformation of Tradition in American Culture* (New York: Vintage, 1991), 618–688.

25. Other such stores cater to "other" specific groups: Koreans, Chinese, Japanese, Armenian, Italian, Indian, etc.

Chapter Four

1. As in the other fieldwork chapters, I have concealed the true names of all respondents to protect their privacy.

2. I borrow the term "hidden transcript" from James Scott, *Domination and the Arts of Resistance* (New Haven: Yale Univ. Press, 1990): "a range of practices . . . [and] discourse that takes place 'offstage,' beyond direct observation by powerholders" (4, 14). The "hidden transcripts" I refer to here are the *palengke*'s linguistic and practiced "disguises" unique to my respondents' conditions, which, in some ways, follow Scott's further clarification of "hidden transcripts" as "the often fugitive political conduct of subordinate groups . . . that [express] dissent

to the official transcript of power relations." (xi, xii, 17). Another way of understanding how this practice works is by situating "palengke" within the linguistic parameters of Taglish.

Most of the Filipino participants in organizational proceedings I attended,
and virtually all first-generation Filipino Americans I interviewed, spoke in
Taglish, especially when there was a chance of being overheard and understood
by strangers. "Palengke politics," as a Taglish term, alerts its speakers and listeners to appropriations that may sound ridiculous or incomprehensible to others, yet are potentially powerful to them. (I discuss the workings of Taglish more
extensively in Chapters 3 and 5.) See Vicente Rafael, "Taglish, or the Phantom
Power of the Lingua Franca," *Public Culture* 8, No. 1 (Fall 1995): 101–126, and
*Contracting Colonialism: Translation and Christian Conversion in Tagalog Society
under Early Spanish Rule* (Durham: Duke Univ. Press, 1993), chap. 2.

3. These rules of conduct, which mostly go unmentioned, are codified in
COPAO's by-laws. As in most associations of this kind, delegates are expected
to abide by them as a condition of membership. Occasionally, conflicts arise as
new members adjust to the practice of such laws.

4. The notion of *pasyensya* is difficult to translate while retaining its idiomatic
nuance. Its literal translation is "patience" (from the Spanish *paciencia*) or "to act
with patience," but it also calls for "a calm bearing of pain . . . or anything that
annoys, troubles, or hurts." Leo James English, *Tagalog-English Dictionary* (Quezon City, Philippines: Kalayaan Press, 1986). I understand it also to mean "for-
giveness" in this particular context, as in: "be patient with and forgive him—let
it go—since he's just new here and is not used to what we do."

5. The words *"po"* and *"ho"* are terms that mark deference and respect (to
elders and the general public, in this context), which I roughly equate with
"please."

6. Part of this history of community organizing among Filipino Americans
is narrated and illustrated in Fred Cordova, *Filipinos: Forgotten Asian Americans,
A Pictorial Essay* (Dubuque, Iowa: Kendall/Hunt, 1983), esp. pp. 175–227. In his
chapter "Community Activities," Cordova begins with: "It has been said that
whenever two Pinoys had gotten together, they formed a club" (175). I have
heard that line from several of my informants as well; community organizing of
this sort is traditionally viewed as uniquely Filipino American.

7. Vargas's estimates concur with my research figures and those in Yen Le
Espiritu, *Filipino American Lives* (Philadelphia: Temple Univ. Press, 1995), p. 25.

8. Such a narrative misses out on numerous immigrants who do not fit into
the wave concept, such as the "Manila men" who settled in Louisiana via the
galleon trade in the years prior to 1898; later generations who intermarried with
other ethnic groups and/or self-identified differently; and, beginning in the
1970s, political exiles fleeing the Marcos dictatorship. See Chapter 2 for a discussion of these issues.

9. At the same time, Yu acknowledges Filipino American organizations in each of the migration waves that she views as unable to sustain coherence and unity across generations. Elena S. H. Yu, "Filipino Migration and Community Organizations in the United States," *California Sociologist* 3, No. 2 (Summer 1980): 76–102.

10. This point also is made by historical, cultural, and literary critics. See, for example, Oscar V. Campomanes, "The New Empire's Forgetful and Forgotten Citizens: Unrepresentability and Unassimilability in Filipino-American Postcolonialities," *Critical Mass* 2, No. 2 (Spring 1995): 145–200; and E. San Juan Jr.'s *Racial Formations/Critical Transformations* (Atlantic Highlands, N.J.: Humanities Press, 1992), esp. pp. 117–130.

11. To Filipinos, speaking in "slang" means speaking like a native-born American, that is, with a twang.

12. I have marked in my translation both *sarili*'s literal meaning (self, individual) and its connotation in this context (group, collective) to highlight the significance of its use as a group slogan. *"Sariling pagsisikap"* obtains its historical currency from its use by the Marcos administration to promote national development and its once frequent utterance in a popular television sit-com in the Philippines. In this show, an upper-class woman always admonished her lower-class son-in-law to be more diligent (*"magsumikap ka!"*). Filipinos I talked to usually alluded to these references, although with the desire to appropriate the term differently in their new situations. Sometimes, the mention and explanation of *"sariling sikap"* slipped into its more humorous (but men's locker-room) register, to connote masturbation, as in relying on oneself for one's pleasure.

13. Alexis de Tocqueville, *Democracy in America*, translated by George Lawrence, edited by J. P. Mayer (New York: Anchor, 1969), pp. 513–514; for an overview of political and social associations, refer to part 2, chap. 3, in vol. 1; and part 2, chap. 4, in vol. 2.

14. This is one thing they have in common with other immigrant associations.

15. See Steven Erie and Harold Brackman, *Asian Pacific Americans: Diverse Paths toward Empowerment* (Department of Political Science, University of California, San Diego, 1993, photocopy; a version of this paper appears in the authors' *Paths to Political Incorporation for Latinos and Asian Pacifics in California*, a report of the California Policy Seminar, University of California, 1993). See also Yen Le Espiritu, *Asian American Panethnicity: Bridging Institutions and Identities* (Philadelphia: Temple Univ. Press, 1992); and Linda Trinh Vo, "Paths to Empowerment: Panethnic Mobilization in San Diego's Asian American Community" (Ph.D. diss., Department of Sociology, University of California, San Diego, 1995).

16. See Tyler Davidson, "Chinese Peaches," *SF Weekly*, 13–19 March 1996, pp. 10–16; and Fennella Cannell, "The Power of Appearances: Beauty, Mimicry,

and Transformation in Bicol," in *Discrepant Histories*, edited by Vicente L. Rafael
(Philadelphia: Temple Univ. Press, 1995), pp. 223–258.

17. Yu, "Filipino Migration," p. 92; also see "Brief History of the Council"
in the newsletter *Pahayagan* 1, No. 1 (November/December, 1974).

18. Reynaldo C. Ileto, *Pasyon and Revolution: Popular Movements in the Philippines, 1840–1910* (Quezon City, Phil.: Ateneo de Manila Univ. Press, 1979), p.
51

19. *Damayan* also recalls a television program in the Philippines, which many
respondents were familiar with. This program helped get financial and medical
support for those in need.

20. Ileto, *Pasyon and Revolution*, 50–54.

Chapter Five

1. The same conditions apply to mainstream newspapers. See, for example,
Sally Lehrman, "Cutting Out the Heart and Soul of Newspapers," *Outlook* 8, 1
(1996): 5–9. However, the capital outlay and maintenance costs of large papers
are size, reach, and nature of their target markets also differ from those of the
smaller papers who choose to serve comparatively smaller ethnic audiences. See
Ien Ang's "Culture and Communication: Towards an Ethnographic Critique of
Media Consumption in the Transnational Media System," *European Journal of
Communication* 5 (1990): 239–260; and Virginia Escalante's "Chicanos and the
Politics of Representation in U.S. Media" (Department of Communication,
University of California, San Diego, July 1996, photocopy).

2. U.S. Bureau of the Census, *1990 Census of Population and Housing Summary* (Washington, D.C.: GPO, 1992). See also Chapter 2.

3. Clint C. Wilson II and Felix Gutierrez, *Race, Multiculturalism, and the
Media* (Thousand Oaks, Calif.: Sage Publications, 1995), 150–167.

4. Robert E. Park, *The Immigrant Press and Its Control* (New York: Harper,
1922), 86.

5. Immigration/citizenship classification has, indeed, been crucial in the
state's construction and imposition of Asian American identities. Lisa Lowe
remarks that "the life conditions, choices, and expressions of Asian Americans
have been significantly determined by the U.S. state through the apparatus of
immigration laws and policies, through the enfranchisements denied or extended
to immigrant individuals and communities, and through the processes of naturalization and citizenship." In *Immigrant Acts: On Asian American Cultural Politics* (Durham: Duke Univ. Press, 1996), 7.

6. There have been rare instances, mostly culled from community gossip,
when TNTs were caught because some other Filipino turned them in as a result
of a personal quarrel. Some of my respondents said such "snitching" is financially rewarded by the INS. My phone queries to INS offices in Los Angeles

and San Diego produced mixed responses regarding the rewards. Some INS clerks said giving out rewards to informers is a practice that is sometimes followed but never encouraged outright.

7. *California Examiner,* June 8–14, 1994, p. 3. Emphasis in the original.

8. One immigration law office that is quite popular among Filipino Americans both in Los Angeles and San Diego frequently uses its lead partner in the ads. Those I interviewed found him contemptible because of his widely known unprofessionalism, his astronomical fees, and his lust for bilking TNTs of their hard-earned money. He writes regularly in the community papers, appears as a guest on Filipino radio talk shows, and hosts a television show on immigration issues. Ironically, I've also seen his photo in the papers, shown donating money to several Filipino American organizations and causes.

9. While the local term for a person without official immigration documents is "TNT," that for those who have them is "sixty cents" (or "sixty-zens")—a play on the pronunciation of "citizens."

10. This is a national estimate of money coming from the United States through banking institutions and personal channels. Including remittances from other countries like Singapore and Saudi Arabia, annual remittances to the Philippines are an estimated $6 billion. See Karl Schoenberger, "Living off Expatriate Labor," *Los Angeles Times,* 1 August 1994, section A.

11. Some of my respondents say driving in both countries is also getting to be more and more the same, with drive-by shootings, recklessness, and discourtesy as familiar in the United States as in the Philippines.

12. In the conclusion to this work, I critique Park's work in specific relation to a theory of assimilation that assumes invariable and irreversible movement from initial contact to total immersion in the dominant culture.

13. This is the fundamental rationale for Park's insistence on framing his study as a project of "control" or management of immigrant populations whose life trajectories focus on their eventual "Americanization." Any deviations from such a course are then seen as threats ("dangers") to the fabric of society. He writes: "Foreign-language newspapers, as we have tried to show in this volume, are a power to be reckoned with in the Americanization of immigrants.... No newspaper is a free agent. It is a product of various influences. If we know what these influences are, and their relative strength, we shall know how to prevent the immigrant editor from being bullied into dangerous courses, and how to give America at least an equal chance with foreign interests." Park, *The Immigrant Press,* 359–360.

14. Park's study needs to be viewed in its historical context as one that was conducted during the period of "Americanization" that followed World War I, not in the context of the contemporary period. I use his work only as an instance of the ways in which immigrant presses have been studied in the past, whose legacy of thinking about immigrant presses within an assimilative framework remains alive in the popular imagination.

15. Research and retrieval of these newspapers are currently and principally being undertaken by the staff of the Filipino American Experience Research Project under the directorship of Alex Fabros. See Alex Fabros and Annalissa Herbert, eds., *The Filipino American Newspaper Collection: Extracts from 1906 to 1953* (Fresno: The Filipino American Experience Research Project, 1994). Also see Enya P. Flores-Meiser, "The Filipino American Press," in *The Ethnic Press in the United States: A Historical Analysis and Handbook*, edited by Sally M. Miller (New York: Greenwood, 1987); and Fred Cordova, *Filipinos: Forgotten Asian Americans, A Pictorial Essay* (Dubuque, Iowa: Kendall/Hunt, 1983) for a more nuanced treatment of the role of Filipino newspapers in earlier communities.

16. Emory S. Bogardus, "The Filipino Press in the United States," *Sociology and Social Research* 18 (July–August 1934): 582–585; Flores-Meiser, "The Filipino American Press," pp. 89–96; and Donn V. Hart, "The Filipino Press in the United States: A Neglected Resource," *Journalism Quarterly* 54 (Spring 1977): 135–139.

17. Jane Rhodes, "The Visibility of Race and Media History," *Critical Studies in Mass Communication* 10, No. 2: 184–190.

18. In regard to these issues, refer to the annotations in Dirk Hoerder, *The Immigrant Labor Press in North America, 1840s–1970s* (New York: Greenwood, 1987).

19. Rosario Briones, "The Price of Assimilating," *Philippine Times*, 15 June 1994, p. 4.

Conclusion

1. An Ilokano is someone from the Ilocos provinces of the Philippines; a Bisaya is someone from the Visayan provinces. I have heard this joke from Filipinos in Washington as well.

2. For a psychoanalytic perspective on jokes and joke making, see Sigmund Freud, "Humour," in *Character and Culture*, edited by Philip Rieff (New York: Collier, [1928] 1963), 263–269.

3. *Webster's II: New Riverside University Dictionary* (Boston: Riverside Publishing, 1984).

4. Robert E. Park, *Race and Culture* (Glencoe: Free Press, 1950); W. Lloyd Warner and Leo Srole, *The Social Systems of American Ethnic Groups* (New Haven: Yale Univ. Press, 1945).

5. Milton M. Gordon, *Assimilation in American Life* (New York: Oxford Univ. Press, 1964).

6. In this section, I borrow extensively from the insightful analysis of the ethnicity-based paradigm in the U.S. context by Michael Omi and Howard Winant, in *Racial Formation in the United States: From the 1960s to the 1980s* (New York: Routledge, 1986), 14–24.

7. Omi and Winant, *Racial Formation in the United States*, 15.

8. Marx and other social theorists predicted that ethnicity and racial divisions would cease to be significant in the modern age. Omi and Winant, *Racial Formation in the United States*, 9; and William Petersen, "Concepts of Ethnicity," in *Harvard Encyclopedia of American Ethnic Groups*, edited by Stephan Thernstrom (Cambridge: Harvard Univ. Press, 1980), 238.

9. In 1944, Gunnar Myrdal, in *An American Dilemma: The Negro Problem and Modern Democracy* (New York: Harper and Row, 1962), argued that the natural and only solution to racial discrimination and national fragmentation was for blacks to assimilate into the core of the nation and for members of the larger society to embrace them in the name of democracy. The consequences of this two-fold process would benefit the entire country. Myrdal's thesis was later applied to other minority groups.

10. Nathan Glazer and Daniel Patrick Moynihan, *Beyond the Melting Pot: The Negroes, Puerto Ricans, Jews, Italians, and Irish of New York City*, 2d. ed. (Cambridge: MIT Press, 1970), 11; Gordon, *Assimilation in American Life*, 4.

11. Stephen Steinberg says that "ethnicity cannot long survive the erosion of the material and institutional underpinnings which was precipitated by the immigrant experience" in *The Ethnic Myth* (Boston: Beacon, 1981), 74. Also refer to Gans, "Symbolic Ethnicity."

12. Park, *Race and Culture*, 50–51. In effect, this cycle was Park's (and his students') operationalization of the "melting pot" ideology prevalent at the time, in which the metaphor provided relief for the "insecure first generation's aspiration to disappear totally, to merge into indistinguishable sameness with 'real' Americans." To some degree, this assertion was instrumental (though not completely successful) in placating the anxieties of immigrant restrictionists of the period. Park's thesis guaranteed that, in time, all "foreigners" would become amalgamated Americans, and all group divisions would become mere *categories.*

13. The preferred mechanism for measuring ethnic identity in this regard was to ask a respondent to specify their "ethnicity" on a 10-point scale, with 1 representing "original" ethnic identity, and 10 representing "full American" identity. Glenn Omatsu, "Asian Pacific Americans: In 'Motion' and 'Transition'," *Amerasia* 18, No. 3 (1992): 84.

14. Omatsu, "Asian Pacific Americans," 83–85; Omi and Winant, *Racial Formation in the United States*, 21–24.

15. Horace Kallen, *Culture and Democracy in America* (New York: Boni and Liveright, 1924).

16. A discussion of this issue appears in Michael Novak, *The Rise of the Unmeltable Ethnics: Politics and Culture in the Seventies* (New York: Macmillan, 1973).

17. A prominent example is Americo Paredes, *With His Pistol in His Hand: A Border Ballad and Its Hero* (Austin: Univ. of Texas Press, 1958). James A. Banks, *Teaching Strategies for Ethnic Studies*, 4th ed. (Boston: Allyn and Bacon, 1987), has a good listing of ethnic and racial studies scholarship in this vein.

18. A discussion of the origins of pluralism in the U.S. context is found in Steinberg, *The Ethnic Myth*, chaps. 1 and 2.

19. Laura Elisa Perez, "Opposition and the Education of Chicana/os," in *Race, Identity, and Representation in Education*, edited by Cameron McCarthy and Warren Crichlow (New York: Routledge, 1993), 268–279; Cornel West, "The New Cultural Politics of Difference," in *Out There: Marginalization and Contemporary Cultures*, edited by Russell Ferguson, Martha Gever, Trinh T. Minh Ha, and Cornel West (Cambridge: MIT Press, 1990), 19–36.

20. This is not to say, however, that criticisms have been lacking. Along with the assimilationist framework, the tenets of cultural pluralism have figured in debates, especially with regard to what they implicitly assume or hide in the rhetoric of acculturation and diversity. The most trenchant critique comes from ethnic studies scholars who claim that both ignore racism as a fundamental element of U.S. society, impacting especially on political, social, and economic relations between dominant (white) groups and people of color. Assimilationists, they say, mask the historical and lasting effects of institutional and systemic racism on the social mobility and political representation of many minorities. Focusing solely on the cultural attributes and behaviors of immigrants (e.g., language and customs), critics say, leaves out the institutional barriers that many immigrants of color face. At the same time, it upholds white culture as the embodiment of immigrant hopes and dreams and downgrades nonwhite culture as something to shed. And last, many have observed that assimilation has not lived up to its guarantee of full acceptance into mainstream society. While racism may not be as overtly practiced as before, its permutations still reach into the everyday lives of nonwhites.

21. Stuart Hall, "Ethnicity: Identity and Difference," *Radical America* 23, No. 4 (1989): 19.

22. Arthur Schlesinger, "The Cult of Ethnicity, Good and Bad," *Time*, 8 July 1991, 27. Other criticisms of multiculturalism appear in Schlesinger's collection of essays, *The Disuniting of America: Reflections on a Multicultural Society* (Knoxville, Tenn.: Whittle, 1991).

23. Schlesinger, "The Cult of Ethnicity," 27.

24. Benedict Anderson, *Imagined Communities: Reflections on the Origin and Spread of Nationalism* (London: Verso, 1983), 15–16.

25. Ernest Gellner, *Nations and Nationalism* (Ithaca: Cornell Univ. Press, 1983), 141.

26. Ibid., 1.

27. Anderson, *Imagined Communities*, 15–18.

28. Benedict Anderson, *Long-Distance Nationalism: World Capitalism and the Rise of Identity Politics* (Amsterdam, The Netherlands: Center for Asian Studies, 1992), 5–8.

29. Ibid., 8.

30. Ibid., 9. Anderson notes, for example, the proliferation of ethnic markers attached to nation markers in multiethnic societies as occurring only relatively recently. Refer to similar observations in Peter Jackson and Jan Penrose, "Introduction: Placing 'Race' and Nation," in *Constructions of Race, Place, and Nation*, edited by Peter Jackson and Jan Penrose (Minneapolis: Univ. of Minnesota Press, 1993), 1–23.

31. Michael Peter Smith and Joe R. Feagin, "Putting 'Race' in Its Place," in *The Bubbling Cauldron: Race, Ethnicity, and the Urban Crisis*, ed. Michael Peter Smith and Joe R. Feagin (Minneapolis: Univ. of Minnesota Press, 1995), 12–17.

32. As I have said before, I in no way condone interethnic violence in support of ethnic "rights" and claims to territorial supremacy and legitimacy. My intent here is to illustrate the usual construction of these forms of nationalism as antimodern and irrational.

33. David Lloyd, "Nationalisms against the State: Towards a Critique of the Anti-Nationalist Prejudice," in *Reexamining and Renewing Philippine Progressive Vision*, Papers and Proceedings of the 1993 Conference of the Forum for Philippine Alternatives, edited by John Gershman and Walden Bello (Quezon City, Phil.: Forum for Philippine Alternatives, 1993), 216. I have benefited tremendously from Lloyd's critical review of the literature on nationalism.

34. Schlesinger, "The Cult of Ethnicity," 27. For Steinberg as well, any resort to ethnic revivalism is bound to fail, because "the more [ethnic groups] restore [their] original culture, the less compatible they are with American society and culture, and the less their ability to attract a large following." Steinberg, *The Ethnic Myth*, 74.

35. Ibid.

36. I say "renewed" because there was a vast tradition of space studies in urban ethnography, cultural anthropology, and physical/social geography to which recent scholars have addressed themselves.

37. Edward W. Soja, *Postmodern Geographies: The Reassertion of Space in Critical Social Theory* (London: Verso, 1989), 31–32.

38. Akhil Gupta and James Ferguson, "Beyond 'Culture': Space, Identity, and the Politics of Difference," *Cultural Anthropology* 7, No. 1 (February 1992): 6–23. I am indebted to the authors' work on space and identity, on which this section is based.

39. Ibid., 7.

40. I am thinking of James Clifford, "Traveling Cultures," in *Cultural Studies*, edited by Lawrence Grossberg, Cary Nelson, and Paula Treichler (New York: Routledge, 1992), 96–112, in this connection.

41. Gupta and Ferguson, "Beyond Culture," 14.

42. George E. Marcus and Michael M. J. Fischer, *Anthropology as Cultural Critique: An Experimental Moment in the Human Sciences* (Chicago: Univ. of Chicago Press, 1986), chap. 4.

43. Gupta and Ferguson, "Beyond Culture," 14–18.

44. These criticisms and prescriptions are not wholly attributable to the efforts of the theorists I mention here. The interdisciplinary nature of space studies relies on multiple borrowings and appropriations from other fields, thinkers, or sources. See Michael Keith and Steve Pile, eds., *Place and the Politics of Identity* (New York: Routledge, 1993).

45. Khachig Tololyan, "The Nation-State and Its Others: In Lieu of a Preface," *Diaspora: A Journal of Transnational Studies* 1, No. 1 (Spring 1991): 6. This viewpoint is echoed by Arjun Appadurai and Carol A. Breckenridge, "Why Public Culture?" *Public Culture: Bulletin of the Project for Transnational Cultural Studies* 1, No. 1 (Fall 1988): 5–9.

46. In this vein, see Arjun Appadurai, "Disjuncture and Difference in the Global Cultural Economy," *Public Culture* 2, No. 2 (1990): 1–24; and George Lipsitz, *Dangerous Crossroads: Popular Music, Postmodernism, and the Poetics of Place* (London: Verso, 1994).

47. Regarding the relationships among space, structure, and identity, I have also benefited from Henri Lefebvre, *The Production of Space*, translated by Donald Nicholson-Smith (Oxford: Blackwell, 1991); Doreen Massey, *Space, Place, and Gender* (Minneapolis: Univ. of Minnesota Press, 1994); Yi-Fu Tuan, *Space and Place* (Minneapolis: Univ. of Minnesota Press, 1977); and Sharon Zukin, *Landscapes of Power* (Berkeley: Univ. of California Press, 1991).

Index